AFRICAN ETHNOGRAPHIC STUDIES
OF THE 20TH CENTURY

Volume 31

THE SOCIAL ORGANISATION OF
THE LO WIILI

THE SOCIAL ORGANISATION OF THE LO WIILI

JACK GOODY

Routledge
Taylor & Francis Group

LONDON AND NEW YORK

First published in 1956 by Her Majesty's Stationery Office, second edition published in 1967 by Oxford University Press for the International African Institute.

This edition first published in 2018
by Routledge
2 Park Square, Milton Park, Abingdon, Oxon OX14 4RN

and by Routledge
711 Third Avenue, New York, NY 10017

Routledge is an imprint of the Taylor & Francis Group, an informa business

© 1967 International African Institute

British Library Cataloguing in Publication Data
A catalogue record for this book is available from the British Library

ISBN: 978-0-8153-8713-8 (Set)
ISBN: 978-0-429-48813-9 (Set) (ebk)
ISBN: 978-1-138-58480-8 (Volume 31) (hbk)
ISBN: 978-1-138-58511-9 (Volume 31) (pbk)
ISBN: 978-0-429-50570-6 (Volume 31) (ebk)

Publisher's Note
The publisher has gone to great lengths to ensure the quality of this reprint but points out that some imperfections in the original copies may be apparent.

Disclaimer
The publisher has made every effort to trace copyright holders and would welcome correspondence from those they have been unable to trace.

A MARKET

Women cooking food for sale

The Social Organisation of the LoWiili

by

JACK GOODY

Second Edition

Published for the
INTERNATIONAL AFRICAN INSTITUTE
by the
OXFORD UNIVERSITY PRESS
1967

*Oxford University Press, Ely House, London W.*1

GLASGOW NEW YORK TORONTO MELBOURNE WELLINGTON
CAPE TOWN SALISBURY IBADAN NAIROBI LUSAKA ADDIS ABABA
BOMBAY CALCUTTA MADRAS KARACHI LAHORE DACCA
KUALA LUMPUR HONG KONG TOKYO

First published 1956
(Her Majesty's Stationery Office)

Second Edition 1967
(Oxford University Press)

Reprinted Lithographically in Great Britain
by Compton Printing Ltd.
London and Aylesbury

PREFACE TO THE SECOND EDITION

The people described in this book occupy the north-west corner of Ghana and the adjacent areas of the Upper Volta and the Ivory Coast, which lie across the Black Volta. They are part of a belt of Dagari-speaking settlements which form a continuum both of dialect and of culture. Indeed there are even fewer distinct boundaries than among the Tallensi and their neighbours, of whom Fortes has written: "there is no 'tribal unity' among the Tallensi in the ordinarily accepted sense of this phrase. They have no fixed territorial boundaries, nor are they precisely marked off from neighbouring 'tribes' by cultural or linguistic usages. ... The 'tribal unity' of the Tallensi is, in general terms, the unity of a distinct socio-geographical region forming a segment of a greater region of similar cultural type, economic organization, and social structure. This region can be demarcated only by dynamic criteria. The Tallensi have more in common among themselves ... than the component segments of Tale society have with other like units outside what we have called Taleland." (1949:1-2).

Among the Dagari-speaking peoples, a similar situation is reflected in the complex and changing mode of identification. The actors recognise the cultural and linguistic differences that obtain in the area, the local variations that exist within a considerable degree of cultural uniformity, and refer to them by 'placing' particular customary acts in relation to two categories, 'Lobi' and 'Dagarti' (Lo and Dagaa), the use of which resembles the English terms 'Westerners' and 'Easterners'. But the outside observer (and in some limited contexts, the locals too) needs a set of fixed, not relative, terms to guide him; indeed one of the great difficulties in the ethnography of this region is the fact that such observers invariably take these relative terms as fixed, 'tribal' designations.

In addition to the relative 'directional' terms, the actors also discriminate areas of cultural similarity, referring to certain features that they deem important, such as matrilineal inheritance of movables and the presence of various types of xylophone. And these areas they sometimes point to by means of other 'tribal' designations, which are usually modifications of the basic directional terms, Lo and Dagaa. The present study is of a large dispersed settlement of LoDagaa who usually refer to themselves by the name of the locality (Birifu) but are sometimes known as the Wiili (Fr. Wilé or Oulé, see Labouret, 1931) or the LoWiili (Duncan-Johnstone, 2nd Lawra District Record Book, p.428, 1918). I have preferred the second of these, in order to conform to the distinction made by the actors between the inhabitants of the Birifu area (LoWiili) and their eastern neighbours around Tugu (DagaaWiili).

Given the terminological complexities, it is perhaps not surprising to find these people largely ignored in standard ethnographies, and, where not ignored, then muddled and confused. For example, Murdock (1959:79) mixes up the pagan, acephalous Wiili with the Muslim, centralized Wala, and includes the Dagari among the Grusi rather than the Mole (Mossi) speakers. The late L. Girault, regarding my scheme as too complicated, throws all the Dagari-speaking peoples of Ghana into one commodious container; linguistically, this may be reasonable, but not ethnographically. The range of social organisation requires more careful

iii

discriminators. The Reverend Father makes the same error as those English speakers who, looking from the other bank of the river, group all the inhabitants to the west under the name Lobi (Lo) and fail to appreciate both the recognized cultural differences and the relative nature of the terminology.

This complex and subtle way of referring to one's own and neighbouring settlements arises from the fact that networks of social relationships have few marked discontinuities; consequently there is no real concept of a 'tribe' (a named cultural unit), much less of a nation (a named political one). The main unit of study is necessarily the parish (or ritual area) which usually comprises a settlement (named area of habitation); and it is the settlements of Birifu and Tom that constitute my 'societies'. The people that Girault speaks of as Dagari (or Dagara) are the same ones that I call LoDagaba, and in this book I refer several times to the LoDagaba settlement of Tom, where I spent some nine months in 1952. Much of my subsequent work has been an attempt to study and explain the differences in the social life of these two communities, differences which, as I have said, are recognized by the actors as characteristic of the wider areas of cultural similarity I refer to as the LoWiili and the LoDagaba.

I make this point in order to establish that these differences in the forms of social action I found in Birifu and Tom are not a question of 'curious discrepancies' in my field notes, as has been suggested (Leach 1961:3; quoted by Southall 1965: 130). 'Discrepancy' carries the pejorative implication of an inconsistency, something there by error or by mistaken observation. Such is certainly not the case. The differences are as concrete as those between the Kachin and the Lakher, and they are substantiated by intensive field observation and confirmed both by local usage and the opinion of other observers. We should not be led astray by the fluidity of the 'tribal' designations; in any case, it is methodologically just as sound, even sounder, to compare differences such as suicide rates or the organisation of descent groups within communities (here 'named territorial groups') as between them. It is precisely the analysis of such 'discrepancies' (read 'variations') that offers the main opportunity for significant advance in the field of comparative sociology, as Leach (among others) has himself shown (e.g. 1961:114ff.).

The elucidation of these variables should not be taken as an attempt to set up a typology of societies or social structures, an undertaking I regard as producing a minimal pay-off. In distinguishing between different kinds of descent groups, and thus differentiating between the 'double descent' systems of the LoWiili and the LoDagaba, I am simply trying to elicit variables, not establish types of society. One source of misunderstanding may be that we often loosely characterize a society by the presence of a particular element and speak, for example, of a matri-lineal society, a pastoral society or a centralised society, although such epithets are more precisely applied to the kind of descent group, economy or government we have under consideration.

In the preface to the first edition, I called attention to the factors that militated against a strictly synchronic study of the social organization of the LoWiili, part-icularly the political system. When British over-rule was established by military conquest, the conquerors imposed a shallow hierarchy of chiefs and headmen upon the previous social system. I claimed at the time that it was still possible to disentangle the past policy from the present, and I chose "to consider the political organization as it existed at the beginning of the century." I am no longer satisfied that it is possible to analyse indigenous political systems relying solely upon the methods that anthropologists normally employ. In general, they remain committed to the twin doctrines of 'intensive fieldwork' and 'structural-functionalism'. One cannot do intensive fieldwork on dead regimes. The procedure that I, like others, adopted was mentally to lop off the more obvious results of colonial rule. On a superficial level this demolition job was not a difficult undertaking, for the administration rarely impinged and the chief had died shortly before my arrival. For the rest, I relied on old men's tales (the initial conquest was less than fifty years away), the District Record Books and other written evidence.

But the lopping-off technique is clearly unsatisfactory on a number of counts. It tacitly assumes that colonial over-rule, the concentration of armed force in the hands of the new rulers, has had a minimal effect upon the local polity. It assumes that if, for the purpose of analysis, you abstract the new role hierarchy and power structure, you can also adequately discount its influence. Such assumptions lead to a distortion in assessing the role of war, raiding, slavery, trading and other aspects of social life; even where it is possible to collect accounts of actual combat, it is difficult to evaluate the part played by the threat of war and the prospect of slave-raids.

There is a further point here which relates to the kind of analysis that social anthropologists undertake, or claim to undertake. I refer to a contradiction in the 'structural-functional' approach, encouraged by students of Malinowski, Radcliffe-Brown, Parsons and others. A social anthropologist supposedly goes into the field to engage in a synchronic study of a particular social system. In any case, there usually is no other way to study kinship behaviour, though it is just possible to resurrect some of the peripheral aspects of terminology from a past era. As far as household composition, divorce rates or marriage patterns are concerned, the basic source for these must be a sociological census based upon interviews, combined with the collection of genealogies.

But when he moves on to examine the political system, the fieldworker usually adopts quite another approach. His enquiries concentrate upon what happens (or happened) in the chief's court rather than at the D.C.'s office or the party meeting, and are mainly directed towards reconstructing what occurred in the pre-colonial era. Looking at my own work, and that of many of my colleagues, I find little or no reference to the actualities of contemporary power. The discussion of such issues is relegated to the study of social change, as if change was a recent innovation in human societies and conquest began with the advent of the Europeans. As in the present study, the writings of Fortes on the political system of the Tallensi or Leach on Highland Burma make little or no mention of the power structure under which we worked and (perhaps significantly) of which we were ourselves a part. Anthropology is the child of European colonisation, and has failed to transcend the limitations of its ancestry. Political anthropology too often boils down to a reconstruction of the pre-colonial past out of the fragmentary memories of old men, an endeavour it euphemistically presents as the analysis of 'the ethnographic present'. But old men are rapidly disappearing, so that the fieldworker's account of an 'indigenous' political system becomes more and more suspect as it becomes more and more hypothetical.

Even such an important contribution to comparative politics, *African Political Systems* (1940), suffers from the ethnographer's classic dilemma. Although carried out in the colonial period, the studies contained in this volume deal not with the contemporary situation (of which little or no mention is made) but with an unspecified period in the past. For want of other evidence, the reader is left to guess that the account refers to the immediately pre-colonial period—though the situations described (or reconstructed) are often perceived as stretching back into the knowable past.

There are two general objections to this mode of procedure. Firstly it makes mockery of the 'structural-functional' approach, since, in giving his overall picture of society, the anthropologist often tries to marry present kinship to dead politics. Part of the trouble here is the implicit assumption of the timelessness of anthropological analyses; for instance, though well aware of the changes which have taken place, some writers seem to think they can disprove the statements of their predecessors by means of data collected thirty or forty years later. In the rapidly changing situation of the modern world, every such supposition should be examined with the greatest care.

The second main objection is that if anthropologists are going in for the business of reconstructing defunct political systems, they need to consider all, not only part, of the available evidence. In other words, they have to make full use of documentary material; in this sense the anthropologist needs to become historian, just as much as the historian needs to become sociologist.

Social anthropologists (unlike some of their sociological counter-parts, such as George Homans) seem reluctant to engage in this task. There is of course a special problem in dealing with acephalous societies, where little information is likely to be recorded either in oral tradition or in written records. But there is certainly a great deal more than one would imagine from most anthropological accounts, though it should be added that much of this material (under the fifty year rule) has only recently been released from archival privacy. But with centralized societies such as the Nupe or Hausa, the Kachin or the Zulu, societies that have long been in contact with fully literate cultures, material on the political institutions of the recent past exists in European archives, in Arabic manuscripts and in other documentary records. Yet even when anthropologists recognize the nature of their reconstructions of past politics, they too often rely upon oral tradition and the more accessible travel books rather than upon a thorough analysis of the whole range of available material. The result is likely to be not so much 'pseudo-history' as bastard history—with a sociological dressing.

The sociologist is bound to have his primary interest in the regularities of process rather than in the chronological record. It is an approach that tends to stress equilibrium mechanisms or the repetitive nature of change, and one that has been fruitfully adopted in a number of studies (e.g. Evans-Pritchard 1940, Fortes 1947, Leach 1954, Gluckman 1954). But the applicability of such assumptions can only be ascertained after a full examination of all the available evidence, and for this fieldwork is of real but limited use. In order to present an analysis of the political system of Ashanti in, say 1890, one has to spend more time in the archives than in the field. With the increasing professionalization of regional studies, any account of indigenous politics must marry the technique and approach of the documentary historian and sociologist. To do otherwise is to court disaster, for neither is adequate on its own.

In other places contributors to *African Political Systems* have presented some of the most valuable analyses of a current political situation in Africa that exist. My point is that these accounts are presented apart from the main body of the material, where the time reference differs for different aspects of the social organization. Present politics are divorced from present kinship, in contradiction to the fundamental theoretical assumptions of the holistic approach to social systems (or culture) that anthropologists propound. And this whole enterprise of presenting an account of an 'indigenous' social system is bound to become rapidly less and less rewarding as the credibility gap grows wider, and orthodox anthropology will stand in increasing likelihood of falling between the stools of sociology and history.

But I am here concerned not so much with the future of a discipline as with the kinds of distortion that are likely to creep into present studies, and which I perceive as detracting, in some measure, from my own earlier account. These kinds of distortion are:

(i)   Insufficient emphasis upon non-recurrent events;
(ii) upon the institutions connected with painful experiences, such as war and slavery;
(iii) and upon external relations (e.g. in connection with trade, the world religions or in communication systems) in contrast to internal networks: combined with
(iv) a tendency to over-emphasize the distinctiveness of groups and their social and cultural cohesion, for example, in the interlocking of symbol, belief and social group.

It would be wrong to give the impression that no progress has been made. 'Conflict' is frequently discussed, though often simply as an alternative mode of 'sociation'. 'Change' and 'difference' are theoretically accepted as worthy of investigation. But in practice anthropologists, trying to avoid the pitfalls of the search for origins of an evolutionary or psychological kind, have failed to appreciate that a system or relationship, whether in the social or natural sciences, can only be fully understood when one understands the conditions under which it is not something else; and if change proves impossible to observe, then at least one can compare—and the more limited the comparison, the more useful it tends to be.

In subsequent writings I have expanded and developed some of the points made in this volume. My paper on "Fields of Social Control among the LoDagaba" (*J. R. Anthrop. Inst.*, 1957) presents an account of the main social groups in the settlement of Tom, while "The Fission of Domestic Groups among the LoDagaba" offers a comparison with the LoWiili (*The Developmental Cycle in Domestic Groups*, ed. Goody, Cambridge, 1958) and explains the differences by reference to the systems of inheritance. The same theme is taken up in the study of "The Mother's Brother and the Sister's Son in West Africa" (*J. R. Anthrop. Inst.*, 1959), where I discuss my material in the context of the theoretical writings of Radcliffe-Brown, Lévi-Strauss and others before elaborating an approach that accounts for differences as well as similarities in matrilateral relationships. The same intention lies behind "The Classification of Double Descent Systems" (*Current Anthropology*, 1961) where I try to deal with some of the variables involved in order to escape from an over-rigid typology. Finally the mortuary customs and beliefs of the LoWiili and the LoDagaba are intensively analysed in *Death, Property and the Ancestors* (Tavistock Press and Stanford University Press, 1962) on the hypothesis that the institutions that centre around death will be closely linked to the system of property relations, since these have necessarily to be re-ordered when the individual dies. In this work I relate certain differences in the funeral ceremonies and ancestor worship to the same 'independent' variable as before, namely, the ownership and devolution of property.

The elucidation of the material which I collected during the two years I lived with the LoDagaa has necessitated some clarification of current concepts and a discussion of various theoretical positions. Polemic breeds polemic and my points have been disputed by several scholars, sometimes (I feel) with an inadequate understanding of my original contentions. But, despite the current vogue, the introduction to such a book does not seem altogether the place to offer either a rebuttal or an apologia.

When I returned to Birifu for a short period in 1965 (while I was working among the Gonja some 100 miles to the south), I was struck more by the continuities than the changes. These latter were much fewer than the presence of a primary school and a literate chief had led me to anticipate. Soon after my arrival I was called to attend a funeral; the stand, dancing, contributions, mourning behaviour, all seemed much as I had known them thirteen years before. The apparent stand-still surprised me, but the explanation seems to lie in the absence of any important cash crop and in the emigration of the educated. The level of literacy within Birifu itself was no higher than when I had lived there; even the educated adults who wish to retain a foot in the neighbourhood build houses in the nearby *zongo* (Hausa for a strangers' quarter) of Babile. In 1952 the *zongo* was inhabited by a few foreign traders, Hausa, Ashanti, Yoruba in the main. But it was strategically sited at a cross-roads and by a large market, and hence ripe for development. In any case the fact that the dispersed settlements of the LoWiili have no real nucleus makes it difficult to locate central services within them. Consequently it was at Babile that the new police station was built and the *zongo* also became the magnet for the educated section of the LoWiili population, whether or not they were employed locally.

The relative lack of change in Birifu stresses one of the major problems for development in Africa and elsewhere, the fact that the roles of literate and farmer are seen as incompatible. Despite nearly 20 years of primary education in Birifu, no boy who had finished his schooling had returned to farming. The only partial exceptions were some who had dropped out of school, and others who had joined the State Farms or the Workers' Brigade as tractor drivers. The last development would be a hopeful sign for the future if only mechanized farming did not at present seem so largely irrelevant to the problem of increased agricultural production in West Africa; and if the individuals regarded themselves as farmers as well as drivers. It is this role incompatibility (deriving from both past and present socio-economic conditions), together with the absence of any important cash crop, that brings about the conservative character of rural life in Northern Ghana and the social problems that arise from uneven development. What the changes have meant, however, is that for any village in the region the field of social relationships extends much more widely than in the past, and any analysis of the social system must now take into account the whole rural-urban situation.

Jack Goody
St. Johns College,
Cambridge,
June 1966

Preface to the First Edition

This is essentially an interim report. Indeed it was written between my first and second tours in the Northern Territories of the Gold Coast.[1] I have since corrected and added to certain sections of my preliminary study as the result of subsequent work but the form of the original has been retained.

It was clearly impossible to give a full analysis of the total social system. I therefore chose to present an outline of the whole and to develop in more detail those aspects of the social structure which appeared to have the greatest interest for theoretical and comparative purposes.

One of the most profitable lines of advance for African sociology lies in the accumulation and analysis of an adequate body of data from communities in which a limited number of variations is accompanied by a large measure of cultural uniformity. The organization of human societies is so complex that it is essential to limit the variables to the greatest possible extent. The peoples of the Northern Territories of the Gold Coast have sufficient in common to make detailed comparison a fruitful procedure. In the earlier chapters, therefore, I have frequently referred to Fortes' work on the Tallensi. The economic system and the domestic organization are shown to be very similar, while the kinship system so confirms his brilliant account in "The Web of Kinship" that I have not in any way aimed at completion but rather concentrated upon the differences, particularly in the analysis of the mother's brother-sister's son relationship. This has some theoretical interest as I believe that Fortes, like most other recent writers, leans too heavily on an early essay of Radcliffe-Brown's.

This attempt to dwell on the points of difference has led to a disproportionate discussion of the system of dual descent and the organization of ritual areas or parishes. I have also considered at some length the problem of "tribal" groupings, as this again raises questions of theoretical interest. For the LoWiili are not a tribe in the usual sense of the word.

Although my main intention has been to examine the social organization of the LoWiili as it exists today, several factors have made it necessary to depart from the strictly synchronic analysis of a single society.

Associated with the lack of a centralized political system is the absence of any accepted designation for these people. Consciousness of their general uniformity of culture is not sufficiently developed to give rise to an accepted tribal name. The names given them by neighbouring communities merely include the LoWiili in much larger groups of peoples who have certain institutions in common, and pay no attention to the distinctive features of their culture. Consequently great confusion of nomenclature exists in the ethnographical studies of the area and I have first attempted to clarify this situation.

The acephalous political system is also accompanied by a fluidity in other aspects of the social structure resulting from the interstitial situation of the

---

[1] I received a grant from the Colonial Social Science Research Council which enabled me to spend nearly two years in the field, from August, 1950 to September, 1951, and again between March and December, 1952. The major part of the second tour was spent among the neighbouring LoDagaba. I am also indebted to the Anthony Wilkin Fund of Cambridge University for an additional grant.

LoWiili between communities inheriting patrilineally and other communities transmitting land and compounds in the agnatic line and certain items of movable property in the uterine line. There seems little doubt that they migrated from an area in which the patrilineal system prevailed and, becoming entangled in the web of uterine kinship, adopted certain features such as the matriclan which are otherwise only found among the peoples inheriting wealth matrilineally. I have listened to an elder explain that the proper person to have inherited the wealth of a man who had recently died was a sister's son, while others present insisted that the children were the rightful heirs. The proverbial sayings in which primitive societies so often sum up aspects of their social life constantly differed from their actual behaviour. What I have presented as static is in reality a point in a process of change. All anthropological studies fasten upon the regularities of a continuing process, but in such a society as the LoWiili the dangers involved in this device may be greater than usual. In order to counteract this I have considered the evidence of recent change and the social organization of surrounding peoples. The institutions of the LoWiili interlock with those of the preceding generation and of the neighbouring societies; they can be fully understood only within this more inclusive spatial and temporal context.

The third factor militating against a strictly synchronic study arises out of European rule. When this area first came under British administration about fifty years ago, a hierarchy of chiefs—known to the natives as "the white man's chiefs"—was imposed upon the previous system. It is still possible to disentangle the one from the other, and I have deliberately chosen to consider the political organization as it existed at the beginning of the century. With this exception the study is concerned with the contemporary situation.

I am indebted to my teachers, Professor M. Fortes and Professor E. E. Evans-Pritchard. The former's experience in a similar society was of great assistance to me. I would also like to thank Cecilia Scurfield for her help with the typing, H. E. Goody for checking the proofs, and the many people in the Administration and in Birifu who assisted me in so many ways.

This book is respectfully dedicated
to my Father and Mother.

A Note on Orthography and Abbreviations

A few religious works have been published by the White Fathers' Mission in the related dialect of Dagari spoken at Jirapa. Local schoolteachers at Government schools are also in the process of producing a written language. I myself have used the script recommended by the International African Institute. I have not indicated tones which are of some semantic importance. The LoWiili often drop the final vowel; the name *Bõyiri*, for example, I have often written *Bõyir*.

The first two letters of English kinship terms are used as abbreviations; for example Fa stands for father and FaFa for father's father. An English word or phrase is placed in inverted commas to denote a literal translation of a Dagari term; thus "brother" means a classificatory brother.

Contents

Preface to the Second Edition iii
Preface to the First Edition v
A Note on Orthography and Abbreviations xi
Chapter 1 The Geographical and Ethnographical Background . . *page* 1
2 The Economic System 27
3 Kinship Relations and the Structure of Residential Groups . 38
4 Descent Groups 65
5 The Territorial System 91
6 The Social System; a recapitulation 106
A Bibliography of the LoWiili 115
Index 119

MAPS AND DIAGRAMS

Figure 1 Climatic zones and language families within the Niger bend *page* 3
2 The distribution of Lobi and Dagari-speaking peoples . . 5
3 Diagram to illustrate the use of the directional names, *Lo* and
Dagaa, for external reference 24
4 Compound occupied by a simple residential group . . . 39
5 Bŏyiri's compound, Tʃaa, Birifu 45
6 The settlement of Birifu 87
7 The distribution of compounds, Tʃaa, Birifu . . . 94

TABLES

Table 1 Goods passing through Bamboi and Ouessa . . . *page* 8
2 Passengers crossing by the Bamboi Ferry 10
3 Main criteria in the use of the name *Lo* 23
4 Distribution of xylophones among the *Lo* and *Dagaa* . . 23
5 Livestock holdings of "Lobi" compounds 29
6 Acreage under cultivation by a farming group . . . 30
7 Land cultivated by three farming groups in Birifu . . 31
8 The composition of the farming group 33
9 Distribution of wives of adult men 41
10 The span of agnates in dwelling groups 42
11 Farming groups and homesteads 43
12 Matriclans and their sub-divisions 83
13 The distribution of patrilineages in relation to Earth shrines . 94

PHOTOGRAPHS

A Market . . . . *Frontispiece*
1. Boys looking after cattle; 2. A new compound . . . ⎫
3. Cooking food; 4. Repairing a compound . . . . ⎬ *Between pages 64 and 65*
5. Poisoning arrows; 6. Funeral of an old man . . . ⎪
7. Bathing an infant; 8. Clearing new land . . . . ⎭

Chapter 1

The Geographical and Ethnographical Background

Below the great northward bend the Niger makes as it flows through Timbuktu and Gao stretches the desert of Asawad, inhabited by the Moors and Tuareg, mainly nomadic peoples speaking Afro-asiatic languages. Further south, as the rainfall increases, the desert gives way to thornland, then to savannah woodland and finally to the dense rain forests of the West African Coast. In the Sudanese Zone south of the desert, roughly bounded by the 15th parallel, live settled agricultural communities, the affinities of whose speech were established by Westermann in his account of the Sudanic languages.[1] Further south, in the belt of rain forest between the coast of West Africa and the 8th parallel north of the equator, live peoples such as the Ashanti, Yoruba, Nupe and Ibo with an economy formerly based on the cultivation of root crops, such as yams and cassava, and speaking languages belonging to the Kwa branch of this same linguistic family. In the centre, in the Sudanese Zone of low trees and tall grasses, the cereals, guinea corn, millet and maize, are the staple crops. It is in this region that the LoWiili live.

The Sudanese Zone is characterized by a well-defined wet season which begins in April and in October is followed by a severe dry season of six months when little rain falls. The vegetation has given rise to a number of descriptive names, orchard bush, tree savannah, sudanese parkland and savannah woodland. It is a country of small, scattered, fire-resistant trees, and of coarse grasses shoulder-high in the rains, no more than a tuft in the dry season when a dust-laden wind, the harmattan, drives down from the desert. The contrast between the two seasons is extreme. During the rains, when between 25 and 50 inches fall, the land becomes covered in a thick green blanket of vegetation; the crops around the compounds reach some ten feet in height and quite hide the buildings themselves. When the rains end and the crops are gathered and the grass scorched by the sun and desiccated by the wind, the country lies dry and bare; from the smallest rise one looks across an expanse of bleached earth, with the mud-compounds scarcely distinguishable from the soil itself.

The first comprehensive ethnographic survey of the Western Sudan was that made by Delafosse at the instigation of Clozel, Governor of the Colonie du Haut-Sénégal-Niger, within some twelve years of the final occupation of the area by the French. Apart from the Moors and Tuareg who speak Afro-asiatic languages of the Semitic and Berber branches respectively, he distinguished "cinq familles de race noire",[2] Tukulor, Songhai, Mande, Senufo and Voltaic. This classification was made after consideration of the established facts of physical anthropology, the "most probable" traditions of the people themselves, affinities of culture and linguistic relationships. The difficulties of such a method were appreciated by the author; but in none of these fields except the last was

---

[1] 1927.
[2] Vol. I, p. 113. He was, of course, only concerned with the areas occupied by the French.

sufficient material available. Delafosse states neither the actual criteria employed nor the weighting to be placed on any one of his general factors. Fortunately, his classification of the peoples coincides exactly with his language families and, in view of his valuable contributions to the study of individual languages spoken in the Western Sudan, it may be assumed that linguistic differentia were not unnaturally uppermost in his mind.

Broadly speaking, Delafosse's classification still stands. His five families form part of Westermann's West Sudanic languages, which Greenberg now suggests should be included together with Bantu in a larger group he calls the Niger-Congo family.[1] The languages known by Delafosse as Tukulor are called West Atlantic by Westermann and Bryan (1952); and Songhai is completely excluded by Greenberg from Sudanic and given an independent status. But with this exception, recent work on the languages of West Africa has largely followed Delafosse's lead.

The peoples with which we shall be concerned speak one of the Voltaic languages, spoken by the vast majority of the inhabitants of that sector of the Sudanese Zone which lies within the Niger Bend. The name is derived from the River Volta, whose three branches drain a large part of the area. To the south lie the Kwa-speaking peoples of the rain-forest; to the north, the nomadic desert dwellers; to the east, the Songhai and the Hausa; and to the west, the Senufo. The last is classified by Delafosse and Greenberg as a separate family within the West Sudanic. Westermann, however, regards it as one of the Gur languages, a term he borrows from Christaller to designate the Voltaic group. The latter had already referred to the Kwa languages as Volta-Sprachen.[2]

Greenberg calls this language group 'Mossi-Grunshi', a term which occurs in Delafosse's earlier "Vocabulaires Comparitifs de plus de 60 Langues ou Dialectes parlés à la Côte d'Ivoire et dans les régions limitrophes" (1904), a work which initiated linguistic studies in this area. Delafosse in his later book sub-divides this family into seven branches, Tombo, Mossi, Grunshi, Bobo, Lobi, Koulango and Bariba. Westermann in his recent work on "The Languages of West Africa" has revised his previous classification; he now recognizes eight sub-groups, including the Mossi (or Mole-Dagbane), Grunshi, Bariba (or Bargu) and Koulango, combining the Lobi, Dogon (or Tombo) and Bobo into one and adding the Senufo, Tem and Gurma groups.

Along the middle reaches of the Black Volta, which up to the 11th parallel forms the boundary between the Gold Coast and the Haute Volta,[3] are a number of peoples speaking languages of the Lobi and Mossi sub-groups of the Voltaic family. The main concentration of Mossi-speaking peoples lies in the area to the east of the White Volta and stretches from Ouahigouya in the north to Salaga in the south.[4] I will refer to this as the Eastern group of Mossi-speaking peoples. To their west lie a series of Grusi-speaking peoples, the Sisala between Lambussie and the Sisili River and, sparsely settled down the valley of the Kulpawn, the Chakalle of the Wa District, the Tampolense and Vagala of Gonja, ruled by immigrant Guang-speaking chiefs,[5] the Degha (or Mo) in southern Gonja and

---

[1]Greenberg, 1949; Westermann, 1927. In an earlier paper (1935) Westermann himself presented evidence for the inclusion of Bantu in the Sudanic group.

[2]1887.

[3]The Cercle de Goua in which the large proportion of Lobi-speaking peoples dwell, has at times been administered as part of the Ivory Coast.

[4]See the sketch-map in Fortes 1945, p. 5.

[5]Guang is a Kwa language.

WEST AFRICA

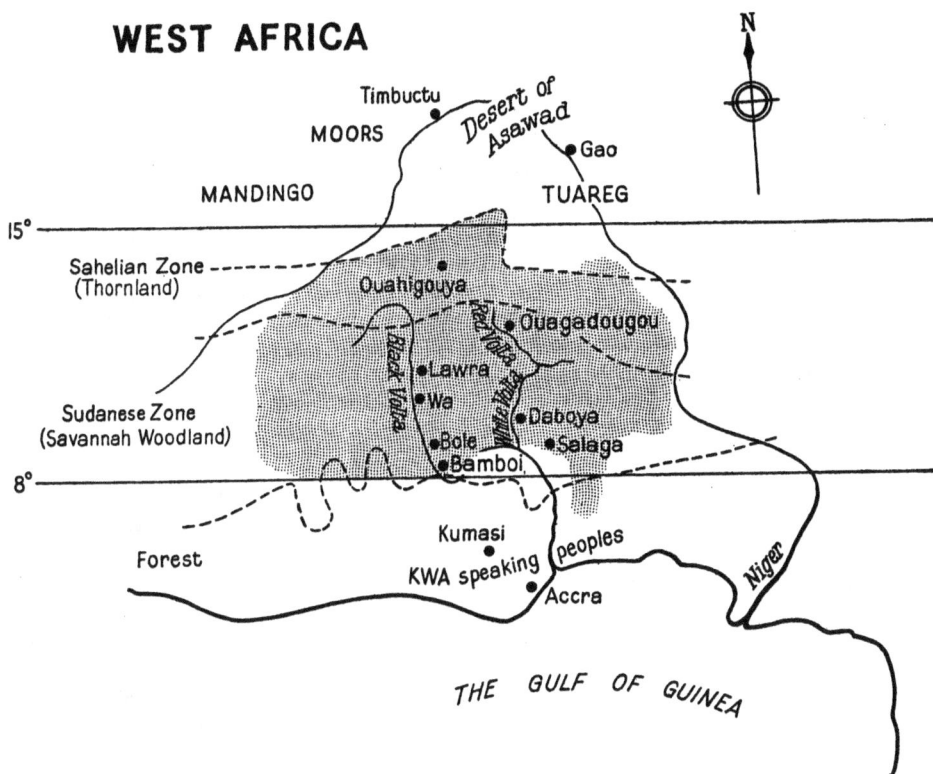

FIG.1. CLIMATIC ZONES AND LANGUAGE FAMILIES WITHIN THE NIGER BEND
The shaded area shows the distribution of the Voltaic speaking peoples

the north-west of Ashanti,[1] and, in the Ivory Coast, the Siti and Degha.[2]

To the east of the Grusi-speaking peoples, and largely bounded by them in the north and the south, live the western group of Mossi-speakers, that is, the Birifor, the Wiili,[3] the LoDagaba and the Dagaba.[4] I refer to these as the Dagari-speaking peoples. Other peoples speaking Mossi languages are found to the south in western Gonja, namely the Nome,[5] the Mara and the Safaliba;[6] these form a

---

[1]Rattray, 1932, gives some account of all except the Mo, about whom he remarks that he collected a word list but lost it. There is an unpublished paper, dated 1948, by H. C. Holmes, in the Chief Regional Office, Tamale, entitled: "Some notes on the Native Customs of the Mos of the Northern Territories". It is unfortunate that no means has been found of publishing these papers submitted by District Commissioners. Ethnographical knowledge of West Africa is not in a position to ignore the most sketchy report; and some of these essays represent substantial contributions to the subject.

[2]The Degha are identified by Delafosse with the Mo, 1904, p. 218. For the ethnography see Tauxier, 1921, pp. 397, 734.

[3]The Oulé, Oulé-Oulé or Dagari Oulé of French writers; the only references in English occur in the 1921 Census Report and in Armitage, 1924.

[4]Rattray, 1932, uses the terms Lober and Dagaba for these two groups.

[5]Armitage, 1924, p. 4. In order to avoid confusing the sketch-map, I have not shown the location of these people who are under the rule of Gonja chiefs. Of the five villages mentioned by Armitage, Nyenyeno is now inhabited only by immigrant Birifor; at Konfosi I was informed that the language, which also belonged to the Mossi group, was called Batigi. Kulmasa and Sonyeri should be added to his list.

[6]These are mentioned by Armitage. Reference to the Safaliba is also made by A. Duncan-Johnstone, 1930.

tongue stretching from Daboya and Yapei to the south of Bole and I include them in the group of Western Mossi speakers with whom they are contiguous.

Situated to the west of the Black Volta are the Lobi-speaking peoples, whose location Labouret has given in some detail.[1] Among the "tribes of the Lobi branch", he includes the Birifor. In attempting to disentangle the uses to which the appellations "Lobi" and "Dagarti" have been put, I am at this stage concerned only with linguistic criteria. I therefore follow Delafosse in classifying the Birifor with the Western Mossi group; their language cannot be comprehended by the Lobi proper and is understood by all the Western Mossi speakers. I would add that the boundary areas are bilingual. A few Lobi speakers have followed the recent Birifor migration into western Gonja where they are known as *Miwɔɔ*.

The sketch map of the territory along the middle reaches of the Black Volta (Fig. 2) gives the situation in its broad outlines.

The distribution map is based on Labouret's work and upon my own enquiries. The tribal nomenclature derives from the names used by neighbouring groups; Labouret's designations are given in parenthesis. I have used Dagaba as a blanket-term, aware that the complexities of the situation are thereby concealed; the continuous series of changes in institutions over the whole region makes prolonged research essential to a satisfactory classification.

The direction of those migrations which have been investigated during the course of the research is shown by means of arrows. In addition to these, former inhabitants of the Lawra District are establishing settlements, such as Piri, Tanina, Ga and Yipaala, along the Wa-Bole road.

The underlined villages in the Wa area (Wa, Dorimon and Wetchiau) are inhabited by 'white' Walas (*Wal piene*) who have a complex system of chieftain-ship apparently connected with the Dagomba, and regard themselves as rulers of the other inhabitants of the area.

The villages similarly marked in the Bole District are inhabited by Voltaic-speaking peoples such as the Vagala, but like those of the Grusi further north, these are ruled by Gonja chiefs. These nucleated villages are quite distinct from the dispersed settlements of the Birifor, Wiili and LoDagaba.

The main towns on the trade routes have a considerable stranger population inhabiting the trading quarter or *Zongo*. In the Lawra District, Babile, Kwŏn-yukwŏ, Lawra, Flyboyiri, Nandom and, on the international frontier, Dapla and Hamile are the most important of these centres.

Camps of Ewe fishermen from the coast are situated on the Black Volta near Lawra, Dapla and Dorimon.

I have been concerned to indicate at some length the whereabouts of the Lobi and Dagari-speaking peoples[2] for the terms are in constant use by the inhabitants to indicate some respect in which their social institutions differ from those of neighbouring groups. But I shall be primarily concerned with only a small section of the Dagari-speaking peoples inhabiting the settlement of Birifu on the bank of the Black Volta, some ten miles south of Lawra, the administrative headquarters of the north-west corner of the Northern Territories of the Gold Coast.[3]

---

[1] 1931, p. 50.

[2] Under Dagari, I include all the languages of the Eastern Mossi group. These are closely related to each other and appear to differ not more than the dialects of English spoken within the British Isles.

[3] The name of the settlement Birifu, which is inhabited by the people I call the LoWiili, should not be confused with the "tribal" name Birifor, a people living in the Haute Volta. The words are phonetically the same (*Birifɔ*). I do not know of any connection between them.

4

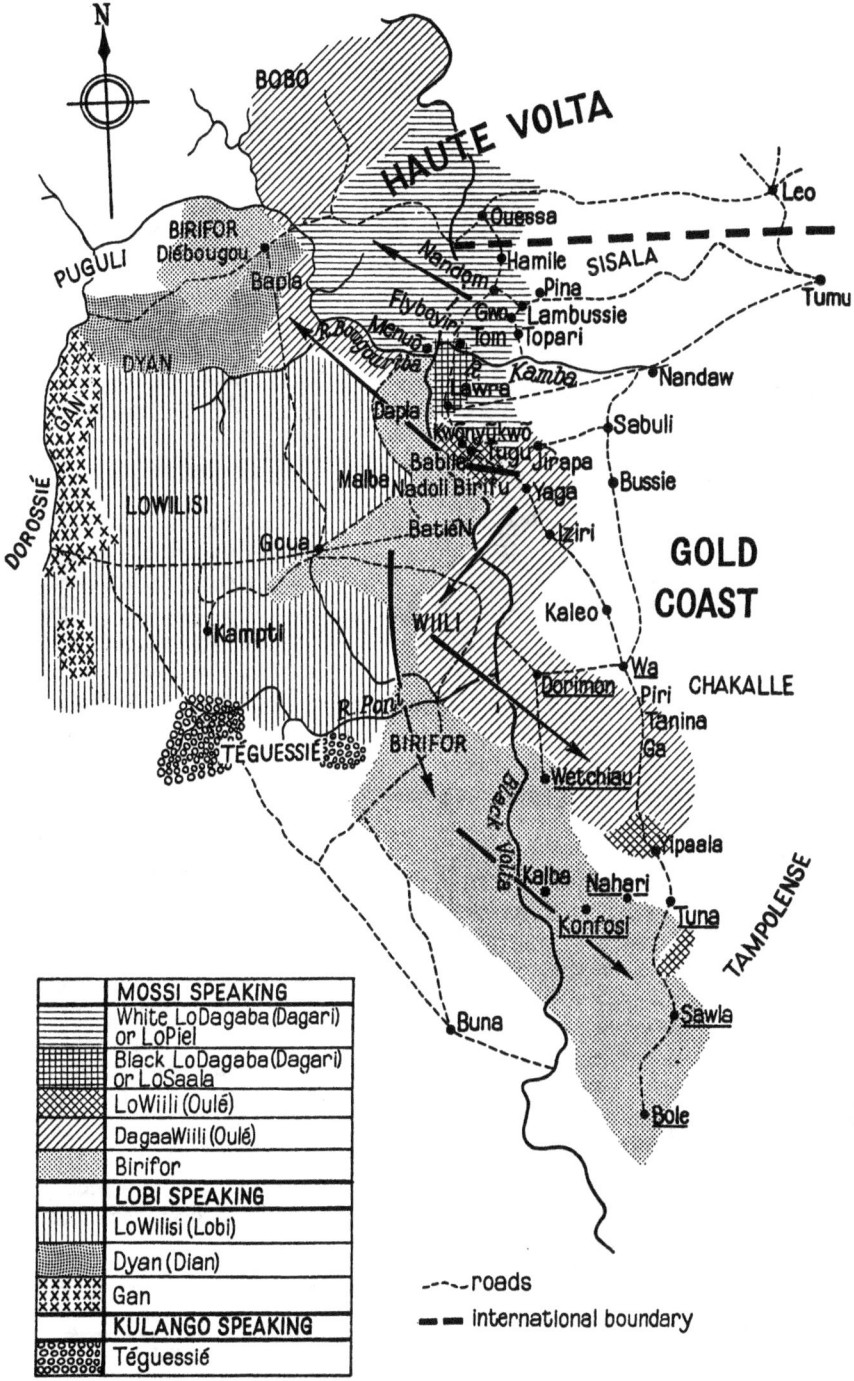

FIG.2. THE DISTRIBUTION OF LOBI AND DAGARI SPEAKING PEOPLES

5

Geological Formations

The physical appearance of the region is typical of the Northern Territories, a gently undulating countryside with broad valley bottoms where, in the wet season, the dried gullies suddenly become violent streams rushing into the Volta.

A belt of a few miles width along the east bank of the river lies on a Lower Birrimian formation and is marked by steep slopes and sudden scarps of red laterite. Further east, the Upper Birrimian is characterized by a flatter, more rolling, landscape where granite outcrops protrude through stoney farmland. Hinds in his "Agricultural Survey of the Lawra-Wa area"[1] maintains that the soils derived from these formations give rise to different systems of agriculture. Over the Lower Birrimian "the bewildering variety", which show a tendency "to become sorted out as soil catenas", cause the farmer "to hunt around choosing land to suit each individual crop . . . unable to get any single large piece of land on which to grow all crops in rotation". But although the population is concentrated on the Lower Birrimian, no doubt because of the presence of adequate supplies of water, the granite appears to provide better farming land. The Lower Birrimian soils tend to form laterite a short distance below the surface; in most farms these rough reddish blocks protrude through the soil and occasionally a flat denuded plateau of solid laterite makes cultivation impossible. Local farming methods, particularly the construction of mounds, are considered to assist the erosion of the top soil. The inhabitants constantly give as a reason for migration the lack of farmland. There is little justification for interpreting this as necessarily indicating exhaustion or erosion of the soil at the previous settlement, although loss of yield due to continuous farming is undoubtedly a factor in present movements from the Lawra district.

Climate

The mean maximum daily temperature is $96 \cdot 4°$ Fahrenheit, the minimum, $71 \cdot 5°$; the rainfall averages $48 \cdot 96''$ a year.[2] The rain is concentrated in six months of the year, April to October, and falls in sudden downpours, preceded by violent atmospheric storms and followed by dry spells of two or three days, even two weeks, during which the inhabitants become more and more anxious about their harvest and resort to various ritual procedures to secure a sufficiency for the growing crops. Rain provides a constant topic of conversation during the farming season.

The sharp climatic break between wet and dry seasons imposes its own pattern of activity. The first heavy rain announces the beginning of the farming season. Except for unwelcome dry spells, most males above the age of twelve are, from May or early June, engaged in farming from dawn to dusk; dancing, sacrifices and hunting fade into the background. Hoeing is heavy work, weeds grow rapidly, agricultural obligations are numerous. Attendance at local markets drops off, even on the day (*ta kwɔr daa*) when hoeing is forbidden.[3]

---

[1] 1951.

[2] These figures, supplied by the Government Meteorological Service, were recorded at Lawra over periods of 13 and 24 years respectively. Readings taken at Babile Agricultural Station during the last few years show an annual mean rainfall of about 45″.

[3] Markets recur every six days on the eastern bank of the Volta; there are no names for the days apart from the names of neighbouring markets, some of which have now ceased to exist although they continue to be used as days of the week. Weekly time is essentially market time.

By the end of August, hoeing is over; many of the young men and boys set off for Ashanti to work as dry season labourers on cocoa farms or on the roads. The tempo of ritual activities quickens; the young men and girls take part in ceremonial and informal dancing; the men attend market regularly; intercourse between villages increases.

Some crops are harvested as early as July but the main harvest of guinea-corn occurs in November after the rains have stopped. Before the pools and ditches near the compounds have dried up, house-building begins; for the water is required for making the mud with which the houses are built.

Vegetation

The size and density of the trees are well conveyed in the phrase "orchard bush". The trees thin rapidly with the increase in population and the length of settlement. When the population density has reached a figure of 50 per square mile, a characteristic selection has been made at the old established villages. Only baobabs (Adansonia digitata—*Tuɔ*) and a few dawa-dawa (Parkia oliveri—*Duɔ*) remain among the edible fruit trees; although shea (Butyrospermum parkii—*Tāän*) are spared outside the limit of continuous cultivation. Within this area, little else is found apart from the occasional Acacia albida (*Guo*), Diospyros mespiliformis (*Gaa*) and silk cotton (Ceiba pentendra—*Gɔ̃*), so great is the demand for firewood, roofing poles, ladders and dug-out canoes. A small cluster of trees will almost certainly turn out to be an Earth shrine (*teŋgaan*) or an altar connected with the hill and water spirits (*kontome*).

In the uncultivated woodland (*wio*) the baobab, dawa-dawa and silk cotton appear to be associated with deserted sites of former habitation. Only fire-resistant trees survive the annual burnings of the bush, an essential preliminary to hunting.

Communications, Trade, and Labour Migration

In pre-European times, the local population appear to have travelled little, although traders continually passed through their settlements and attended local markets.

The river system is little used for communication; dug-out canoes can be employed only for crossing rivers and even this short journey is surrounded by considerable dangers in the wet season. During the last thirty years, however, Ewe fishermen from the coast have established camps in the district, from which, in the dry season, they make trips lasting four to six weeks. The fish is dried and sent by lorry to Ashanti markets.

The arrival of Europeans found a long-established trade route passing through Wa, Lawra, then crossing the Volta at Menuõ to Diébougou; salt, 'mossi' cloth and cattle came from the north, kola and manufactured trade goods from the south.[1]

The coming of motor transport and the construction of a bridge over the Volta in French territory have diverted the Diébougou traffic through Nandom and Ouessa. Although the volume of trade has increased immensely with the new means of conveyance, its character has remained basically the same. The imported goods which Delafosse reported in the market at Wa in 1901 are essentially those to be found today on a Zongo trader's stand anywhere in the Northern Territories. The extent of trade can be judged by the records kept at Bamboi where a ferry

---

[1] *v.* Binger, 1892, Vol. I, p. 372; 2nd Lawra Record Book, p. 268.

crosses the Black Volta, which forms at this point the administrative boundary between Ashanti and the Northern Territories. The figures for the most important goods, given in Table 1, were supplied by the Department of Agriculture.

Table 1

GOODS PASSING THROUGH BAMBOI AND OUESSA

NORTHBOUND	Bamboi		Ouessa
	Tons 1943	Tons 1949	Tons 1951 (Jan.-June)
Kola Nuts	294·0	817·4	470
Oranges	·4	70·4	
Salt	372·0	741·1	

SOUTHBOUND	Bamboi		Ouessa
	Tons 1943	Tons 1949	Tons 1951 (Jan.-June)
Fish (smoked) . . .	17·4	390·3	140
Groundnuts	133·8	1,286·3	
Groundnut oil . . .	·2	35·9	
Guinea Corn. . . .	1·2	26·4	
Kapok floss	2·4	46·9	
Meat (smoked) . . .	—	49·0	
Millet	—	30·7	
Shea butter	61·5	163·6	
Beans	—	181·2	107
Yams	50·5	411·4	
Livestock			
Cattle	880	2,714	
Fowls	9,060	35,820	
Goats	23	11,094	7,500
Sheep	4,212	15,813	4,000

The third column shows the amount of goods which passed through the French customs post at Ouessa during the six months January to June, 1951. It may be assumed that the foodstuffs not mentioned in that column were mainly purchased in the Northern Territories, and, apart from the shea butter and yams, in the Lawra district. In Babile market, one of the largest centres for the sale of food-stuffs in the north-west, groundnuts and beans are the main local crop sold to traders, the former being regarded as the cash crop *par excellence*. The grain offered for sale in this market has nearly all been carried across the Black Volta; few of the local inhabitants have themselves any to spare, but the sparser population in the Ivory Coast can practise shifting cultivation and obtain better

8

yields. This appears to have been true for many years past; a number of stories are told of people who were sold to the Lɔɔri ("Lobi", in this case the Birifor) in time of famine and yet few instances are found where they themselves were in a position to acquire slaves (s. gbaŋbaa). The prospect of abundant farmland undoubtedly led to migrations from the east to the west of the river before the arrival of the Europeans at the turn of the century.

Although most of the goods which pass through the north-west are the subject of transactions which take place outside the area, local markets thrive, particularly in the dry season. The selling of groundnuts and beans to traders, pots and baskets to other women and cooked food and beer for immediate consumption, is a woman's task. The local men may be seen trading kola, tobacco, calabashes and various wooden objects, but mainly they just go to drink beer and talk. The social occasion plays a dual rôle in announcing common interests in the economic sphere and emphasizing cleavages of a territorial nature. At Babile market in the past, men from the surrounding settlements of Tanchera, Tugu and Birifu sat down to drink in their own sectors of the market place, with bow and quiver to hand; for a fight might easily start, particularly as the market dispersed. Early records of the Administration and tales of the older men make the special association of the custodian of the Earth shrine (teŋgaansob) with the market place quite comprehensible, for here violence was most likely to occur and this would result in breaking the prohibition of the Earth against the shedding of blood.

These small markets are the centres for the distribution of European goods as well as of local produce. Rarely does one find a woman nowadays who cannot produce at least one towel or cloth; and hoe blades, hurricane lamps and matches are now considered as necessities by the men. The purchase of these and other goods, and the payments of taxes levied by the Native Authority, are made within the framework of an agricultural economy that present conditions and accounts of the past suggest has had difficulty in producing a sufficiency of food, quite apart from a surplus.

The main factor in increasing the volume of goods exchanged has undoubtedly been seasonal labour migration. In the early days of the Administration, the local chiefs established by the British Administration were encouraged to supply recruits for work in mines and on the railways. As a result, numbers of the young men came in contact with the achievements of a more developed technology and earned the money to acquire some of its products. The time required to cover the 300 miles to Kumasi meant that these recruits were not available during the farming season. Although there was little or no immediate economic gain to the community, the foundations of future developments were laid.[1] The migration thus set in motion continued under its own momentum. The arrival of motor transport in the middle twenties enabled young men to travel down to Kumasi when they had done their share of the heavy farm work and return in time for the next wet season. Economically the community profited, for little "productive work" is done by the men after the guinea corn harvest.

The numbers involved in the annual migration are considerable, the vast majority working on Ashanti cocoa farms or as temporary labourers on the roads. Labour in the mines is less popular, particularly now that the inhabitants associate

[1] See the complaint of Chief of Zinni about the absence of the young men, recorded in the Lawra District Diary for 23rd June, 1923, to which the Commissioner replied: "Very aggravating, but it is really the first steps towards this country coming to a further state of civilization."

9

a persistent and sometimes fatal cough with work underground. Some return after as little as four months, bringing a wooden box with a padlock holding a length of cloth for themselves and other clothes for their kinsfolk. The goal is a bicycle, but this requires self-denial and continuous employment for a good half year. Table 2 gives the records of the Bamboi ferry check showing the numbers of passengers for the post-war years; the columns show the total for a calendar year and therefore those dry season labourers going south in any one year should be included in the northbound travellers of the following year.

Table 2

PASSENGERS CROSSING BY THE BAMBOI FERRY

	1945	1946	1947	1948	1949
Southbound					
British subjects . . .	8,443	19,134	21,620	35,684	36,198
French subjects . . .	9,899	7,252	15,872	24,205	35,154
Northbound					
British subjects . . .	4,435	24,791	21,476	35,503	38,129
French subjects . . .	3,975	3,642	11,454	23,352	24,294

Total (1945–9): Southbound . 213,361 Northbound . 191,031

Of a sample[1] of 122 Birifu men and youths over sixteen, at least twenty had been to Kumasi the previous dry season; two others had remained during the next farming season. In addition, another eight had been absent for longer periods. The 1948 Census records that of 159,646 "Lobi" and "Dagarti" in the Gold Coast, 14,179 or 9% were living outside the Northern Territories in February, 1948. By February, the cocoa has been harvested and the dry season labourers have usually returned to their villages. This percentage is higher than for any other tribe indigenous to the Northern Territories.[2] This annual migration has had comparatively little effect as yet on the organized social life of the community, for the average age of these labourers cannot greatly exceed twenty. Indeed, during my stay, a number of boys of between fourteen and sixteen succeeded in "running down to Kumasi", and a number of others attempted to go but were stopped trying to board a lorry. The south proves an irresistible temptation to expelled schoolchildren, to those who have completed their primary education without having been selected for further training and to many others attracted by the possibility of a life other than that of farming. Tensions within the domestic family provide an additional reason for migration. I once saw an elder pass his own stool for his "grandson" to sit on; the latter was wearing a cloth which he wanted to keep clean. I protested that this was unseemly behaviour and was later told by the old man, who had laughed nervously at my words, that if he failed to treat the boy well, he would run off to Ashanti. A sister's son living and farming with his mother's brother appears more likely to go than a son farming with his father, a situation which seems at first sight incompatible with the freer relations between adjacent generations of matrilateral, as compared with agnatic kin. But sisters' sons actually living with their mother's patri-kinsfolk are tied by a number of additional rights and duties, those which operate

[1] Consisting of all males over 16 in a patriclan sector.
[2] Compare Fortes' estimate of 7% for the Tallensi, 1949, p. 72.

10

among members of a residential group, the inhabitants of one house, whether or not they are agnates. At the same time they are not bound to the head of the house, as are his sons, by joint title to a common patrimony.

Contact with other societies

The recorded history of the Lobi and Dagari-speaking peoples begins with the advent of the European military forces in the last years of the nineteenth century. The empires of the Western Sudan had their Arab historians but references to the Voltaic peoples are confined to the Dogon, to the Gurma, and to the Mossi who in 1333 are said to have sacked Timbuktu and penetrated the desert beyond.[1] According to Bovill[2], the great empire of Ghana obtained slaves, for sale on the North African litoral, from the "primitive forest tribes beyond the southern frontier". Delafosse writes of the "Lobi", shortly after the occupation of their country, "ils échangent leur or contre du sel provenant du Sahara; ils n'en fabriquent aucun bijou et ne le montrent jamais".[3] Certainly the trade in slaves and gold formed the economic basis for the wealth of these Niger empires, and the penetration of the Mandingos into Western Lobiland is not unconnected with this fact.

The subjects of the Wala and the Gonja apart, such contact as there may have been has had little effect on the segmentary societies of the region. In Wa there exists a tradition of migration from Dagomba as the result of a quarrel over the chieftainship and indeed the political organizations of these peoples bear strong resemblances to one another. On their arrival in the district, the Wala relate, they encountered the "Lobi" (*Lobisi*) who moved westwards across the Volta.[4] A Hausa manuscript[5] claims that the Mamprusi "brought under subjection the Grunshi, likewise the Moshi, the Dagombawa, and the Gurmawa. The men of Gambaga ruled over the Lobi and as far as the country of the Kolansawa". Of such a state of 'subjection' no trace remains in the oral traditions of the subjected. When Delafosse visited the Koulango in 1901, the "King of Bouna" claimed his kingdom extended over the "Lobi" dwelling between his capital and Diébougou and tried his utmost to dissuade the International Boundary Commission from proceeding further north on the grounds that "les Lobi sont des sauvages qui ne reconnaissaient aucune autorité, ni la sienne, ni celle des Blancs, et qui vous lanceront des flèches empoisonnées dès qu'ils vous apercevront".[6]

The traders passing along the kola route through Bole, Wa and Lawra also left little mark on the social organization of the inhabitants. Even today the Zongos, or trading quarters, maintain but slight contact with the people around them outside the sphere of monetary transactions. I know of two instances of men who, after years in the army, adopted the Mohammedan faith on their return and went to live in the trading quarter. Mohammedan celebrations give these mixed communities a sense of homogeneity. Although Islam long ago penetrated the Voltaic region, its influence is important only in the centralized states such as Wa, Gonja, and Dagomba. Rattray suggests that the immigrant

---

[1] Bovill, 1933, p. 75.
[2] op. cit., p. 62.
[3] 1908, p. 182. Also Bovill, 1933, p. 248.
[4] The non-Mohammedan inhabitants of Wa are referred to as *Wala Dagaba*. They call *Lobisi* not only all Lobi speakers but also the Dagari speakers who live to the west of them, that is, the Wiili and the Birifor.
[5] J. Withers-Gill, 1924, p. 9.
[6] "Les Frontières . . .", p. 139.

founders of some of these states were "conversant with the rudiments of Mohammedanism"; certainly Islamic influences stimulated political centralization.[1] Missionary efforts were concentrated upon the ruling classes; the segmentary systems in the north-west gave little opportunity of successful entry. The elders of two Dagaba lineages maintained that forefathers had formerly "prayed to God" (*pure Nà'aŋmin*) but that they now no longer did so; both these groups claimed to have migrated from the vicinity of Wa. Outside the strangers' quarters, little evidence of Islamic influence remains.

Contact with Europe

In 1854, Barth penetrated the Niger bend and recorded his careful observations; but he touched only the fringe of the Voltaic peoples. The Arab travellers of the middle ages were concerned with the impressive Niger towns and the trade routes to the north, not with the country to the south. Timbuktu and the Niger remained the goal of European explorers of the late eighteenth and nineteenth centuries, such as Park, Laing and Caillé. Despite this activity, no successful approach to the Volta basin from the north was made until the French military missions to Ougadougou in the early nineties.

The desert in the north and the tropical forest to the south created such difficulties for the European that, although the empires of the Western Sudan had been known through the works of the medieval Arab writers, and the Guinea Coast had been the scene of some of the earliest 'factories' or trading posts, the Voltaic region itself remained virtually unknown.

By 1876 Europeans had explored the south of the present Northern Territories from Ashanti. Dr. Gouldsbury reached Salaga in that year; Captain Lonsdale's journey took place in 1881.[2] Some years later (1886-7) G. A. Krause, travelling alone from Togoland and carrying his entire belongings on his back, reached Dienné, Bandiagara, 'Mossi', 'Grunshi' and finally Kintampo. The following year another German, von François, travelled to the south of Mossiland and down to Salaga.

The greatest exploratory voyage of the period was that made by Binger[3] through western Lobiland, southern Mossi and Dagomba during the two years 1888 and 1889. Basing himself on the methods and experience of Barth, he assembled the detailed and accurate statements about the country and its inhabitants that had made the German explorer's account so important a contribution to knowledge of the Western Sudan. Binger travelled to the west and north of the Dagari speakers, crossing the territory of the Lobi-speaking people. But his map first indicates the position of the "Oulé", the "Dagabakha", the "Dagari" and the "State of Wa".

The activities of the French at this time caused some concern to the Governor of the Gold Coast, Sir William Maxwell, and in 1889 G. E. Ferguson was dispatched to negotiate treaties with chiefs on the eastern side of what became the Northern Territories. This was followed by a second mission to the western side during which treaties were signed with Buna and Wa[4]. He does not, however, appear to have penetrated into the present Lawra District.

---

[1] 1932, p. xii.

[2] Cardinall, "The Gold Coast, 1931".

[3] See "Du Niger au Golfe de Guinée", 1892.

[4] Labouret, 1925, p.349, and Cardinall, "The Gold Coast, 1931", p. 30. Cardinall gives a short biography of this African survey officer, explorer and political agent of whom Northcot , first Chief Commissioner for the area, wrote: "The map of the Northern Territories owes its outline to the astronomical observations and road traverses of the late Mr. Ferguson . . ."

In November, 1896, a military expedition under the command of Lieutenant Henderson was dispatched to Bole and Buna which were then occupied by the forces of the Mandingo freebooter, Samori, whom the French had recently driven from the north. Henderson reached Bole without difficulty and moved on to Wa. The inhabitants of Buna, who had fled to the Birifor village of Dokita when Samori's son and chief military leader, Saranti Mori, sacked the town, asked for the assistance of the British force. The British accepted this request and were defeated by the enemy, a defeat which led to the death of Ferguson, Henderson's capture and the evacuation of Wa. Nevertheless, the east bank of the Black Volta had been virtually freed of slave-raiders for, previous to the Dokita episode, Henderson had made his way along the Wa-Tumu route, interviewed Babatu,[1] the Zaberima leader of a largely Grusi slave-raiding band, and persuaded him to exclude first 'Dagarti', then 'Grunshi' from the area of his activities. A few years previously, in 1893, some of Babatu's Grusi followers had rebelled as a result of the Zaberima continuing to sell the women of their country as slaves; they then formed another band under one of their number, Hamaria, known at the time as "King of the Grunshi".[2]

The inhabitants on the right bank of the Volta suffered considerably from Samori's forces, while the Lawra district was visited by Babatu and by other raiders. Birifu itself escaped. The story is told that eggs were thrown into a stream to the north which flooded its banks to such an extent that the Zaberima were unable to cross.

Around the town of Ulu a defensive wall was built, of the same sort Henderson had remarked on his journey from Wa to Tumu[3]; this served as an operational base for a local freebooter, Boyon, a Dagaba modelling himself on the Zaberima pattern. Henderson[4] refers to "Grunshi" (i.e. the area occupied by Grusi-speaking peoples) as a series of "independent village communities, bound loosely under the protection of large towns". There are other suggestions of such a pattern in the early District records, associated with the area in which the activities of Babatu and Hamaria were concentrated, along the trade route between Wa and Tumu which leads to Ouagadougou, the southern capital of the Mossi.

Slave-raiding in the Lawra District was most severe where it adjoins Grusi territory; travelling only a little further north, Binger expressed surprise at seeing a Grusi village which had escaped pillage by the Zaberima.[5] The Grusi were the real prey both of the Zaberima and the Mossi[6] slave-raiders. The south of the Lawra district lay on the periphery of their sphere of action and incursions were consequently infrequent. At the rumour of their coming or at the sight of headless bodies drifting down the Volta, the inhabitants would rush across the river, abandoning their granaries to the horsemen; at dusk the men would secretly creep back to collect some food and when sufficient confidence had been regained the population would return to their homes. Slave-raiding left little trace of any permanent effect on the institutions of the Lobi and Dagari-speaking peoples.

---

[1]About 1860, Alfa Kazaré, referred to by Henderson and Delafosse as Gandiari, gathered a band of plunderers from Dzerma, on the banks of the Niger, and some twenty years later was raiding "Grunshi" from within; after his death in an attack on the Kipirsi, his place was taken by his deputy, Babatu. Labouret, 1925, p. 344.

[2]See the dispatch from the Governor to Secretary of State, 31st March, 1897, Public Records Office.

[3]1898, p. 491.

[4]p. 490.

[5]Binger, Vol. II, p. 4.

[6]Binger, Vol. I, p. 485.

Shortly before the departure of Henderson's expedition, French forces entered Ougadougou, the seat of the Mogho-Naba, paramount chief of the Mossi,[1] and subsequently established themselves in Wa. By the end of the following year, another British force had been sent to Wa to occupy "Dagarti".[2] Reconnaissances were then made further north but even in Northcote's report of 1899 no town in the Lawra District is marked on the map; all is shown as "Grunshi". Actual contact with the British was made between this date and the visit of the Boundary Commission in 1901.

Europeans had previously been known to the peoples of the Voltaic basin by the trade goods which circulated along old established routes through the hands of Mande and Hausa merchants. Binger and Henderson both comment on the interruption to this trade caused by the slave-raiders, and assumed that their journeys had coincided with periods of exceptional turmoil.

Military occupation rapidly followed exploration and the area was divided between the two conquering powers. The Administration established a hierarchy of chiefs, sub-chiefs and headmen where none existed before. The imposition of a centralized system which disallowed the use of armed force except on its own conditions made travel safer; the area of social intercourse widened considerably. From the first, young men were encouraged to join the military forces or go to work in Ashanti and the Colony. The establishment of a system of law and order over a wide area led to greatly increased contact with other African societies and later to the introduction of missions, schools, courts and dispensaries. A series of fundamental changes spring from the initial fact of European rule and these have only begun to impinge upon the social life of the inhabitants.

In view of later political developments, it is important to realize that although chiefs in the Lawra District were officially appointed by the Administration, there was a real sense in which their authority was delegated by their subjects. If a majority of the people consistently disobeyed a chief, the Commissioner would usually ask them to choose another whom they would agree to follow. The chief, therefore, occupied a double position, at the apex of a system of delegated authority and as a link in the controlling organization established by the conquering powers. The interlocking of these two systems was possible because both were of the pyramidal type. Although the elements of delegation and control are present in any political system of this hierarchical kind, the distinction made depends upon a recognition of the degree of emphasis placed upon these two aspects in any particular case.

History of the Lawra District

Scattered on small hillocks and scarcely perceptible rises in the ground throughout the Lawra District are to be found numerous reddish grey pottery fragments covered in a rouletted decoration and quite distinct from the black ware now in use. Among the sherds are handles and hollow bases, features which do not appear on present-day pots. These fragments are invariably ascribed to the *Dʒanni* who formerly dwelt on and "owned" the land, migrating to Diébougou (*Nyibu*) when the present inhabitants arrived. The sites of their former compounds are well known; indeed, in the bush one often finds small farms deliberately made on such mounds because of the beneficial effect of human

---

[1] On the 1st Sept., 1896, according to Dim Delobsom, "L'Empire du Mogho-Naba", Paris, 1932, p. 36. Labouret, 1931, gives an account of French movements at this period.

[2] Dispatches received by the Secretary of State on 7th Jan. and 11th Feb., 1898, Public Records Office.

detritus on the crops. This tradition of earlier occupation by the Dyan, a Lobi-speaking people, is confirmed independently by their own migration histories.[1] Pottery examined in Diébougou was identical with the surface fragments collected in the Lawra District. At one site, Tobil (at Flyboyiri, near Nandom), I found examples of similar pottery, on which a regular pattern consistently appeared, to a depth of seven feet. The disintegration of mud-built houses creates a greater overlying deposit than would be the case with other building material, and an estimation of age is therefore difficult.

In their migration stories, the Dagari-speaking peoples, who now occupy the region, recall at least the settlement in which their ancestors previously dwelt and will sometimes give the names of a series of villages extending some fifty miles away. In nearly every case investigated, the named villages contained members of the same exogamous patriclan, holding in common a clan name, the concept of descent in the agnatic line from an unspecified ancestor (*saakum*, "grandfather"), the obligation to render assistance in war, and ideally, in terms of the actor situation, a totemic animal or other prohibition. Each local sector of these patriclans has its own migration story; a known ancestor, from two to four generations removed from the present elders, abandoned his former home because of lack of farming land, a bad harvest or, very occasionally, because of pressure from another group, in order to occupy new land usually discovered while hunting in the bush[2]. In certain cases the local sectors of two patriclans now living together maintain that they did so in their previous settlement, and that one founding ancestor followed the other. This may be explained in terms of clanship, the clans standing in a joking partnership to one another as the result of which the presence of both was essential to the well-being of each, or in terms of kinship, the founding ancestor of the second clan sector to arrive being a sister's son of the first settler.

The generation depth between the founder of any local descent group and the present senior representative is two to four generations. Labouret gives five generations back as the point when the Lobi-speaking Dyan, "Tuna" and LoWilisi abandoned the left bank of the Volta.[3]

Eyre-Smith[4] maintains that the "Lobis and Dagaris from around Wa and the Janni (i.e. Dyan) people from what is now the Lawra District" were driven out by "bands of marauders armed with Dane guns, consisting of Dagombas . . . , Tampoulimas (i.e. Tampolense), and possibly Gonjas". The Dane guns arrived from the Coast during the later part of the seventeenth century, coinciding with the rise to power of the Ashantis and the establishment of the Gonja state. This "tremendous invasion of the north-west of the Northern Territories" began from Daboya, a town of great importance on account of its salt flats and "the centre from which Ashanti levies radiated in search of slaves". Eyre-Smith's fanciful association of place names does not create great confidence in the evidence he presents. But the expedition from Dagomba forms part of the Wala traditions and their expulsion of the Birifor appears to coincide with the north-westerly movement of the other Dagari-speaking peoples. Local traditions tend to confirm the

---

[1]Labouret, 1931, p. 24, "Les Dian".

[2]I have heard it stated in several such stories that the Dyan left only after the arrival of the new-comers.

[3]Labouret, 1931, p. 23 *et seq.* The estimated date of 1770, based on the assumption of thirty years to a generation, would seem reasonable. A large baobab grew out of the debris of a Dyan house at Tobil; a forestry officer suggested this tree was between 150 and 200 years old.

[4]1933(b), p. 12.

supposition of a general movement of peoples as the result of pressure from the south.

A distinction must be drawn between this type of movement, set in motion by military pressure and involving the expulsion of the previous inhabitants from their farmland, and the piecemeal migration of individuals and small groups into bush areas from the thickly populated settlements. Labouret has described the Lobi as "très mobile". Some hundred miles to the south, the Birifor, who claim to have come from the vicinity of Wa five generations ago, are now recrossing the Volta into the sparsely inhabited areas of Western Gonja. One of the oldest of these settlements is Kalba; an entry under this name in the Record Book for Western Gonja, dated 1919, remarked on the twelve recently built "Lobi" compounds. The 1948 census gives the "Lobi" population of Gonja as 7,333, the great majority of whom have arrived in the last forty years.

Men still decide to leave their natal settlements for new areas where land is plentiful and higher yields can be obtained owing to the increased fertility of land left fallow. These moves take place over a considerable distance. Before the European came, inhabitants of Birifu were settling at Bapla, south of Diébougou, a distance of some twenty miles. The establishment of an international boundary along the Volta discouraged this general trend of movement from south-east to north-west, which was also apparent at Lawra and Nandom. Later, resistance to the French Administration, the subsequent repressive measures and the higher level of taxation required to develop a poorer colony led to considerable migration of Birifor and DagaaWiili into the thinly inhabited areas of Wa and Gonja. The early pressure upon the Administration for labour in the south and the coming of motor transport led to the discovery of, and movement to, the land along the Kumasi road between Wa and Bole, now settled mainly by migrants from within the Gold Coast, the more densely populated areas of Lawra and Jirapa.

The reason given for past moves is almost without exception in terms of lack of food or farmland. But examination of contemporary instances reveals inter-personal conflict situations in the context of which the decision to migrate is made.

There is reason to believe that a general movement of population, partly invasion, partly migration, has placed limiting factors on the use of genealogical connections in organizing social relationships; it is a question which will be returned to later. The organization of local groups must in any case be capable of dealing with the individual migrations and of providing a framework in which descent groups of diverse depth and span can co-operate.

Tribeship

I have mentioned that the community with which I shall be mainly concerned is the Dagari-speaking settlement of Birifu, situated on the eastern bank of the Black Volta some ten miles south of Lawra, the administrative centre of the north-western district of the Gold Coast. I have called these people the LoWiili, a name under which I include a few other people living nearby. The name LoWiili is not one used by the people themselves nor by any of their neighbours. How and why I adopted it I will explain in the following pages.

I went to West Africa looking for a "tribe" called the "Lobi". Previous writers had reported the existence of such a people in the border regions of the Gold Coast and the Haute Volta. In fact I never found a group of people who replied to my questions, "We are Lobi". The word Lobi, or variations of it, is known throughout the area; I shall use the root form *Lo* to avoid the difficulties arising from these differences of dialect. When I first asked, the *Lo* always appeared to live in some settlement other than the speaker's. It gradually became clear that *Lo* (*Lɔɔr*, *Loba*, Angl. Lobi) and *Dagaa* (*Dagari*, *Dagaba*, Angl. Dagarti) were a pair of words used throughout the area by a congeries of peoples to refer to their neighbours and occasionally to themselves.[1] There are no individual "tribal" names, for indeed there are no tribes in the accepted sense of the word.

Nadel has defined a tribe or people as "a group the members of which claim unity on the grounds of their conception of a specific common culture"[2]. The existence of a name is the criterion of the consciousness of unity in this, "the widest, loosest unit in the hierarchy of communities". These designations consist of two types, actor names, those applied by the group to itself, and observer names, those used by neighbours. An actor name emerges when one major group requires, in a large number of verbal contexts, to dissociate itself from its neighbours, that is, where there exists a pronounced hiatus in social relations between the groups concerned. This hiatus may arise in connection with the reckoning of descent, spatial discontinuity, political allegiance or cultural differences.

In the North-West of the Gold Coast, there are few marked discontinuities. Unilineal descent groups are widely dispersed among peoples of different language and social organization. Compounds are scattered unevenly across the countryside in such a way that it is difficult to tell where one settlement ends and the next begins. There was no centralized political system before the advent of the British, nor does any group crystallize around a cohesive ritual institution such as the Great Festivals of the Talleñsi[3]. Cultural changes take place imperceptibly like dialects merging into one another. Group nomenclature, the actor's conceptualization of the social system, reflects this gradual merging. In other areas, names are normally found to be individual to each particular major group; these point to their differences by means of a series of mutually exclusive tribal designations.[4] But when we examine the system of group designations used in this region, we find that it is based not upon a series of exclusive tribal names but upon a "directional" system in which a number of contiguous peoples refer to themselves obliquely by means of two names.

It will be obvious that such a system introduces many complications for the outside observer. To a member of a western European society, it is almost inconceivable that a person should not be aware of his "nationality", whether he is French or Italian, Fulani or Ibo. Therefore, in making enquiries among these peoples, the responses of their informants have often been channelled into a similar mould. I shall first examine the usages of previous writers in order to clarify the ethnographic picture and to see where the difficulties lie. I shall then discuss the way in which this pair of words is used by the actors themselves and by the LoWiili in particular. The name LoWiili has been adopted in order to isolate a group of people who have certain common cultural features. The selection of the cultural features is based upon local usage, upon the manipulation of the words *Lo* and *Dagaa*. But the name itself I have "invented". In

---

[1] I use the words Lobi and Dagari with a purely linguistic reference.

[2] 1942, p.17.

[3] Fortes, 1945, p.28; 1936c.

[4] Mutually exclusive in a relative sense, for where there are several criteria of eligibility, the composition of the group may vary according to which is considered relevant in the particular context. See Goody, 1954(a).

acephalous societies, the lack of such a name is not as uncommon as often appears, for ethnographers have often adopted that used by their neighbours. In this case, the neighbours usually employ the same words *Lo* and *Dagaa*, and it becomes impossible to offer a classification on this basis. I have therefore had to make up names for these groups. In so doing I have chosen words which are sometimes used in the region, but never in the definite form I have used them here. A fuller explanation of this occupies the final section on tribeship.

In dealing with this question of "tribal" nomenclature, it is impossible to avoid treating the region as a whole and referring to the usages of neighbouring Lobi and Dagari-speaking peoples. Only in limited respects can the LoWiili be considered an isolated unit. The clarification of the ethnographic situation therefore requires a fairly lengthy discussion. This detailed treatment has another and more general application. If "tribal" names were more often examined in the context of the situation in which they were actually used, they would I think reveal that this is no singular example. The same sort of positional terminology may often be involved in names such as "easterners and westerners", "upper and lower people", "insiders and outsiders". From the reports of ethnographers it would seem that these have often enough been translated or adopted by them as "tribal" names. Quite apart then from the complexity of the situation, an extended discussion of this mechanism is perhaps merited by the possible generality of the phenomenon and by the absence of such discussions in previous accounts.

i *Usages of previous writers*

The descriptive nomenclature used by writers on this area has been extremely confused and the ethnological data consequently difficult to assess. The earliest known European traveller in these parts, Capitaine L. Binger[1], whose information was largely gathered from the Dagomba at Wale-Wale in 1888, records the supposed position of the State of Wa, the "Oulé" (Wiili), the "Lobi", the "Dianné" (Dyan), and the "Lama" (Sisala, who are known to the Dagari-speaking peoples as *Laŋbε*); the Sisala are shown to occupy the whole of the Lawra District. Mention is also made of the "Dagari" (LoDagaba) and the "Dagabakha" (Dagaba) who are assumed to be one and the same; the latter are placed in territory occupied by the Birifor.

Henderson, the commander of the first British expeditionary force to reach Wa, refers to the Birifor, of the village of Dokita, who sent for protection against the Mande slave-raider Samori, as "Lobi"; the whole of the area between Gonja and "Grunshi" (i.e. those speaking Grusi languages) he calls "Dagarti, of which Wa is the capital"[2]. This is the position in Northcott's map of the Northern Territories of 1899[3]. In the earliest Record Book at Wa, the first administrative station in the north-west of the Gold Coast, the Wiili and the LoDagaba living in the Wa and Lawra Districts are known as "Lobi" as distinct from the "Dagarti" (Dagaba) to the east. No distinction was therefore made between the Wiili, the LoDagaba and the Birifor of the Haute Volta and all were grouped with the Lobi-speaking peoples still further west, under the all-inclusive name "Lobi". Rattray's chapters on the "Lobru" in his survey of the tribes of the Northern Territories[4] were written as the result of field work carried out partly around Lawra, and

---

[1]1892, Vol. II., p.35 and map.
[2]1898, p.489 and p.496.
[3]Northcott, 1899.
[4]1932.

18

partly in the village of Tiole, south of Wetchiau on the borders of Wa and Gonja, that is, among the two groups I refer to as the LoDagaba and the Birifor. His account was written up as if it pertained to one culturally homogeneous group, known officially as the "Lobi", whereas the institutional activities and social structure of these peoples are by no means the same. Labouret recognized the distinction between these two groups in his book on the tribes of the "Lobi branch", in which he included the Birifor but excluded the "Dagari" (LoDagaba)[1]. These "Dagari" of the French writers are, in fact, the people referred to as "Lobi" by the English; indeed it is a blanket name often used by the French to cover all the Dagari speakers in the Gold Coast. Meanwhile, to the English, the LoDagaba, LoWiili, Birifor, and LoWilisi of the Haute Volta are all known as "Lobi". The English restrict the name "Dagarti" to the most easterly group, the Dagaba; the French limit "Lobi" to the most westerly, the LoWilisi. Rattray, misled by the accepted English designation "Lobi" which included the Birifor and the LoDagaba, confused the two groups in his account. Labouret, while distinguishing these, was misled by the western use of the name "Dagari" to confuse the LoDagaba with the Dagaba.

ii *Actor names*

The apparent discrepancies in these reports arise from local usage. Neither of the names "Lobi" nor "Dagarti" (Fr. "Dagari") refers exclusively to one group; they are anglicized versions of two local words, which I have translated by the roots *Lo* and *Dagaa* in order to avoid the complications of the dialectal variations and are used by a series of peoples living to the east and west of the Black Volta, when referring to their neighbours and, obliquely, to themselves. They are not mutually exclusive names indicating individual groups. The reason for the existence of such a system appears to be the lack of any pronounced hiatus in the social relations of neighbouring peoples sufficient to arouse the consciousness of unity necessary for the emergence of a group name. For there are no effective groups larger than the parish (the ritual area of the Earth cult) which are characterized by "territorial unity and exclusiveness".[2] There is no build-up of these units into more inclusive groups because there is no centralized authority system, geographical discontinuity, or any extensive ritual collaboration outside the parish. In warfare the association of these local units appears to have altered and never given rise to permanent alliances.

The inhabitants of neighbouring ritual areas are exclusive to one another only in so far as they belong to congregations sacrificing at different Earth shrines. Social relations between members of adjacent areas may, if geographical and kinship factors insist, be more intensive than within the area itself. Descent ties operating between local sectors of the dispersed patriclans cross-cut ties of contiguity realized in the form of the Earth cult. As Fortes has made clear in his analysis of the Tallensi, we are dealing in the Northern Territories with a continuous intermeshing of social relationships; there are few discontinuities between neighbouring groups. The interlocking of social relationships is paralleled by a gradual and continuous change of culture over the whole area; there are no distinct "cultures", but a slow merging as of linguistic dialects.

In the north-west, people recognize their affinity with some neighbours in matters, for example, of bridewealth payments, but will dissociate themselves from this group and identify themselves with another in relation to some other

---

[1] 1931, p.45.
[2] Evans-Pritchard, 1940, p.278.

feature such as the xylophones they play, just as the inhabitants of a ritual area, or even the members of a constituent descent group, combine in warfare on one occasion with their eastern against their western neighbours, and on another reverse the alliance, depending upon ties of contiguity, ties of descent, and the particular *casus belli*. Even within a limited area such as Birifu, cultural differences were observable and recognized; for example, in Biro, in the south-east, people were considerably more proficient at the leaping funeral dances of their *Dagaa* (DagaaWiili) neighbours, but the inhabitants of Tʃaa in the north-west regarded them as beginners in the *Kobine* dances which take place between the end of hoeing and the harvest of the guinea corn and are widespread among the *Lo* (Birifor) to the west of them. The inhabitants of Birifu have no designation which distinguishes them from any of their neighbours; indeed the question which Europeans are so inclined to ask, "What do you call yourselves?" is hardly meaningful within their frame of reference. In response to such a question, they would in all probability give a name derived from that of the settlement, *Birifuole*. Self-applied designations arise only in the context of a particular social fact, as they have no general referent of a political or geographical nature. They emerge with reference to a unit of customary action by which a certain group of people differentiates itself from another. At a funeral, the people of Birifu will watch the leaping dances of the inhabitants of Tugu (DagaaWiili) and smile at their *Dagaa* ways (*dagaa tomo*), automatically associating themselves with the dances of the *Lo* (Birifor) to the west of them. Or, hearing that the cows of a dead clansman in Kwõnyũkwõ (LoDagaba) have been taken by his sister's son, they deplore this *Lo* practice (*lɔɔri tomo*), now placing themselves in the opposite camp, this time among the *Dagaa*. Thus, if one asks the question, "Are you *Lo* or *Dagaa*?" the answer is only meaningful in relation to the context of custom in which the hearer conceives the question to have been asked. A LoWiili, if he took the question as referring to the matrilineal inheritance of wealth would reply *Dagaa*; if he thought you were referring to dancing he might say *Lo* (*Lɔɔr*).

These same names are used to refer to individuals and groups by all the peoples dwelling between Kampti in the Haute Volta and Hian in the Gold Coast, a distance of two hundred miles from west to east and three hundred from north to south. As I have said, they are not divided into tribes, for no constituent group has consciousness of unity sufficient to give rise to a tribal name. Broadly speaking, they acknowledge only place names, the names of settlements, which correspond to the parishes of the Earth cult. On the other hand, a pattern can be observed in the ways in which the terms *Lo* and *Dagaa* are manipulated. Groups of parishes emerge on the basis of the fact that they apply the two words in the same way to their neighbours and to themselves. They point to the same features as being characteristic of the *Lo* and the *Dagaa*. The main criterion pointed to is the relative stress given to matriliny and patriliny; the *Lo* in the west are matrilineal, or rather double unilineal, while the *Dagaa* in the east are patrilineal.

On the basis of these common usages, one can classify the peoples of the area, for this in fact will differentiate them by reference to the cultural differences which they themselves recognize as important. The reasons for this classification will be clarified in the following paragraphs but meanwhile it is necessary for me to list the subdivisions I am using, and have used throughout this book, to enable the analysis to proceed. The actual position of these people is given in Figure 2, and diagrammatically in Figure 3. The designations are more or less invented, though they have some local connotations.

In the extreme west are the LoWilisi, the true "Lobi" of Labouret, the only ones to speak a language of the Lobi group. As in the case of the Birifor, I have followed Labouret's map of the distribution of these people. We can regard the LoWilisi as placing most emphasis on the matrilineal descent group; they have a dual system of inheritance and descent groups based on both lines. Land is inherited patrilineally, marriage is virilocal, at any rate in its later stages, but wealth passes matrilineally. Owing to preferential patrilateral cross-cousin marriage, the matriclan of a founder of a settlement tends to be that of his grandson, so that specific areas within a settlement become associated with a certain matriclan. In any case, the population density is lower than in the Lawra District.[1] Land is plentiful, and the preferred system of shifting cultivation encourages mobility. Moving to a new area, a man will tend to settle with his matrilineal clansmen.

The Birifor to the east have a similar dual system but place less emphasis on the matriline in matters of residence. Like all the other groups to the east of them, they speak a Mossi language which is unintelligible to the Lobi-speaking LoWilisi.

The LoDagaba, which include the LoPiel (lit. white Lo) or white LoDagaba and the LoSaala (lit. black Lo) or black LoDagaba also possess fully-fledged dual descent systems, but there is increasing emphasis upon the obligations of patriclanship. The matriclan is less important among the LoPiel than among the LoSaala.

The LoWiili, with whom I am here mainly concerned, recognize descent groups based on both lines but property of all kinds is inherited patrilineally and consequently matriclans play a comparatively subsidiary rôle.

The DagaaWiili only have patrilineal descent groups but in certain ways, such as the prohibition on a son inheriting his father's wives, they are distinct from the Dagaba proper and closer to the groups previously mentioned.

The Dagaba themselves, the most easterly of the cluster, are emphatically patrilineal.

In general, these peoples have no nomenclature individual to themselves. For both internal reference (actor names) and external reference (observer names), they make use of dialectal variations of the two names *Lo* and *Dagaa*. At the two poles, the LoWilisi and the Dagaba consistently refer to themselves as *Lo* and *Dagaa* respectively. The Dagaba refer to all groups to the west of them as *Lo*, the LoWilisi refer to all groups to the east of them as *Dagaa*; and the intermediate groups refer to their neighbours in the same way. But the referents of the names *Lo* and *Dagaa* are not fundamentally groups but aspects of culture, the most important being the relative weight placed upon matrilineal or patrilineal descent. That is to say, a statement such as *ti loba ib* (LoDagaba), "our *Lo* way" is, in the absence of other contextual implications, to be taken as referring to the existence of the matrilineal inheritance of wealth. Thus, those who inherit wealth in this way will sometimes use the term *Lo* for self-reference when this issue is under discussion. But matrilineal inheritance of wealth is not the only referent of *Lo*, nor is patrilineal inheritance the only referent of *Dagaa*. Only the groups at the two poles use one name consistently for self-reference in every context. When the Birifor speak of their language in opposition to that spoken by the LoWilisi, they can call it *Dagaa*, thereby placing it among those Mossi dialects spoken by the people they call *Dagaa*, those dwelling to the east of them.

The process is seen most clearly when we examine the usage of the two names for external reference. The example of the LoWiili speaking of the dancing of the

[1]Labouret, 1931, p.54.

21

DagaaWiili and of the inheritance system of the LoDagaba illustrates the mechanism whereby the intermediate groups define their own institutions by opposing them to those of their neighbours on one side, and by associating them with those of their neighbours on the other. Such unity as characterizes any one of the groups to which I have given distinctive names, such as DagaaWiili, or LoDagaba (names which would have little or no meaning for the groups concerned), emerges only in situations where certain common features of their culture require to be distinguished from those of their neighbours; it is unity in juxtaposition. Of the Nuba, Nadel writes "in a few groups tribal consciousness is not intensive or clear enough to have evolved a common tribal name which·the group would itself use, though the group would be known by such a name to its neighbours. The consciousness of unity, of varying intensity, must be the basis of the definition of the tribe."[1] Definition by opposition does not in itself constitute consciousness of unity. The group to which I have given the name LoDagaba emerges as a group only in so far as it employs the terms *Lo* and *Dagaa* in the same contexts; its members refer to the same people as *Lo* and *Dagaa* on the basis of certain criteria of cultural differentiation. This means of course that there is a uniformity in regard to these specific criteria within the group employing these verbal symbols in a particular way, but this does not give it a consciousness of unity sufficient to require a group name. It is a reflected unity, a positional unity.

For internal reference the groups intermediate between the two poles employ both *Lo* and *Dagaa* to characterize various features of their culture. But in their use of the names for external reference, neighbouring groups are either *Lo* or *Dagaa*. The reasons given for so describing a group vary; if the usage is questioned, a particular criterion will be indicated linking the designated group with the other peoples lying in that cultural direction. Attention is particularly directed to the diminishing emphasis on the matriclan from A. to G. (Fig. 3). The main criteria are recorded in Table 3. They are not, however, the only ones employed. For other institutional features are associated with the central referent, the method by which movable property, wealth, is inherited. Xylophones, for example, include *Lo* and *Dagaa* types. The distribution of these among the groups we have differentiated is given in Table 4. The lack of the *Dagaa* xylophone among the LoSaala is often pointed to by the LoPiel as the reason for their being classed as *Lo*. It is the act of pointing at such indices which gives the group its unity—a consciousness of what it is not. These subsidiary criteria may conflict with the central referent of matrilineal descent. I know of only one case in which this happened and that was when I was living in a LoDagaba community and speaking of the LoWiili to my cook, Timbume (literally, *teŋgaan bume*, thing of the Earth shrine). He came from Tom, near Nandom, whose inhabitants I have classified as LoPiel or white LoDagaba, and had worked for many years in the south. There, language is the main referent of the two names because the important fact among migrant labourers and their employers is what they speak and not how they inherit. Thus the name *Lo* tends to be restricted to the LoWilisi. It has pejorative implications, particularly in these days, when the gourd discs inserted in the lips of women and girls arouse considerable derision from outsiders. Timbume at first insisted he was *Dagaa*; only later on, when I pointed out that members of his patrilineage inherited wealth matrilineally, did he reluctantly agree that in this respect they were *Lo*. He agreed to this, but remained resentful at the implications, not only because of the reason I have mentioned above, but also because his father, a comparatively rich man,

---

[1] 1947, p.13.

Table 3

Speaker's Group	Group referred to	Criteria pointed to
B.	A.	Language of *Lobi-Dogon* group
C.	B.	i. Emphasis on matrilineal inheritance of movable property ii. Heavier bridewealth payments
D.	C.	i. Emphasis on matrilineal inheritance of movable property ii. Use of *Lo* xylophones in dances
E.	D.	Matrilineal inheritance
F.	E.	i. Emphasis on matriclanship ii. Use of *Lo* xylophones in dances
G.	F.	i. Sons cannot marry widows of lineage members of adjacent generation (i.e., "fathers") ii. Dialect resembles that of those who inherit wealth matrilineally

H. and I. also refer to those to the west as *Lo* on grounds of dialect resemblance. For the names of the groups corresponding to the letters, see **Figure 3**.

Table 4

DISTRIBUTION OF XYLOPHONES AMONG THE LO AND DAGAA

		Xylophones (*Gil*) in order of size			
		Dagaa Gil	Lo Gil Kpɛɛ̃	Lo Gil Prumo	Gbin
Dagaba		X			
DagaaWiili		X			
LoWiili		X	X	X	X
LoPiel	} LoDagaba	X	X		
LoSaala			X		X
Birifor				X	X

had died in his youth, while his mother's brother, from whom he would inherit, was still middle-aged and something of a spendthrift. Counter-attacking, he maintained that the LoWiili were also *Lo*. He pointed to their use of the *Lo* xylophones, to their dialect and to the particular dance (*Kobine*) with which they celebrate the end of hoeing. It is true that in these respects the LoWiili are more like the Birifor than are the LoPiel of the Nandom area; this is related to their geographical position between the DagaaWiili and the Birifor. To this extent they are out of cultural alignment, for these features do not coincide with the absence of matrilineal inheritance of wealth. This usage was later confirmed only by listening to the way the LoWiili were referred to in ordinary conversation. Direct questioning by an outsider tends to be misleading, for a man's response will depend upon his interpretation of the question. This was the only time I

23

have heard a neighbouring group referred to as *Dagaa* in one context and *Lo* in another, the reason being that elsewhere the criteria are consistent with one another and no conflict arises. When I first came to Lawra, and asked about a "Lobi" community outside the administrative centre itself, the LoWiili were mentioned; it was some time later that I realized I had been directed to what for my purpose was the wrong community—as they did not inherit wealth matrilineally—but only towards the end of my fieldwork there that I understood why. As terms of external reference, *Lo* and *Dagaa* are normally used consistently by one group to its neighbours; but for internal reference, the group may employ either term according to the context.

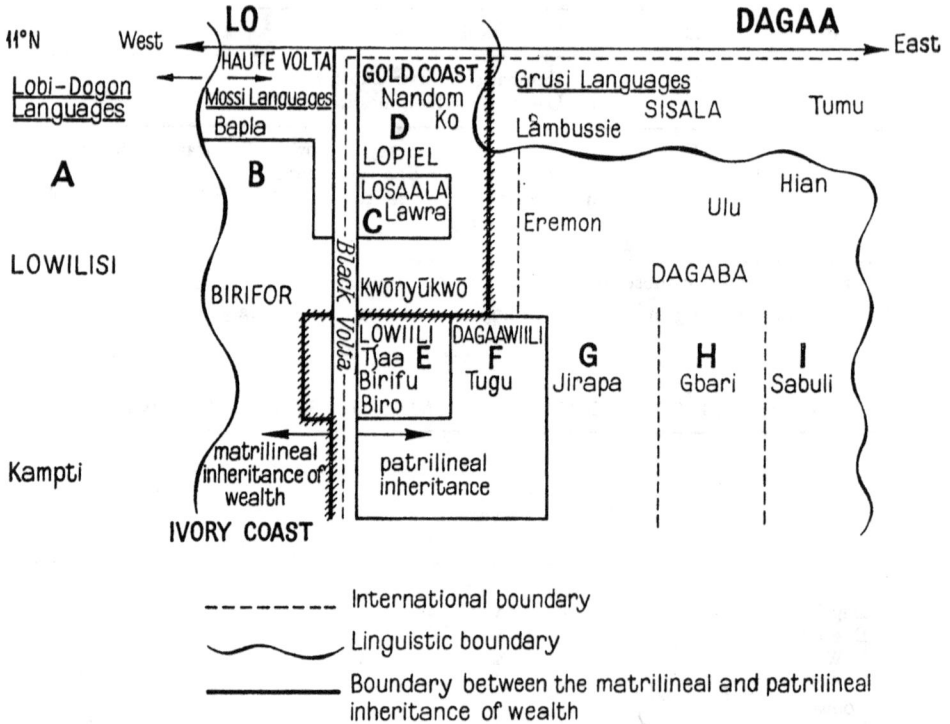

FIG.3. DIAGRAM TO ILLUSTRATE THE USE OF THE DIRECTIONAL NAMES, LO AND DAGAA, FOR EXTERNAL REFERENCE

The group, unable to visualize its unity from within, defines itself in opposition to the surrounding peoples, who are considered in relation to the two cultural poles, *Lo* and *Dagaa*. This conceptual mechanism resembles our employment of the directional terms, North and South, for their use is determined by the speaker's situation in relation to two poles; indeed, the words were once translated as West and East by an educated person from the area, whose attention I had drawn to this phenomenon. This view corresponds to the sociological reality, for the polar cultures have inevitably a spatial aspect and the groups are strung out on the East-West axis. But there is a closer parallel to the use of directional terms. If we employ the term westerners to refer to all those

24

living to the west of us, we automatically include ourselves among the easterners. This is how the cluster of peoples in this area use *Lo* and *Dagaa* in relation to their own institutions and to those of their neighbours.

This mechanism provides a means of dealing with, that is to say, of accounting for and referring to, a multitude of cultural differences within and without communities; it places institutions in relation to the speaker and its use is always relative to his position between the two poles. This relativity explains why the LoDagaba, for example, are called "Dagari" by French writers and "Lobi" by the English and why Delafosse regarded the inhabitants of the Wa and Lawra districts as all "Dagari".[1]

An attempt has been made to elucidate the uses of the terms *Lo* and *Dagaa* and, in the absence of "tribal" names, to present some typology of peoples in the region. I have already mentioned that the names chosen for these groups have some significance locally. As far as the peoples living in the Haute Volta are concerned, I have adopted both the nomenclature and the distribution given by Labouret, except that with regard to the latter I have indicated in Figure 2 the pockets of LoWiili and LoSaala which exist in the Haute Volta adjacent to their Gold Coast counterparts, and with regard to the former I have preferred to avoid the term "Lobi" as a name for a social group owing to the great confusion which has centred around its use. I have therefore called his "Lobi" LoWilisi, a name which is sometimes heard among the Dagari-speaking peoples to indicate that sub-class of *Lo* whose language is unintelligible to them. The name Birifor is that given by Labouret. The LoDagaba he calls "Dagari". One sometimes hears the term *Dagara* used by the LoDagaba for internal reference, whereas they speak of the Wiili and Dagaba to the East or patrilineal side of them as the *Dagabr* (s. *Dagaba*). But I was told that this was a recent adoption of a name by which they were known to a neighbouring people, the *Puli*, presumably the Pougouli mentioned by Labouret, a Sisala-speaking group living to the west of Diébougou; in other words, a name of external reference applied to the group has been taken over as a name of internal reference. This usage is far from frequent. I have preferred to give the word Dagari, like Lobi, an exclusively linguistic connotation and to use the compound LoDagaba for the social group. The LoDagaba are subdivided into the LoSaala and the LoPiel. The first of these is sometimes used by the remaining LoDagaba and others to distinguish the people living within a mile or two of Lawra itself, who throw more weight on matriliny. I have heard etymologies which derive this from the place-name and alternatively from the epithet "black". Within the Voltaic region, the colour terms, which can only roughly be translated "red", "white" and "black", are often used to differentiate related groups. The adjective "black" usually carries a pejorative significance relative to "red" and "white". The name for the other sub-group, LoPiel, means white *Lo*; I heard it used occasionally in Birifu to distinguish these other LoDagaba from the LoSaala and the Birifor. The name I have given to the inhabitants of Birifu, the LoWiili, would not be recognized by them. However, a group of former inhabitants of the parish who migrated to Bapla, south of Diébougou in the Haute Volta, are sometimes referred to by their neighbours as the Wiili. This is the name of one of the central settlements of the DagaaWiili near Tugu in the Gold Coast, and is only used by these people as a place name. On the other hand, they are aware that the name is sometimes given to them.

---

[1] 1908(b), p.168. Labouret, 1931, p.23, speaks of both "Dagari" and "Dagaba"; he does not apparently realize however that they are structurally distinguishable nor that the two names are variations of each other.

Most of the people spoken of as Wiili in the Haute Volta differ somewhat from the inhabitants of Birifu, certain of whose customs are closer to those of their westerly neighbours, the Birifor, than are those of the Wiili around Tugu. Indeed, they refer to each other as *Dagaa* and *Lo* respectively. I therefore divide them into two groups, the LoWiili and the DagaaWiili.[1]

The name Dagaba is in fact the name by which these people refer to themselves. On the other hand, they sometimes refer to Dagaba to the west of them as *Lo* (Figure 3). There are certainly some differences, for example, in the lay-out of settlements, between the Dagaba of Ulu in the east and those of Eremon in the west. But before any sub-division could be attempted, a detailed investigation would have to be made. It is for instance also used in the centralized state of Wa to the south, where both "black" and "white" Dagaba are recognized.[2] Meanwhile, I retain the blanket term Dagaba.

In this introductory chapter, I have considered not only the ethnographical and geographical background of the LoWiili but have also discussed certain problems of nomenclature which arise in this highly diffuse political system. These problems will be dealt with from a different point of view when we consider the system of local groups.

---

[1]French writers use the name "Oulé". According to Delafosse, 1912, vol. I, p.141, the Dyulas, Mande speaking traders scattered throughout the region, know them as the "Dagari-Oulé" or "red Dagari" to distinguish them from the "Dagari-Fing" or "black Dagari" (i.e. the LoDagaba). I have not heard this Mande version but only the name Wiili; I assume "Oulé" to be a bad transliteration of this.

[2]Goody, 1954(a).

Chapter 2

The Economic System

The population

The LoWiili live on the banks of the Black Volta, concentrated mainly in the settlement of Birifu; others live immediately across the river in the Ivory Coast. In all, they do not number more than 5,000. This calculation is based on the census reports which give the following figures for Birifu:

1948 .. 2,939   1931 .. 2,335[1]

Included under Birifu are the ritual areas of Birifu (phonetically *Birifɔ*, and its inhabitants, *Birifuole*) and of Biro, covering in all about nine square miles, a density of 330 compared with the 81 per square mile for the Lawra District as a whole and the figure of 100 which Fortes estimates for the Tallensi.[2] The LoWiili who inhabit the Ivory Coast are more widely dispersed and their system of agriculture differs in consequence. Labouret[3] puts the population of this area at 40 to the square kilometer, that is roughly 100 to the square mile. The remainder of the LoWiili live in Babile and in Kumansaal, which for administrative purposes forms part of Kwõnyūkwõ. The increase since 1931 has been considerable, despite the high infant mortality. The introduction of medical services and the limited extension of European ideas of hygiene, the opportunity to buy imported clothing and medicines, the absence of famine conditions in recent years, have all contributed to the increase.

Local records give no evidence of famine even during the early years of the century, but District Commissioners made considerable efforts to persuade farmers to cultivate a larger area and to diversify their crops by growing yams in case the cereals failed. Travelling across Gurma, Barth observed that concentration on a single crop, millet, made food shortages of a local character inevitable; his account also points to disturbed conditions being partly responsible for the failure of supplies. A more forceful index of scarcity lies in the number of recorded instances of men who sold their close agnates as slaves in such times. I have heard of only one season within the last twenty years when such a situation could possibly have arisen; the institution of chiefship, introduced by the Administration, created an alternative method of meeting minimal requirements of food, the chief's obligation to assist in such circumstances being a corollary to the right of exacting labour on his farms. Communal labour provides him with a clear surplus over consumption, stored until the following harvest and then sold. But the main reasons for improved supplies are, firstly, the wider political system which has established alternative methods for settling disputes and prevented the attacks of slave-raiders from without, and, secondly, the larger acreage now cultivated by each household.

---

[1]The report gives 2,395 but the records show this to be a mistake.

[2]Fortes, 1945, p.4. Fortes' work on the Tallensi constitutes the only detailed study of a people living in the Northern Territories of the Gold Coast; linguistically and culturally they are similar to the LoWiili. I therefore use his data for comparison.

[3]1931, p.54.

27

The introduction of cheap European-made hoe blades has made an important contribution to increased productivity. Previously, a blade, manufactured from locally smelted iron, would cost 5,000 cowries, equivalent to the price of a cow; poor men could not always afford to buy a hoe for each of their sons and these might have to take turns at using their father's. Nowadays, the money gained by wage labourers both locally and in the south provides an additional insurance against localized famine by making possible the purchase of food from neighbouring communities. And the advent of motor transport has made possible the rapid transfer of surplus production from one region to another.

Food supply[1]

The LoWiili are typical of the Voltaic peoples in obtaining food mainly by hoe agriculture, the emphasis in this region being on guinea-corn (sorghum vulgare: *tfi*), with late millet (pennisetum typhoides: *ziɛ* or *tfi ziɛ*) as the main subsidiary; maize (zea mays: *kamana*), groundnuts (arachis hypogea: *simiɛ*), yams (dioscorea sp: *nyuu*, pl. *nyiɛ*), farafara potatoes (coleus dysentericus: *pierɛ*), bambara beans (voandzeia subterranea), sweet potatoes (ipomea batatas: *nanyiɛ*), rice (oryza sp: *mui*) and various types of beans (vegra sp: *beŋe*) are also grown. The variety of crops may appear to belie Barth's remarks, but some of these are quite clearly recent introductions. The Lawra District Diary indicates that yams have only been cultivated on any scale since 1920; the natives regard both maize and rice as new arrivals and as luxury crops.

Specialization in other activities

Apart from the sons and dependents of the late chief and five others permanently employed as labourers by the Government or the Native Authority, the inhabitants of Birifu gain their living by subsistence farming, selling some beans and early groundnuts to traders in order to purchase salt and other commodities, and in order to meet their annual head and cattle tax. There are a number of part-time specialists but the only man who does not consider himself primarily a farmer is a Mossi leather worker, a former soldier, who settled there on his way north when he was demobilized in 1945. Ritual specialists, such as diviners, grave-diggers and medicine men, will not be considered here, although their services are not given for nothing. Certain women possess greater skill in brewing beer and making pots. Certain men display more ability in decorating drinking gourds, weaving baskets and in the three pre-eminent specialist activities, smithying, woodcarving and xylophone making; in connection with all three, shrines are established, principally to protect the individuals concerned. In most cases a son or, even more likely in the native view, a grandson, will continue a man's craft. These part-time specialists are not separated into castes as in some West African societies[2]. The sexual division of tasks can more appropriately be discussed in another context.

Other sources of food

Unlike less densely populated areas of the Northern Territories, wild fruit provides a negligible part of the diet of the inhabitants of Birifu. For trees are scarce near the settlements and even for firewood women may have to walk six or eight miles.

---

[1]This report deals only briefly with the agricultural system itself as this aspect of social life has been the subject of detailed research by J. H. Hinds. Fortes' account of Tallensi agriculture shows the two societies have basically the same economic system.

[2]See Paulme, 1940, p.185. Among the southern Voltaics, neither the Tallensi nor the LoWilisi have endogamous specialist groups. Among the various Mande speaking peoples, there exists a caste of blacksmiths called the Numu.

Hunting, a subject of much discussion and considerable preparation, and a prestige-conferring activity surpassed only by war, brings little reward in terms of food. However, Birifu is more fortunately situated than many settlements in the Lawra District, for the more thinly populated areas across the Volta provide hunting grounds within easy reach.

The keeping of cattle and other domestic animals is regarded by the inhabitants as essentially peripheral to farming; their possession creates a reserve of wealth to be used for marriage payments and for sacrifices to shrines. Although the index of riches, cattle are left in the charge of the youngest boy available and the milk is consumed only by the boys herding the animals. Meat itself is not considered 'food' (*bunderi*) for it cannot sustain a man in the way that guinea-corn, either as porridge or beer, does. With the exception of guinea fowl, domestic animals are never slaughtered for consumption alone. A goat might be provided for the farmers brought by a son-in-law or occasionally killed for sale at a market, a funeral or a house where beer was being brewed. But sacrifices and funerals constitute the main occasions for the distribution and consumption of meat. The cattle population, largely "short-horns", has risen sharply since the introduction of vaccination against rinderpest, a disease which was previously said to decimate the herds every fifteen years.[1] The riverine tsetse which caused the evacuation of the banks of the Kamba, north of Lawra, and certain areas to the east of Jirapa is less dangerous to cattle than another species, Glossina morsitans, dependent upon the presence of game. When the population density exceeds fifteen to the square mile Glossina morsitans is rarely encountered as most of the wild animals have been either shot or driven away. Despite the sleeping sickness epidemics in the north-west, the presence of tsetse has not seriously interfered with cattle rearing.[2] Hinds[3] gives the following average holdings for "Lobi" compounds; the samples were taken among the LoDagaba, the LoWiili and the DagaaWiili.

Table 5

LIVESTOCK HOLDINGS OF "LOBI" COMPOUNDS (AFTER HINDS)

	Average	*% of compounds possessing*
Cattle	4·0	57
Sheep	5·9	81
Goats	5·8	93
Poultry	16·0	100

In 1948 the ratio of cattle to human population in the Lawra District was 1 : 2.5, compared with Hinds' figure of 1 : 3 for 1945; the livestock census shows a rise since 1948 from 35,500 to 40,000. Detailed enquiry indicates that the census tends to understate the actual number of cattle held.

---

[1] Lawra District Diary, 13/3/1922.

[2] T. A. M. Nash, "The Eradication of Glossina morsitans by the Planned Development of a Territory", Farm and Forest, Ibadan, Vol. 10, 1950, gives the density above which this fly is infrequently found as forty to the square mile. For the Gold Coast, see K. R. S. Morris, 1946, 1949 and 1950. I am particularly indebted to Dr. Morris, through whose work the incidence of sleeping sickness has fallen to a negligible figure. He pointed out that there was a problem of underpopulation as well as overpopulation under these ecological conditions. A rapid depopulation in the Kulpawn valley appears to have followed the attacks of slave-raiders and the later labour migrations occurred because numbers were insufficient to maintain agricultural activity in the face of the ravages of disease and the destruction by wild life.

[3] Pt.2., p.13.

The wealth accumulated by chiefs as a result of the new dispensation can be seen in their completely atypical holdings both of cattle and of women. The late chief of Birifu was said to have 200 cattle; 33 wives were formally separated from him at his final funeral custom.

Cattle are regarded as an investment of the gains made by farming rather than as means of increasing wealth or of maintaining life. Guinea-corn remaining in the granary at the end of a good year will be sold to purchase livestock. And such a cow acquired by farming (*kukur naab*, cow of the hoe-handle) is nowadays killed at the death of every adult male who is not a pauper, a tribute to his success in the central activity of existence. A man's cattle are viewed as the embodiment of his skill as a farmer, not as a cowherd. Indeed, no grown man would consider herding cattle himself unless in very straitened circumstances. Many of them find it difficult to tell whether a stray animal belongs to their herd or not. There is little emphasis on cattle in song, in folk tale or in vocabulary. Outside Birifu, Fulani herdsmen are occasionally engaged by the larger owners to look after their herds. In return for their services they retain the milk and the manure. A certain resistance to the introduction of plough farming by the Agriculture Department originates in this evaluation, "it is a cow farming, not a man", they maintain. Looking after cattle is a job for children and foreigners.

Agriculture and Population Density

Most of the Lobi and Dagari-speaking peoples practise a form of shifting cultivation. Their main farms lie at some distance from the compounds[1] and are cropped for three or four years and then abandoned for another seven to ten years.[2]

Among the densely-settled LoDagaba and Wiili in the west of the Lawra District the emphasis is laid on permanently cultivated farms in the immediate vicinity of the homesteads. Hinds calculates the average area under cultivation by a farming group to be 9.82 acres among the LoDagaba and Wiili, 19.26 acres among the Dagaba; in addition the yield per acre was considerably greater among the latter. Table 5 shows the breakdown of these holdings.

Table 6

ACREAGE UNDER CULTIVATION BY A FARMING GROUP

Farm	LoDagaba and Wiili	Dagaba
Compound	3·62 (37·2%)	1·75 (9·1%)
Periodic Fallow . . .	4·10 (41·7%)	4·12 (21·2%)
Bush	None	12·90 (67·0%)
Swamp	2·10 (21·1%)	0·17 (0·9%)
Yam	Small patches under trees	·32 (1·8%)
Total . . .	9·82	19·26

In the case of the three farms which Hinds investigated in Birifu itself the average strength of a farming group was as follows:

---

[1]Labouret, 1931, p.138.
[2]Hinds, Pt.II., p.5.

Acreage farmed	Supported by Farming Group			Farming strength of Group
	Men	Women	Children	Men and Youths
7·87	3	3·3	3	2·3

My own survey of fifty such groups among the LoWiili gives the following results:

Supported by Farming Group			Farming strength of Group		
Men and youths	Women	Children	Total	Men	Youths 15–18
2·62	2·98	4·61	2·42	1·94	·48

Hinds' sample groups contain a larger number of men incapable of farming and a smaller number of children. But if we accept his groups as representative, the land under cultivation is seen to be roughly one acre a person. This suggests that within the confines of Birifu there remains a considerable area of unused land. This is so, but such land cannot be used under present conditions. The river annually floods its banks and when the water subsides the bare clayey soil bakes hard; all this land is unemployed. Gulley erosion has eaten into existing farms. On the laterite plateau little or no top-soil remains, while some of the side slopes of the scarp and hillocks are considered worthless.

On the other hand, Birifu is well favoured by the wet season streams which run down to the Volta and create swamp land in which some of the more valuable cash crops such as rice and tobacco can be grown. At one point where the water seeping below the scarp issues in a perpetual spring, some twenty-five acres are kept sufficiently moist to allow two or even three crops during the year with the help of simple irrigation. From September to February, sweet potatoes are grown and from then until June, groundnuts; maize is sometimes planted when these have been harvested.

A much greater proportion of the farmland is under continuous cultivation than among the LoDagaba. The figure of 9.82 acres cultivated by a LoDagaba farming group includes 4.0 acres of periodic fallow farm; that is to say a total holding of 17·82 acres is required on the basis of four years cultivation followed by a rest of twice that period. Table 6 shows the acreages of the different types of farm under cultivation in the three Birifu examples which Hinds recorded.

Table 7

LAND CULTIVATED BY THREE FARMING GROUPS IN BIRIFU

	Malka	Pore	Na'um	Average
Compound farm and contiguous farms under continuous cultivation	5·2	4·3	5·2	4·9
Swamp and irrigated farms . .	2·5	2·7	—	1·7
Periodic fallow farms . . .	—	—	3·6	1·2

These figures reveal a higher percentage under continuous cultivation than among the LoDagaba and Wiili as a whole, which accords with my own observations. Seldom did I see the Birifuole breaking new land. I can recall only five of the fifty farming groups in Tʃaa who did so at the beginning of the rains in April, 1951. This continuous cropping results from the high density and consequent shortage of farmland.[1]

The preoccupation with compound rather than bush farms, with continuous rather than shifting cultivation, is a direct consequence of population pressure and the exceptional ecological conditions. Individuals who leave to farm in the less heavily populated districts of Wa and Gonja at once adopt a system of fallow farming.[2] The comparatively poor soil of LoDagaba and Wiili areas can only sustain the high population density under continuous cultivation and the use of manure. The inhabitants themselves are conscious of these facts. The gain of fertility after a fallow period, the better results obtained by manuring, the richness of soil where rotting vegetable matter has lain, these are clearly understood by the indigenous farmer. A sure index of how many farming groups a homestead contains is to be found in the number of middens outside. Here is thrown the waste left after brewing guinea-corn beer, the heads of millet and maize, the sweepings of the rooms and faeces of infants; all of this the women later transfer to the growing crops.

The fertility of the earth and the rain (saa) are central to the success of the harvest, and both are matters of great concern. For the rain, adequate as it may seem by European standards, falls at times so heavily that the water rushes quickly off the surface, taking the topsoil with it. A downpour such as this may be followed even during the wet season by a dry spell up to a week or ten days. The rôle of these two basic prerequisites of food production is metaphorically conceived as the male sky (saalõ) sleeping with the female earth (teŋgaan).[3] When drought causes anxiety about the harvest, this is expressed in sacrifices at rain shrines (saa do), as well as at the central Earth shrine (teŋgaankpẽ). Concern about the land's fertility is more diffuse but arises in its most specific form after the harvest has been gathered, when the annual sacrifices to the ancestor and medicine shrines (bomaaldãã) and to the Earth shrine (teŋgaandãã) are made to ensure the soil's continued productivity.

The high density of the population and the uncertainty of harvests appear to be general factors behind contemporary migrations. New settlements are being established seventy to one hundred and fifty miles to the south, along the main lorry route to Kumasi. In these new areas, the various Dagari-speaking peoples from the Lawra District intermingle with one another. This type of migration is continuous and is not controlled by segmentation of the genealogical structure. Close agnatic kin of the same generation, classificatory "brothers" (yebe, pl.

---

[1]M. and S. L. Fortes, 1936, p.243, give tentative figures for cultivated areas among the Tallensi:

Compound farm	..	..	3.36	
Bush farm (5-10 acres)	..	..	7.50 ?	
Total	..	..	..	10.86 ?

In comparing the amount of land required by a farming group, one must not only consider the larger area actually under cultivation during any one season, but also the fact that the methods of shifting cultivation employed in bush farms increase the amount of land required for each group.

[2]Hinds points to this in a note on periodic fallow farms, which "among Dagartis occur only at Sentu where congestion is degrading bush farms to this type" (Table III, pt.II, p.2).

[3]I do not wish to suggest it is a recurrent theme in LoWiili speech; but it appears in the origin myth which I recorded.

yɔɔr), tend to follow one another. Territorial dispersion creates two separate and independent clan sectors whose members after two generations will cease to trace their relationships genealogically. Common descent continues to be recognized diffusely through the bond of patrilineal clanship. Individuals migrating under the pressure of land shortage can be assimilated only where specific unilineal connections are not the prime mechanism for integration into the local system.

The earlier and more general movements discussed in the introductory chapter may also have been caused by land shortage, although complicating factors of a military and political nature were also present. In both cases the result has been to place an upper limit to the possible generation depth available for the elaboration of genealogical ties.

The farming group

The scattered farms are cultivated by small groups of close agnatic kinsmen and their wives and children; this unit of food production I have called the farming group. The Table below indicates the composition of fifty such groups:

Table 8

THE COMPOSITION OF THE FARMING GROUP

		Effective strength of farming group						
	Females only	No. of males over 15						
		1	2	3	4	5	6	7
No. of groups so constituted .	2	15	11	12	6	2	0	2

Of the fifteen who farm alone, one is considered insane and lives completely on his own. He gets his food mainly by grubbing through groundnut farms after they have been harvested. Another, unable to walk, drags himself out to cultivate a small patch. Excluding these and the two women living by themselves, also highly abnormal cases, the average farming strength is 2.6.

The two women who live alone both left their husbands and have been allocated land as members of the patrilineage. At their husbands' homesteads women have only the right to plant vegetables amongst the maize and guinea-corn in the immediate vicinity of the house. This, the most fertile part of the whole farm, is usually called the *seman* or *dondor puo*. The phrase "compound farm" I have used to describe the immediate surround. The inhabitants often extend the term to include the whole area under continuous cultivation, excluding the swampy land (*bãã puo*) but I have used the term home farm for this. These vegetables which the women grow form the basis of the sauce which accompanies the habitual meal of guinea-corn porridge (*saab*) and in the preparation of which a woman takes considerable pride; the provision of vegetables and condiments is the responsibility of the woman except when she provides food on her husband's behalf for the workers his son-in-law is obliged to bring.

A woman only possesses rights of use as the wife of her husband, for farmland is inherited patrilineally through males. The LoDagaba, the Birifor and apparently all the Lobi-speaking peoples, transmit land in this way, although, in these societies, unlike the Wiili and Dagaba, movable property passes along the uterine line. Although the Birifuole speak of a certain area as belonging (*so*) to a certain patriclan (*dɔɔro*), referring to the local sector of a clan, effective rights of

33

usage are held by the senior members of farming groups. These are obtained from their nearest agnates by inheritance or by the division of existing holdings. The senior member holds such rights on behalf of those who farm with him. He is said to "own" (*so*) the farm (*puo*); but if anyone wishes to break away, he must be provided with land. This nominally occurs only between siblings. However, children whose father is dead and who are farming with a paternal uncle can form their own productive unit when they feel themselves able to stand on their own. They will then claim their dead father's land, although they are not always able to make this claim effective.

The main cleavage occurs between siblings of different maternal origin, although if the mothers are full sisters their offspring are regarded as full siblings. This tendency of agnates to divide with reference to their maternal origin is recognized in the inheritance of farmland. On his death a man's farm may continue to be worked as a whole for a few years; when fission occurs, the fertile *seman* or compound farm will be divided equally, not among the sons, but among the groups of full siblings. The three children of one wife will together be allocated the same as the only child of another. The portion given to a group of siblings is thought of as that in which their mother grew her vegetables. Land in the home farm is divided on an individual basis.

It sometimes happens that conflict between a father and his eldest son may lead to the establishment of independent economic units. The younger sons remain with the parent, for theirs is a special obligation to support him in his old age, while the eldest will probably be joined by his other brothers born of the same mother. The farm cannot be divided (*puon*) during the father's lifetime; he can only "cut" (*ŋman*) a portion for the son to use. This is an important step in the fission of a residential group. The farm "cut" for the eldest son may later be augmented at his father's death. This was fiercely denied by an elder whose judgment was greatly respected in the community, but as his eldest son was farming on his own it was generally recognized that his opposition arose from hostility towards that unfortunate individual. The principle that "only brothers can divide" limits the wider social consequences of such conflicts between father and son.

Bush farms (*mwo puɔ puo*), the LoWiili maintain, "we cannot divide"—*ti kantwõ puon*. Rights of usage are held more loosely. Another member of the lineage (the genealogical segment of a clan) could in theory start hoeing an uncultivated plot without even asking the farm owner himself. What this means in practice is that if one member of a lineage has more such land than he is capable of farming, another will approach him and ask permission to hoe a part. Such a request could not be refused. If the original 'owner' requires the land when his children are capable of farming, it will be returned. Where the population remains constant, this method of land tenure permits a continual readjustment of the relationship between the numerical strength of a farming group and the amount of land at its disposal, between the unit and its means of production.

The word *so* is used in both these cases to express the rights a man has over the land and the range of meaning is but inadequately conveyed by the English "own". It is said that "the ancestors own the land and the crops"; they first cleared the bush and only by virtue of their efforts does the present generation farm the land today. It is in this sense that they refer to the land as being "owned" by a patriclan; the land farmed by the members of a patrilineal group, or lineage of maximum depth, is regarded as having once been farmed by their founding ancestor. Hence when *Nonε*, a member of a lineage of the *Ɖmanbili* patriclan, decided to join his younger brother at a new settlement in the Wa area, his farm-land was divided equally between the five other farming groups descended from the common ancestor. The lineage as a whole have the reversionary rights.

The ritual leader of the community (*teŋgaansob*) may also be said to "own the land", *o la so a tiuŋ*. This formulation indicates his special duties within the settlement, which is essentially an area of ritual collaboration or 'parish'. His position gives him no power over the distribution of farming land. For there is no such land which does not have an "owner" in whom are vested rights of tillage; a stranger has to beg land from this individual himself. Pogucki calls the rights of the *teŋgaansob*, as representative of his lineage, "alloidal"[1]. In Birifu he has the power to expel a recalcitrant member of the settlement but he acts on behalf of the ritual community as a whole, not merely on behalf of his own descent group. While the office is generally associated throughout the north-west with the patrilineal group or matriclan of the first settler, such a system of succession to office gives neither the *teŋgaansob* nor his descent group any special position with regard to rights of tillage.

Three primary levels of rights and duties in respect of land are indicated by the word *so*. The position may be summarized as:

(i) Rights of tillage and duties of ritual supervision in relation to farm shrines are vested in the senior of a farming group on behalf of the other members.

(ii) Rights of bestowal and duties of ritual supervision in relation to the ancestor cult are vested in the lineage elder on behalf of the other members.

(iii) The duty of ritual supervision in relation to the Earth cult is vested in the *teŋgaansob* on behalf of (*a*) the lineage, patriclan and matriclan of the first settler, (*b*) the settlement as a whole.

As in any social system, rights over land are distributed at certain significant points of differentiation. The owner of freehold land in English law is restricted by rights vested at various levels in the political organization. The misunder-standings arise from the failure to appreciate a different system of distribution. An intelligent elder once remarked that "according to the white man the land has no owner". This idea may have derived from the fact that the Government originally assumed certain overall rights over land. On the other hand, it repre-sents a widely-held opinion among strangers and no doubt arises from the fact that the selling of land, an integral feature of our conception of "ownership", is wholly inconceivable to the native; such an act would be sacrilegious both to the ancestors and to the Earth shrine (*teŋgaan*). Retribution would inevitably follow; "it would be the soil (*tiŋsɔɔ*) you trade". The descent group cannot alienate the property, the means of production, on which its corporateness is based.

Although the sale of land is out of the question, it is possible for someone outside the patrilineal group to obtain the right to farm a piece of land by asking (*zɛlɛ:* request) the owner. The secondary rights so granted may be restricted by a time limit; such is the case should the request be made by a fellow clansman or a member of an adjacent group with whom the owner or his close agnates had ties of matrilateral or affinal kinship. Alternatively, the grantor, having discussed the question with the senior members of his lineage, can declare "*n ŋman ko*", "I cut and give you", in which case the rights pass to the children of the man who made the request. Land is granted in this way to a sister's son (*arbile*) who as a child

[1] 1950.

35

has accompanied his mother when she returned to her father's house as a result of divorce or the death of her husband. It would be unthinkable for anyone to ask for this land back again; in any case, the original kinship bond will have been strengthened by intermarriage in every generation. And although the mother of any specific agnatic descendant of the original sister's son may not belong to the grantor's lineage, the whole patrilineal group will continue to be known collectively as *ti arbile*, our sisters' sons. Moreover, an individual has, in an extenuated form, the same right to expect favours from the patrilineage of his father's mother and his mother's mother as in the lineage of his own mother's brother. The ancestors would not stand idly by while one of their patrilineal descendants did an injustice to a sister's child. The children of female members of the lineage have quite specific rights which extend throughout the patriclan; rights vested in agnates are transmitted in a diluted form through females. With the children of sisters' children the rights derived by them as offspring of a daughter of that clan die out. Two generations represent the limits of reckoning matrilateral relationships; an individual is normally only aware of the patriclan affiliations of his mother's mother and father's mother. In the case of the descendants of the sister's son who settled amid the compounds of his mother's brother's lineage, such ties never cease for, as I have said, they are reinforced by intermarriage in every generation.

In the case of these derived or secondary rights of usage, the land if left uncultivated reverts to the members of the lineage from whom it was begged. While it remains in use, the grantor or his successor continues to collect the fruit from certain trees growing there; or, alternatively, the borrower of the land may gather the fruit and send half to the grantor. These rights to the produce of fruit trees gradually fall into disuse. I have noted a number of instances in which they existed only in the memory of an elder. When he dies the full rights of tillage would be regarded as vested in the secondary user; the second, or lineage, level of primary rights would inevitably be transferred to his own patrilineal group as these derive from the obligations of a particular farmer to the other descendants of a common ancestor. The third level of rights, those of the custodian of the Earth, remain as before, if the stranger has actually transferred his residence from one settlement to another. Where a farmer has begged land from a neighbour living in an adjacent ritual area, I am of the opinion that the boundaries of that area will eventually alter; but this is a matter on which one can offer little definite evidence.

Common rights exist over water. Once a stranger has drunk the water or eaten the soil, he is a member of the political community in the sense later defined, being placed in the same relationship to the Earth shrine as all those owing allegiance to it; he can no longer be killed by a member of that settlement without the murderer bringing automatic retribution on his whole patrilineal group. Important rights exist over trees; rights in respect of fruit trees, a valuable source of food in famine, are held by the 'farm owner' (*puosob*); rights over other trees are less specifically conceived, although no-one would cut down a tree in another farm without obtaining permission. In the case of trees in the bush (*wio*), anyone can cut firewood and obtain roofing poles, although the members of the ritual community feel they have first claim. One cause of the outbreak of violence between Nadoli, whose inhabitants regard themselves in certain contexts as LoWiili, and the Birifor of Malba is commonly said to be that the people of one village broke the pots full of cowdung which had been left in the bush by members of the other settlement to collect white ants, the proper food for young chicks.

Common rights in 'parishes' other than one's own cannot be defined abstractly; they vary with the degree of friction existing at any one time between the two settlements. Rights of grazing, particularly important in a country where water is scarce in the dry season and cattle often roam some distance, are of the same nature. A debt between members of different clans might lead to the seizure of such roaming cattle, thus abrogating common rights which the debtor conceived his lineage to possess. Secondary rights of tillage also have to be considered within the framework of self-help.

In the Northern Territories the individualisation of farming rights tends to increase with the density of the population.[1] Western Gonja, with a density of four persons per square mile and a shifting agriculture, is "marked by an absence of an idea of ownership of a right to use land linked and bound permanently to a particular parcel of the land"; only "land actually under cultivation" is the subject of succession.[2] The LoWiili are typical of the northern parts, where a dense population requires a more precise systematization. The comparative lack of emphasis on the rôle of the *teŋgaansob* in the distribution of land, and certain statements I have quoted which reveal a dichotomy between ideal and actual patterns in relation to the inheritance of bush farms, should also be viewed in this context.

---

[1]Pogucki, 1950, p.99. As G. I. Jones has shown, the same is true of the Ibo.
[2]pp.52-3.

Chapter 3

Kinship Relations and the Structure of
Residential Groups

The Compound

A system of relatively settled agriculture and the inheritance of rights of tillage by close agnatic kin[1] leads after a number of generations to the formation of a group of compounds inhabited by males descended from a common patrilineal ancestor and constituting a unilineal descent group with specific genealogical connections. This is how the inhabitants see it, as they presume an increasing population.

In Birifu a typical patrilineage inhabits some seven large compounds (s. *yir*) situated about a hundred yards apart from each other.[2] The eight-foot high walls of these compounds are built entirely of mud. They are divided into a number of rooms (s. *diu*) roofed with timber and covered in puddled earth (*tene*).[3] The entrance to these rooms is from a long central chamber (*tfaara*) which abuts on an open semi-circular yard (*davra*, a patio) surrounded by a wall of the same height as the compound itself. Such a group of rooms forms a self-contained section of the house; I have seen openings connecting them with other similar sets only in the case of two full brothers who farmed together and in one other instance referred to later. Otherwise one can only get from one to the other by means of the roof. The one doorway in the outside wall leads into the cattle byre and provides no access to the remainder of the homestead.

The cattle byre (*naab zɔ*) is the most important room in the compound. When a new house has been completed, three stones from the minor Earth shrine are laid in a trench dug across the entrance of the byre and a sacrifice is made to ensure the future well-being of the occupants. In a corner of the room are placed the ancestor shrines, anthropomorphic figures cut in wood. Here a woman in her final labours is taken to deliver her child. It is the room consecrated to the continuity of the lineage.

The entrance to the byre usually faces west. Close by is the ladder which leads to the roof—the only means of access to the rest of the house. Climbing to the roof, the occupants then descend by another ladder into their respective patios which serve as kitchens during the dry season. In this open kitchen are the pots containing the infusion for bathing infants, the women's urinal and perhaps the firewood stacked for use in the rainy season. In the long room leading from the open yard, the women carry out much of their daily work when the sun is hot, and men may sit and drink guinea-corn beer (*dãã*). In the furthest depths stands the main granary (*buur*), square at the base and with rounded sides ending in a bottle-neck which protrudes through the roof and is capped with a conical covering of woven grasses. In front of the granary will be placed a few small

---

[1]Inheritance is within farming groups. Where this consists of "brothers", the surviving full brother or senior half-brother will become farm-owner; he must provide land for his dead brother's children when they desire to farm by themselves.

[2]See Fig. 7.

[3]See Figs. 4 and 5.

conical clay mounds which form another kitchen for the wet season, when the heat of the fire also helps to preserve the grain.

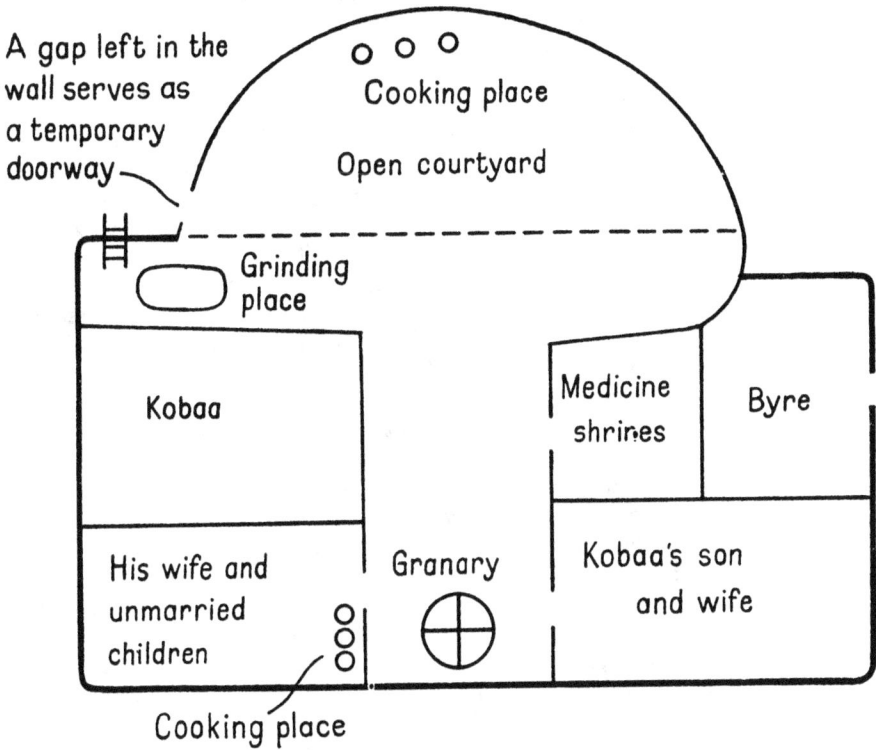

FIG.4 COMPOUND OCCUPIED BY A SIMPLE RESIDENTIAL GROUP

Kobaa's house, ʏʄaa, Birifu — a newly built compound

On both sides of the long room are the smaller rooms in which a woman and her children sleep. A married woman with a child desires to have her own room as soon as possible; in a newly-built house she may have two, one for sleeping and one for storing pots and for cooking, in case the communal cooking places are being used by the senior woman in the yard or in case beer is being brewed, an operation which takes up two days. It may in fact be some time before a man's first wife has a room of her own; at first she joins her husband in his mother's room. In a large compound this situation may continue for several years as it is often difficult to construct additional rooms as desired. The husband himself normally has no room of his own but keeps his possessions and personal shrine to the hill and river sprites (*kontome*) in the room of his senior wife, the wife he first marries. Her children who also sleep there, are his senior offspring, although there may be an older son by a junior wife; her first born male will carve his ancestor shrine at the last of the funeral ceremonies. The Birifuole generally sleep on the roofs of their houses except during the wet weather. The plan of the rooms is exactly traced by the party walls themselves, which project about a foot above the roof itself. One sits, works and sleeps on the roof of one's own rooms.

39

There is another type of living room, not known by the generic name *diu* but as *kampil*; it is a conically-roofed hut, thatched with grasses. These huts, which usually adjoin the patio, strike the observer as additions to the main building; indeed, work is never started on them until the rest of the house has been completed. I have the strong impression that they have spread from the north and east, partly through the influence of the traders' villages; they are rarely found among the Birifor across the Volta.

Such huts are coveted by youths and young married men, particularly those who have been to work in Ashanti, as a place to entertain friends, store their wooden box and cloth—the first essentials of any labour migrant—and sleep with their wife. A father hastens to provide such a room for a son who shows a desire to run south. Older men will sometimes build a similar type of hut (*kampil garo*) above their senior wife's room. A widower can build another type of roof hut (*bo pie*) by filling in his dead wife's room with earth and rubble and then constructing another above it which is entered directly from the roof. Although only a widower can build this room, it may be used after his death by his son who continues to refer to it as his father's.

House-building begins after the guinea-corn harvest in November. The senior members of the local clan sector gather together. The plan of the house is first marked out on the ground with a hoe; a guinea-corn stalk serves as a measuring rod, broken to the correct length against the walls of a room in the old house. And then, while the women fetch water, the men hoe up the soil, mix it into swish and hand it to the girls to carry to the site itself where other men are building the walls of the house. This first stage takes place on the particular market day—*Nakwol daa* or *ta kwɔr daa*, day of no farming—when all sacrifices to the Earth shrine are performed and all hoeing forbidden lest rain should cease to fall.[1] On this day the Earth shrine is especially propitious towards activities under its aegis and especially dangerous to those who have neglected its prohibitions; any person who dies on this day is considered a witch and can only be given the customary mourning rites after his close agnatic kin have made a payment of animals and cowries to the shrine. With earth the basic material, house-building is the particular concern of the Earth shrine.

The work group consists primarily of members of the local clan sector who offer their services on the principle of reciprocity; beer, an essential of all social occasions, is provided in good measure.[2] A much smaller group of helpers will arrive, at least on one or two of the opening days, from any patriclan still having an obligation as affines to farm for the compound head or a close agnate living in the original compound.

The building of a homestead may take from two to eight weeks, from marking out the foundations to actual occupation. During this period a "new house shrine" (*yipaala tiib*) is specially constructed, at the place where the soil is to be dug, out of swish and wood from a tree closely associated with the Earth shrine; this maintains a close watch until the day the ancestor shrines are transferred. After that the house must not be left unoccupied. In a wider sense, the task of house-building is never complete, for the continuously changing composition

---

[1] The week consists of six days named after near-by markets, some of which no longer exist; *Nakwol daa* or market is one of these. The word *daa* also means a day and the plural, *daar*, a week.

[2] I had to be careful of visiting a compound unannounced, for the head of the house might be so overcome with shame if he could not provide me with a pot of beer that my questions would be met only with mumbled apologies and a parting gift offered before the conversation had begun.

of the residential group has a much more direct effect on the lay-out than in any society employing more permanent materials such as stone. The more durable the material, the longer do buildings continue to structure the social relationships of the occupants in accordance with past patterns.

The occupants of a compound

The simplest dwelling group consists of an elementary monogamous family, a man, his wife and their children. Although polygamy is the ideal norm of the LoWiili, the majority of men are monogamous at any one time; only 25% of married men in the sample summarized in Table 9 had more than one wife at the time of the census. I have included the Tallensi figures in this table for comparison.

Table 9

DISTRIBUTION OF WIVES OF MEN OVER 18

SINGLE MEN			MARRIED MEN				
Not married		*Widowers and deserted*	*Number of wives*				
Under 20	Cripples, Lepers, Blind		1	2	3	4	5
5	4	5	63	18	6	—	2
Percentage of sample i Birifu . . .			61%	17%	6%	—	2%
ii. Tallensi . .			46%	20·5%	4·1%	4·8%	0·7%
Percentage of married men i. Birifu . . .			71%	20%	7%	—	2%
ii. Tallensi . .			60·4%	27%	5·4%	6·3%	0·9%

	Composition of sample		*Percentage*		*Ratio men-women*
	Men	Women	Single	Married	
Birifu	103	127	14	86	1·233
Tallensi . . .	146	178	24	76	1·247

The survey was made in a specific area (Tʃaa, Birifu) and headmen were included; in fact it is the present and past headmen who each have five wives. As in Fortes' table (1949, p. 65), I have shown the distribution of "effective wives", a category which included all wives living with their husbands. Wives nominally inherited by, but not living with, their late husband's "brothers" have been excluded from the figures. So have young girls, betrothed as infants but still living with their fathers. Both these categories are referred to as "wives" in certain contexts.

The emphasis on monogamy is more marked than among the Tallensi; there is a more even distribution of women. However, the lower percentage of unmarried men may be partly due to the difficulties involved in estimating ages in African societies possessing no age-set system. One elder insisted to me that he was two hundred years old. I myself enjoyed only comparatively junior status until I added one hundred years to my age calculated according to the European calendar. Most people are quite unclear about 'dates' more than two years from the present.

Of the 103 married men referred to throughout this chapter, only one lived in a compound with his wife and children alone. He had left the house of which his paternal half-brother was the head only six months before the date of the survey. There were two other residential groups among the thirty-one compounds in Tʃaa which consisted basically of an elementary family; three other houses were inhabited by the 'abnormal' personalities previously mentioned

Dwelling groups can be considered in terms of the relationship of the other males to the head of the house (*yirsob*). The results show nine groups of which the head was the father of the other adult males and sixteen groups of which the head was the senior brother of one or more of the other adult males.[1] There is no half way stage in the fission of a dwelling group such as is represented by Fortes' "domestic family", which has its own gateway within the compound. I know of no house in Birifu having more than one byre doorway (i.e. *dondor*, door) although one compound has two ladders. This I believe to be an index of approaching fission, a hypothesis which can only be tested over a period of time; it has not sufficient significance in this continuous process of separation to justify the demarcation of a distinct phase. This fact makes comparison with the Tallensi material difficult as Fortes has constructed certain tables around the domestic family, "the inhabitants of one gateway"; here the basic unit is a group occupying a dwelling variously referred to as a homestead, house or compound.

These dwelling groups are organized on the basis of agnatic descent; the agnatic joint family consisting of several close male agnates, their wives and children living in one compound is the normal pattern. The table below shows the distance in generations of the common ancestor from the most junior member, an index of span.

Table 10

THE SPAN OF THE AGNATES IN DWELLING GROUPS

	Common Clan	Common patrilineal group	Order of Segmentation		
			1 (common Fa)	2 (FaFa)	3 (FaFaFa)
Number of homesteads	2	2	5	10	9

In these twenty-eight homesteads[2] were also living eleven "sister's children" (*arbile* or lit. *ti yepule biir*), including three adult males with a total of three wives and two children. Children of unmarried women, or of sisters rejected by their husbands, are included as lineage members; this is how the Birifuole consider such a "housechild" (*yirbie*), although disabilities as well as privileges are attached to his position. The Birifuole see nothing contradictory in clan and lineage membership passing through females, although these groups are primarily organized on the basis of agnatic descent. The offspring of an illegitimate child (*yirbie*) are full members of the lineage. In Tʃaa there are two married "house-

[1] Compare Fortes, 1949, p.64.
[2] The three 'abnormal' households are not included.

42

children", two youths and one small boy, all members of the clan.[1] To summarize the position, the dwelling group is organized on the principle of agnatic descent; its modal form is a joint family the males of which have a common grandfather. This, however, represents a point in a continuous process of family development which leads to the fission of the dwelling group over a cycle of roughly three generations.

The dwelling group and the farming group

The thirty-one compounds of Tʃaa house fifty farming groups as indicated below.

Table 11

FARMING GROUPS AND HOMESTEADS

Farming groups per homestead .	1	2	3	4	5
Number of homesteads . .	20	6	3	1	1

Average: Birifu: 1·6 Tallensi: 1·3

The average composition of a homestead is 4 males, 5 females, and 7.45 children, a total of 16.45 compared with the figure of 17.4 for the whole of Birifu, according to the 1948 Census Report,[2] and 14.5 for the Tallensi.[3] The most simple dwelling group consists of an elementary family where the father cultivates the land with the help of his wives and young children.

His wives sow the seed and may, in so small a unit, assist with the weeding. Among the LoDagaba, women often clean a groundnut field before planting, but they do none of the heavy hoeing; this involves building the mounds on which cereal crops are usually planted, except when fallow land is first re-sown. The LoWiili regard this as a *Lo* practice: a stronger emphasis exists on the women's contribution within the area in which matrilineal inheritance of wealth obtains.

When the sons marry they continue to farm with their father. Within a few years of his death, the group splits along the line of fission already indicated; the children of one mother will farm together. When this happens, the house remains united for most ritual purposes; the senior son as head of the house is custodian of the ancestor shrines. There is only one cattle byre in a house, although farming groups nowadays often construct their own kraals separated from the compound itself. And it is in the byre that the ancestor shrines are kept.

Independent food production means independent consumption; each farming group has its own granaries. But in time of shortage, the grain would be regarded as available to all living under one roof. The splitting of one compound into different farming groups is often explained as a means of obtaining greater productivity; one lazy individual, not contributing his share of labour, causes them to hoe separately. Between two or more farming groups of "brothers" in the same homestead, a high degree of co-operation continues to exist: "We don't farm together but we all eat together; we have one hoe". The suggested commensalism must be understood metaphorically as an expression of interdependence. For when a man's wife cooks separately, he will eat alone with his offspring; this often

---

[1]These figures are probably too small as I may not have been made aware of the child's status in all cases.

[2]p.349.

[3]Fortes, 1949, p.74.

happens as soon as his first child is weaned. The patrilineal group, the members of which can trace their descent from a named ancestor by genealogical steps, is also said to eat together and have one hoe; the meaning of this assertion is brought out at the regular offering made to the ancestor and medicine shrines at a certain time of year (*bomaaldǎǎ*) as well as at the sacrifices which arise from specific difficulties linked by a diviner to agricultural activities (*kur bɔɔre*). In some lineages, all farming groups make the yearly offerings at the ancestor shrine of the founding ancestor, and in others, at the ancestor shrines of the homestead. In the second case, the founder's name will first be called.

The food available to a particular farming group is not limited to the contents of its own granaries nor to those of the compound; the recognition of any kinship tie involves an obligation to provide food in need although this may come into operation only when the kinsman arrives as a guest. Within the lineage, the conception of the interavailability of supplies is more developed, arising as it does from the idea of the land and its fruits being inherited from a common ancestor. The statement that the lineage has one eating place (*dibzie*) is a recognized expression of genealogical ties rather than an axiom of conduct; outside the context of sacrifices and the preparation of wild animals, it could emerge as a norm of overt behaviour only in famine conditions. I have a record of a man who sold himself to a fellow patriclansman for a cow at a time of extreme hunger. The concept of supplies held in common by the members of a lineage prevented the acquisition of another member as a slave; in this case the "one hoe" had a practical application in regard to food. The group in which certain rights over land are vested by virtue of common descent from a named ancestor who first hoed the area appears to hold supplies in common, at least in times of emergency.

Although sometimes viewed as a method of increasing food production, the existence of two farming groups in one compound represents a distinct phase in the process of fission. The death of one of two brothers who lived together but farmed separately will lead, if the children are too young to farm by themselves, to the reconstitution of a single agricultural unit. But as soon as they feel themselves able, the sons will ask for their father's land, or as much of it as they can farm. Before doing so they may wait a number of years, for women are required to perform their special duties in the fields, and children to look after the cattle and scare the birds from the growing crops. The next stage in the process is the establishment of a separate compound, a grave step involving diviners, senior members of the lineage and the ritual leader of the Earth cult who must first approve the new site. The status of compound head (*yirsob*) confers heavy ritual responsibilities. With the agreement of the dead ancestors the head of a newly-built house removes his father's shrine from the byre and places it in his new compound. Henceforth a failure on his part to conclude successfully the essential ritual performances will bring retribution upon any or all of the occupants; as the requirements are revealed by the diviner only after the catastrophe, the burden will not lightly be assumed by young men.

The building of a new house constitutes a significant point in the segmentation of a descent group as well as in the life of an individual. A limited fusion of dwelling groups operates side by side with fission. On the death of the adult males, the widows disperse either in leviratic union or by marriage outside the lineage, the small children following their mothers, the older ones remaining under the guardianship of their close agnates; meanwhile the walls crumble, the roof falls in and the house becomes a ruin (*dabuo*: an uninhabited house; a former compound site). The dispersal of local lineages through slave-raiding and the

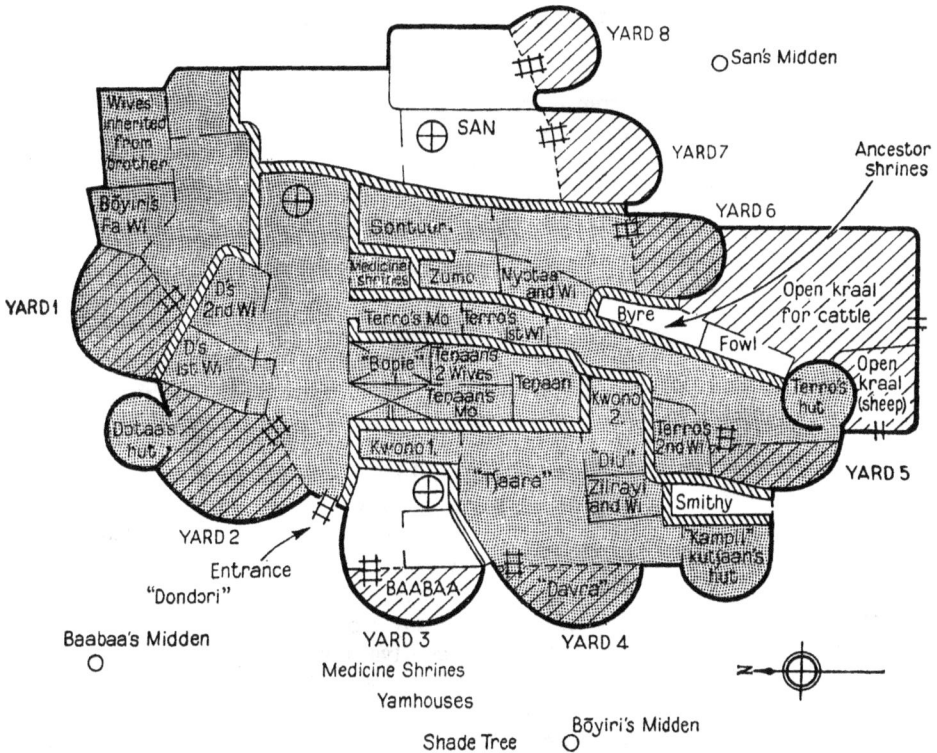

FIG.5. BŌYIRI'S COMPOUND, TʃAA, BIRIFU. BUILT BY HIS FATHER

Fig. 5. BŌYIRI'S COMPOUND, TʃAA, BIRIFU

Rooms occupied by *Bōyiri's* farming group. His eldest son, *San* (Yards 7 and 8) and a clansman who had fled from the Ivory Coast (Yard 3), both farm by themselves.

The main granaries of each farming group; subsidiary granaries are built in most long rooms.

Ladders.

Kampil, grass-roofed hut. (The local names of the different rooms are shown in parenthesis for Yard 4).

Open access to long room (*Tʃaara*).

Limits of sets of rooms.

Rooms on roof.
  (i) *Betʃaara*, open on the south side, and used by *Bōyiri* for entertaining strangers and for divining.
  (ii) *Bopie*, used by *Bōyiri* as a sleeping room.

Unroofed courtyards and kraals.

Bōyiri's own polygynous family is discussed in the text.

The occupants of the yards are :

Yard 1. *Bōyiri's* father's widow and two wives inherited from a brother.

Yard 2. His senior wife and her sons, *Dɔtaa* and *Teŋgaan*.

Yard 4. His favourite wife, *Kwono* and her sons, *Ziirayi* and *Kutʃaan*.

Yard 5. His second wife and her son *Terro*.

Yard 6. *Sontuur* is *Bōyiri's* Si Da Da, the widow of a "son, ", of whose children *Bōyiri* became guardian. She has two sons, *Nyotaa* by her first husband, *Zumo* by *Bōyiri's* "son".

45

more recent activities of European administrations has led to the establishment of dwelling groups of a wide genealogical span, for such migrants usually seek out their patrilineal clansmen. Two houses in Tʃaa[1] had given hospitality to a clansman under such circumstances. In another homestead resided a younger sister of the compound head's senior wife; her husband, temporarily working in Ashanti, had also moved eastward across the Volta. Accretions from a residential group broken up through the death of the senior males accounted for the two compounds whose members were linked only by the founding ancestor of the maximal lineage.

Farming groups and the consumption of food

The granaries of a farming group, like the farms themselves, are under the control of the senior member. While decisions among the adults will be made only after discussion, he will bear the final responsibility for the distribution of food. A young boy or girl is asked to descend into the granary and fill a number of baskets with heads of guinea-corn or millet, which the senior wife then arranges to have threshed. The grain is brought up on to the roof again to be divided among, and in the presence of, the cooking groups each according to its strength (*dirbɛ*—eaters). A polygynous family may consist of more than one cooking group. *Bõyir*, an old man of some wealth as he had been a paid 'headman'[2], had five wives. Two of these, whose relations with their husband had never been firmly established, were inherited leviratically from his paternal half-brother. They lived with his father's widow in one courtyard, No. 1 in the sketch (Fig. 5). These three women were all past childbearing, had no male children, and together formed a single cooking group. *Bõyir's* other three wives each had separate courtyards of their own where they lived with their married children. The senior wife had two sons both with two wives, and their polygynous families formed two independent cooking groups, the mother attached to the group of her younger son.

Bõyir's next wife had one son and until 1951 they had shared a courtyard with the senior wife; when her son took a second wife, a new yard (5) and long room were built, but there still remained an opening between the two. A separate cooking group now occupied its own set of rooms within the compound, although the sons mentioned farmed with their father.[3] Characteristically, the split occurred not between the two older sons, who had one mother, but between those two sons and their younger brother by a different woman. The establishment of two apartment groups is a definite stage in the fission of the polygynous family. The common bond in a joint family is patrilineal; matrilateral filiation supplies the lines of cleavage. This stage precedes the setting up of separate farming groups. Of the fifty farming groups in Tʃaa, only one shared a set of rooms with another farming group. In this case a woman had been inherited by her husband's younger brother; when they grew up and married, the dead man's children decided to farm by themselves but continued to live in the same apartment as their mother and her husband. Although the LoWiili say that a separate *davra* could be built if co-wives continually quarrelled, in every observed case a polygynous family had more than one set of rooms only when the women's sons had married.

---

[1]Table 9., Column 1.

[2]A European-created official for whom Dagari speakers use the English word.

[3]I call this an apartment group, the inhabitants of a *davra*, literally a yard or patio, but by extension the set of rooms entered by the ladder which drops into it.

Food consumption and the differentiation of the polygynous family

When a man first marries, his wife becomes a member of his mother's cooking group. She sleeps in her mother-in-law's room, uses her pots, grinding stone and utensils, does the heavier tasks and generally acts as her daughter; she prepares food for her husband on behalf of her mother-in-law whose responsibility it has hitherto been. Gradually she is left to do more and more of the work and even at this stage may accumulate her personal food supplies by helping at her father's harvest and by picking groundnuts on the farms of her own and her husband's patrilineal kin. These supplies, kept in earthenware pots sealed with cow dung, serve to augment those distributed by the head of the farming group. With the birth of a child the husband may build her a room; a girl's first marriage is regarded as highly unstable until she has given birth. The likely duration of a marriage at any one time increases in proportion to the number of children.

A wife accumulates wealth of her own by brewing beer, by trading, and, in a few cases, by pot-making. In order to buy the original grain to re-sell or brew, she borrows cowries from her husband, creating a debt which she has to repay in the event of divorce. With her trading profit she purchases pots and gourds, the basic requirements of an independent cooking group; eventually she may get herself a grinding stone (*nier*).

The LoWiili regard sexual intercourse with a woman who is breast-feeding a child as likely to impede the flow of milk and the satisfactory development of the infant. As children are regularly breast-fed for two to three years, until they are proficient at talking, the husband tries wherever possible to acquire a second wife. In the beginning the newcomer occupies the room of the senior wife and even when she has her own, culinary tasks are still shared. A common allocation of grain is made and a portion of the cooked food sent to their husband from the wives jointly; of the remainder, some is eaten with the smaller children, and the rest preserved in a pot containing a bitter preserving infusion (*kwõ miiru*) to provide food until the next distribution of grain. It is around the contents of this pot that quarrels develop and cooking groups divide. The children of one woman may so harass their mother for food that she will go to the common pot and take out some of the cold porridge without reference to her co-wife (*yentaa*) who may arrive later to find nothing left. It is in this way that the LoWiili conceive the setting up of independent units of food preparation—a simplification, for the question of separation is not decided by reference to food alone. The temperament of the wives concerned has a considerable influence on the length of time a cooking group survives. But at every turn in domestic life the LoWiili are aware that the breach in a polygynous family occurs through the children of different mothers. Childless women, or those whose only children are married daughters, frequently cook together; a man's mother and his wife will normally continue to share duties, the younger woman gradually taking over responsibility. But fission occurs when two women are both looking after children, for a woman's first duty is to feed her own offspring.

Dɔtaa and *Teŋgaan*, two of *Bõyir's* sons[1], occupied a set of rooms with their old mother. Each had two wives and when grain was distributed both the senior wives received shares for their respective polygynous families, the mother eating with the younger son's wives. In another yard in the same house, *Bõyir's* youngest and favourite wife, *Kwono*, lived with her three sons, two of whom had recently married but had as yet no children. The women all cooked together; the domestic

---

[1]See Fig. 5.

personalities of the young wives were submerged in that of their mother-in-law. *Kwono* provided her husband with food (*saab ni la ni zier:* porridge and bowl of relish), as did all her co-wives, whenever a distribution of food was made.

The regular distribution of grain does not begin immediately, but some time during the dry season. Until then a woman cooks the grain she has acquired through her own resources and from her husband at harvest. This is called *pobo tfi*, "women's guinea corn" and consists of those heads not expected to keep. The husband may provide a special granary for his wives (*pobo buur*) into which they can put the grain they have acquired but this is rarely done among the LoWiili.

Where two co-wives cook together, the one whose turn it is to sleep with her husband generally cooks for him. A wife deprived of the sexual attentions of her husband can refuse to prepare food for him; the two obligations are treated reciprocally. In a polygynous system stress situations often develop around the lack of balance in the sexual activity of married men and women. Here this is reflected in the refusal of a wife to cook for her husband.

Marriage

The elementary family is established through marriage; polygyny creates a number of elementary families centred on one man. The desiderated state of male existence includes a plurality of wives and an abundant progeny. However, as the ratio of men to women in the Lawra District is 1 : 1·075[1] and there is no access through purchase or capture to brides from other communities, the majority of men at any one time are monogamous, although the longer married life of women makes the incidence of polygyny greater than the ratio suggests.

Marriage being virilocal, a woman has to leave her own father's house and join the compound of her father-in-law; henceforward she lives apart from the main body of her agnatic kin. In the case of marriages arranged in the girl's childhood, the transfer takes place with the consent of both her parents. The weight of opinion is behind sending a daughter, in any case a woman's first-born girl, to marry the mother's brother's son; matrilateral cross cousin marriage also being permissible, her brothers support their mother's resolution to send the girl to her patrikin, as satisfactory relations may assist them to secure a wife from that lineage. A husband, moreover, regards the return of his daughter to her mother's kin as a general obligation contracted in marriage, depending for its fulfilment on satisfactory relations with his in-laws.

Infant betrothal to persons other than the girl's matrilateral kin may occur in specific situations, in return for assistance rendered in preserving the girl's life through the timely administration of "medicines" (*tɨ̃*) or with a stranger who first greets the parents after the birth of a female child. Such an understanding permits the future husband to refer to the child playfully as "my wife" (*n pɔɔ*).

The second type of arrangement for first marriages is elopement, which occurs about the age of puberty. The man persuades the girl to escape to his home; alternatively she may be seized by his "brothers" at a dance and forcibly brought to his house, although this would only be done with her consent. If the girl elopes without loud protest, she will be called a bitch. Her sexuality will not have been alienated to outsiders in the particular manner which the social structure demands; she has given herself freely to the first comer, like an animal on heat. The girl's parents, one of whom has probably been in the son-in-law's confidence, express their anger; they thereby free themselves from the accusation of having condoned the marriage and deliberately broken an existing pledge or

[1] 1948 Census Report.

48

obligation. The element of force persists even in arranged marriages; the actual move to the husband's home may take place, for example, after a funeral in the bride's house when the girl is taken away on the grounds that she requires solace in the bereavement she has suffered. These acts constitute formal expression of the transfer of rights over a woman from one group to another; they represent dramatically the change in her social position and the conflict between her filial and conjugal ties.

Marriage under the rule of clan exogamy sets up a series of kinship ties between members of two different patriclans. Among the agnatic kin of his mother a man is always welcome; on the other hand, the obligations entered into at marriage are the source of continual friction between the husband and his wife's guardian.

The transfer of rights over the bride is accompanied by a transfer of property from the groom's group. The first instalment of bridewealth consists of a placation gift of a cock and guinea-fowl to the in-laws, and a sum (*pɔɔ libie*) equal to that given for the girl's mother, in Birifu nowadays about 20,000 cowries. The essential element in this bridewealth payment consists of three hundred and sixty cowries which are known as *libie tuo*, the bitter money. These are taken by the father or proxy father of the groom and placed before the compound's ancestor shrines. By this act, the rights over women acquired by the transaction are vested in the lineage as a whole, in its dead as well as its living members, and the fertility of its wives is placed under the aegis of the ancestors. Any abrogation of these rights has henceforth to be expiated by a sacrifice at their shrines and adultery payments are in effect offerings to the ancestors exacted from the adulterer.

All the 20,000 cowries are then carried to the bride's home by a group of the groom's agnatic "fathers", patriclansmen of the senior generation, who are accompanied by two witnesses, members of another clan and usually matrilateral kinsmen of the groom who may be called upon at some future date to testify to the amount transferred. Once they have reached his house, the cowries are spread on the rooftop and counted out in piles of one thousand. On their first visit the amount is never correct and the groom's kinsmen are sent home with the cowries and asked to come again bringing a sum adequate for their daughter. They return some days later only to be again turned away. On the third occasion the money is finally accepted. These acts are to be related to the phenomena of marriage by capture, for which Radcliffe-Brown has provided a sociological interpretation. It is possible to regard both of these expressions of what may be called institutionalized reluctance as arising from the sudden change in a woman's rôle from that of daughter to that of wife, a change which is particularly violent where marriage is virilocal and one which is a corollary of the incest rule whereby men have to deny themselves their own sisters and daughters in order to acquire wives.

When the bridewealth is at last accepted, certain cowries are again set aside for special purposes. First they are shown to the ancestor shrines and some are used to purchase a black fowl which is then sacrificed to the deceased members of the lineage. A small amount, usually one hundred, is distributed among the lineage "brothers" of the girl present at the sacrifice. This serves to confirm the fact that the payment which has been received at her marriage can be used only to marry a wife to one of her "brothers", never to one of her 'fathers'. A further hundred is given to the old woman, a wife of a lineage member, who has brought the perineal bands of goat hide which the girl will henceforth wear as a married woman. It is usually this same old woman who has excised the girl's clitoris at about the age of puberty, an act which is considered essential to fruitful intercourse. A further sum of eighty cowries, that is, the customary contribution of twenty multiplied by the female number, four, are given to the girl's guardian spirit which has looked after her from childhood.[1] At the same time a fowl is sacrificed to its shrine, which may be the Earth, the hill and water sprites, a specific ancestor, the clan guardian spirit or any of the numerous medicine shrines. This sacrifice normally occurs not at the time of the marriage itself but when she has borne her first child. It is in effect a thanksgiving offering for having protected the girl until she has proven her reproductive powers, for having watched over a girl until she has become a mother.

This payment establishes the clan membership of any child conceived after the acceptance of the money by the close agnates of the bride's father. Rights over a woman's procreative powers are thereby transferred from her own to her husband's lineage. Any child conceived before the transfer of the bridewealth is a 'house-child' (*yirbie*) attached to the mother's agnatic lineage.

A man's father, or the inheritor of the father's wealth, is responsible for finding the bridewealth payments for the sons and for any other person farming with him; anyone who ceases to hoe with his father takes upon himself the responsibility of providing the bridewealth for any wife other than the first. Among the LoDagaba, where the inheritance of wealth is matrilineal, the responsibility of the father or his inheritor ends with the bridewealth for the first wife; the gifts for the second are contributed by the mother's brother. A corollary of this is the division. of the cowries received when a daughter marries, called *poɣ tʃεra libiε* by the LoDagaba, between the father and the mother's brother, the latter having the larger share. These cowries are considered roughly equivalent to one cow.

A son-in-law's obligations to his father-in-law include the provision of ten to twenty men to clean and hoe his land at least three times during the rainy season. A prospective son-in-law may bring labourers before the girl has moved to his compound, or, if living there, before she has reached puberty, in order to ingratiate himself with his in-laws (*kob zεlε*). The wife's father supplies beer and, on the final occasion, soup, porridge and meat or a small quantity of cowries for each of the labourers. They consume the beer and food on their own, the son-in-law himself only drinking beer because of the 'shame' (*vĩ*) he would feel were he to eat food at the house of his in-laws.

I have never attended a gathering of this nature where some disagreement over the interpretation of recognised obligations did not arise. On one occasion blows were only avoided by an elder constantly repeating that "a man and his son-in-law cannot fight, only brothers-in-law can" (*diem ni diem kantwõ ziorε; dakyiε bε na ziora*). The word *diem* is employed reciprocally between children and parents-in-law and *dakyiε* between siblings-in-law of the same sex. The relationship between in-laws of adjacent generations (*diem*) is characteristically strained, constant difficulties arising in the fulfilment of rights and duties. Although the term can include the entire first ascending generation of the wife's clan, these difficulties usually develop only with her guardian, the person primarily interested in the fulfilment of the obligations.

Concerning the relationship between brothers-in-laws, among the Wala, a neighbouring people, Rattray was told: "You may abuse your wife's brother . . . because he cannot take your wife from you".[2] This is also true of the LoWiili.

---

[1] These payments vary, but the core is usually the same, eighty cowries and a black fowl.
[2] 1932, Vol. I, p.8.

Freedom of address between affines is specifically associated with the absence of rights and duties. This relative lack of tension in personal contact with in-laws where no obligations intervene is a corollary of the respect relationship existing between in-laws of adjacent generations. The LoWiili say that brothers-in-law can abuse each other. They can play (*diena*) but are not joking partners (*lonluore*), a term which implies the exchange of cathartic services. Friendship exists because both find themselves in conflict with the senior generation; in a quarrel between a man and his son-in-law, I have seen a son come to the defence of the latter. The friendly relations cease when the brother-in-law becomes responsible through his father's death for ensuring the fulfilment of the obligations contracted by marriage. The dual situation of brothers-in-law, which Fortes noted among the Tallensi,[1] is therefore present but perhaps not emphasized to quite the same extent; the people themselves speak of a 'convention of joking', (*dakyiɛ dieno*, sibling-in-law play) but this is not in much evidence between brothers-in-law. It applies rather to the joking between a woman and her brother's wife whom she will jokingly address as 'my wife' (*n pɔɔ*). The explanation offered for this remark is "If I had been a man, would she not have been my wife?" Here the unity of the sibling group, or lineage, conflicts with sexual differentiation. This situation relates to the whole problem of the rights and duties which a man possesses in his mother's agnatic group.

The most unstable period of marriage is the early years when a man farms for his father-in-law, who, if dissatisfied, may persuade his daughter to return to his house until the obligations are met to the full. The son-in-law continues to hoe for some three to five years, and, if required, to repair his in-laws' house during the dry season; at the end of this period, the precise length of which depends upon his relations with his father-in-law, he is asked for a 'hoeing sheep' (*ko pir*) to be used, his in-laws say, to obtain substitute help on the farm during the following season. At this point the wife has become an established member of her husband's family; she pays less frequent visits to her father's house and holds increased responsibility in her husband's. The next formally demarcated stage occurs when she has borne about three children. By calling his daughter to his house, the father automatically presents a demand for the 'cattle payment' (*doɛ*) consisting of a cow, the calves of which are used in further marital transactions, and a bull, the daughter's bull (*pɔɔyaa naab*) or bull of child-bearing (*bidɔɔ naab*) which is sacrificed to the founding ancestor of her lineage, either at his own shrine or at the homestead shrines. It is said of a woman who possesses three or more children that "she builds the house" (*o men a yir*); she has now "entered the house" (*kpen a yir*) and may peer into her husband's granary without offence. It is a matter of considerable comment if a woman of this standing leaves her husband; she it is who loses (*lona*, falls) for when her children grow she will want to return to be near them. The second bridewealth payment of cattle marks a woman's increased separation from her family and her full incorporation into her husband's domestic group. She has now proven her fertility; the transfer of her procreative powers to her husband's lineage is confirmed. As a formal index, the LoWiili point to the fact that once the cattle have been sent, any wild animal the woman kills—a most unlikely happening—now belongs to her husband's and no longer to her father's lineage. It is said that formerly the male lineage members would be entitled to remove the dead body of one of their married "sisters" if this payment had not been made, and bury her in their own cemetery.

---

[1] 1949, p.120.

On arrival at the funeral, they would overturn the xylophone and throw some ebony leaves upon it. The ceremony could not proceed without the matter having been set right; for ebony has a special association with the Earth shrine whose anger would be provoked by any attempt to continue mourning. The lineage threatened to carry off the body unless payment were made; however, a joking partner would usually persuade them that "a putrified corpse was not worth the trouble of removing."

In theory, a final payment of a cow (*naab baara*) should be made when the woman ceases to be capable of childbearing and when bridewealth cattle have been received for her daughter. When the preferred patrilateral cross-cousin marriages take place, the 'final cow' and the bridewealth are exchanged between two lineages at the same time. A man does not, however, normally ask for this 'final cow' if his daughter has married within the ritual area.

A woman who has finished childbearing is most unlikely to leave the house. On the death of her husband she remains with her sons, although nominally she might be considered the "wife" of her husband's nearest agnatic kinsman of the same, or an alternate, generation. After the menopause she "changes to a man" (*o lieba daba*). Her whole life centres around her husband's house. She visits her own kin only for funerals. She has become a woman elder (*pɔɔ kpɛ̃ɛ̃*), knowing the detailed rituals of the main medicine shrines (*daanyuur kpɛ̃ɛ̃*, the great tree roots) of her husband's clan better than many of the younger men. At the first of the series of *Bɔɔre* ceremonies,[1] the initiation rites of a 'secret society', she not only receives a share of the food allotted to her husband's lineage, but is even permitted to sit among the men to eat her portion.

The successive payments of bridewealth mark stages in the integration of a woman into her husband's domestic group. These gifts are essentially tied to the birth of children and confirm the transfer of rights over the procreative powers of a woman from a lineage of one clan to a lineage of another. Sterility automatically dispenses with the need for further gifts. Although the clan membership of the children and the transfer of rights over the sexual powers of the woman are established by the first payment, subsequent payments are made only when her fertility is proven. In contrast to the immediate transfer of rights in the woman as wife, *uxor*, rights in her as *genetrix* can only be effectively exchanged when her powers have been confirmed.[2]

Although rights *in uxorem* normally form a unitary category in patrilineal societies, where virilocal marriage is the rule, it is useful for comparative purposes to consider the rights transferred at marriage under the following heads:

    (i) rights over a woman's procreative powers (*in genetricem*);
    (ii) rights over sexual services;
    (iii) rights over domestic services;
    (iv) rights over economic services;
    (v) rights of co-residence.

(i) Bridewealth payments other than the first may be regarded as validating the transfer of the rights over the woman's procreative powers as evidence of these is provided by the birth of children; this has already been discussed.

(ii) Marriage always involves a transfer of rights over the sexuality of women; this is the constant element—the other sets of rights may or may not be involved. Among the LoWiili the first bridewealth payment immediately validates the

---

[1] *Bagre* among the LoDagaba and the Birifor; see Labouret, 1931, p.461.
[2] See Laura Bohannan, "Dahomean Marriage: A Revaluation", Africa, XIX, 1949, p.273.

transfer of these rights. Payments to the husband's ancestor shrines become due from the offender if the wife subsequently commits adultery; this fine can be used by the lineage, but not by the husband himself. He cannot himself consume any of the flesh of the sacrificed animal, lest it might be said that he was profitting from this alienation of his wife's sexuality. These rights of the lineage derive from factors previously discussed, especially its position as a land-holding group, an economic unit in relation to agriculture. Wealth, the surplus of agricultural production over consumption, belongs, like land, the basic productive resource, to the ancestors. In this sense the mere payment of the bridewealth, the alienation of wealth, is the concern of the ancestors, quite apart from their interest in maintaining the continuity of the lineage.

(iii), (iv), (v) Rights over a girl's domestic services are acquired by the husband directly she resides with him. This may be before the bridewealth transaction takes place. In the case where eligible girls are living in the compound of their future husband, for example, a sister's daughter, or a wife's unmarried sister brought in to look after one of the latter's offspring, there is no precise transfer of these rights, which are the function of co-residence under the virilocal rule. Although economic services are acquired by the husband, the woman's father retains the right to call his daughter to his house in order to help when her husband brings people to carry out the farming services involved in marriage. She may return for the day at harvest time; but in this she pleases herself. If she goes, it will be in order to visit her parents, and to acquire a little wealth of her own, for she will be given some of the crops she helps to harvest.

The question of how often and for how long a woman should visit her parents is a difficult one; frequent visits indicate dissatisfaction and a long visit may easily widen into a permanent separation, for which the husband's only remedy is to demand the return of the bridewealth. Essentially, marriage is virilocal.

The transfer of rights in a woman is not completed by the first payment; indeed, important aspects of ritual and jural authority remain permanently vested in her patrilineal group. Although a woman is drawn closer and closer to her husband's lineage in a process marked by successive payments of bridewealth, she can never become a member of that lineage, nor cease to belong to her own. The series of funeral performances sums up the social personality of the deceased; a woman is buried among her husband's lineage, of whose continuity her male children are the guarantee, but at the final ceremony a stick cut in her name is carried ceremonially to her father's house where it joins the ancestor shrines.

The husband also has certain obligations towards his wife, namely, to provide her with food, shelter and such medical treatment as the diviner may specify.

The dissolution of an elementary family. 1. Through death

The break-up of an elementary family through death or divorce has important consequences in relation to descent groups, for such an event may re-define the position of the offspring of the marriage in regard to those groups.

If a woman dies, her unweaned child is taken by her mother or close uterine kinswoman, who looks after it until strong enough to return to the father's house. Before the husband's lineage can claim its offspring, fermented guinea-corn, fowls and a young goat have to be sent to the lineage who have taken care of the child, so that they may prepare beer and sacrifice at their minor Earth shrine (*teŋgaanble*). This is an upbringing or fostering payment. When the grandmother first collects the child after the mother's death, she will give it water in which was sprinkled a little dirt from around the homestead in which she lives. The act of eating the soil places the infant under the protection of that Earth shrine. Failure to make this thanksgiving offering, the fostering payment, is held to account for the interstial position of the *Ŋmanbil-Maale* lineage between Ŋmanbili and Tʃaa. This lineage acts in most respects as a member of the *Ŋmanbili* clan sector but their homesteads are entirely situated within the ritual area of Tʃaa and it is at that minor Earth shrine that they sacrifice. "They are children of our Earth shrine (*teŋgaan bir*)", say Tʃaa, "because their clansman did not make the necessary offerings". The existing territorial distribution is confirmed by a story which explains how a sister's son, the founder of *Ŋmanbil-Maale*, was at his mother's death taken to live with her patrilineage. The descendants of the sister's son are prohibited by the ancestors from referring to themselves as *Ŋmanbili* or *Tʃaale*. Instead they call themselves *Ŋmanbil Maale* or *Ŋmanbil Tʃaale* and observe the taboos of both clans. These cases show that the rights held over a woman as *genetrix* are not absolute; the descent group affiliation of a child can be modified under the circumstances mentioned above as well as when a woman is rejected by her husband, that is, divorced by him on insufficient grounds.

The question of transfer at the death of the mother does not arise with children who have been weaned. If the marriage is dissolved while the mother is alive, it is usual for children under the age of seven to accompany her. Otherwise the children remain in the care of a co-wife, a classificatory 'mother'. It is true that in a polygynous family, and this is particularly so where classificatory kinship is generalized to the boundaries of the unilineal descent groups, relations between a mother and her own born are more diffuse, less intense than in a simple conjugal family; a woman may suckle the child of a co-wife who has some specific task in hand. But the LoWiili realize that these services are based on the principle of reciprocity; otherwise a co-wife tends to neglect children other than her own, and motherless children come off badly. For these reasons, they claim, "it is good that our in-laws take away the young children". Other situations arising out of the dissolution of elementary families show the importance laid on keeping the mother and child together during at least the first three years. It is not until he is weaned and can walk and talk that a child has a complete social personality, that he is a real human being. Only after that period has passed is he entitled to a proper burial. If the death of the mother makes it impossible to keep mother and child together, the best alternative, in terms of their social structure, is the closest uterine kinswoman of the deceased.

Death involves the redistribution of rights in a man's widows. This occurs after the final funeral ceremony when he has been formally admitted to the company of ancestors (*kpiin*, pl. *kpime*, lit. dead). The thirty-three widows of the late chief of Birifu remarried as follows:

Main inheritor (a younger full brother)	4
Other members of the compound	7
Other members of the lineage outside the compound	2
Sisters' sons outside the compound	3
Other non-clansmen	9

In addition eight, most of whom had finished childbearing, declared they wished simply to remain in the house without marrying anyone else; nominally, they are wives of the inheritor. In all, fourteen left the homestead after their husband's funeral.

Widows may be taken by any member of the lineage, without any further bridewealth transactions, a corollary of the rights in a woman held by the patri-

54

lineal group. The issue of such a union continue to belong (*so*) to the deceased; if he left no male offspring, a son of a widow taken in leviratic marriage would cut his ancestor shrine, a service he could not perform for his actual begetter. The person on whose behalf the bridewealth payment was made owns the child (*libie sob, ola so a bie*). The same principle applies when a sister's son marries a man's widow without repaying the bridewealth. Thus rights *in uxorem* pass to any lineage member or even sister's son, but rights *in genetricem* continue to be vested in the dead husband until a bridewealth payment is made.

If a widow marries outside the compound, the young children may accompany her and return to their own lineage at about the age of ten when they are capable of fending for themselves. A widow who has ceased childbearing is unable to find a husband other than a lineage member who has an existing obligation to care for her. Of the younger widows, those who have adult male children are the most likely to remain in the compound, for their future security lies in their sons. Occasionally, a woman who has no sons may go to live with a married daughter after the death of her husband.

The death of the mother or father may result in a child being raised among other than agnatic kin; the death of the former may lead to a redefinition of lineage affiliation of the offspring.

The dissolution of an elementary family. 2. *By divorce*

The failure of a man to feed and shelter his wife, to take the necessary steps to cure her sickness and resolve her ritual difficulties, or of a woman to fulfil a wife's allotted economic and domestic duties, the refusal of either to join in sexual intercourse, these are held to be grounds for divorce. Adultery is normally settled by the provision of the required sacrifice for the ancestor shrines; although the resulting conflicts may later cause the marriage to be dissolved, it is not in itself held to be grounds. At divorce a woman returns to her father's home until she finds another husband. If she leaves her husband of her own accord (*o zona*, she runs), either openly by hanging forbidden leaves over her buttocks or secretly by removing her pots and breaking down her shrine to the hill and water sprites (*kontome*), she has no doubt already made an arrangement with another man. The children remain members of their father's clan although the younger ones accompany their mother to her new home. The new husband pays the original bridewealth to his in-laws who then return it to the former husband.

If the woman is cast out (*o zɔɔra baar*, he rejects her utterly) by her husband breaking her cooking place (*dɔɔn*) or throwing away her sleeping mat, no bride-wealth is returned until she remarries, which in view of the prevailing ideal of polygyny and the restricting demographic factors[1] she is likely to do within a few weeks. In this case children who accompany her enter her clan as 'house-children' (s. *yirbie*), grafted to the agnatic line through a female; by the formula of rejection, the husband abdicates his position as *pater* or legal father of the children. It should be added that a recent judgment of a District Commissioner has altered this situation. He maintained that in this case the begetter of the child should be its legal father and this is now generally accepted by the LoWiili living in the Gold Coast. It was once maintained to me that the children of a rejected wife would change their clan affiliation only if the bridewealth had been repaid to the husband; if the woman did not remarry this would have to be done by the wife's father himself. Changing conditions make it difficult to check this interesting point.

---

[1] See Fortes, 1943, p.99.

55

Formerly, if a wife ran away, remarried and then returned to her first husband, the young children by the second husband would be attached to the clan of the first, although the payment of bridewealth at the appropriate times might appear to give the second husband the right to his children. A second qualification must therefore be added to the rights *in genetricem* conferred through bridewealth transactions.

Maalo and *Dʒato* were living in a compound in Tʃaa and I took them for lineage members; later it was whispered that they were not clansmen. The story was a complicated one; what had happened was this. The mother of their father, *Domuo*, was from Tʃaa; she married at Naayili but the union proved sterile. She then ran to a '*Yoŋyuole* man and, after bearing three children, returned with them to her first husband. It was whispered to me that *Maalo* and *Dʒato*, *Domuo's* sons, were not really *Tʃaale* at all, but *Naayili*, the clan of the first husband. I later found this was not so, for during a famine the latter had rejected his wife, who took the children to her father's house. The children became attached to her lineage as "house children" (*yirbie*), but the grandchildren are now full members and trace their descent through males to its founding ancestor. How they do so will be explained when the position of the "house child" is discussed in greater detail after we have considered the relationship of a mother's brother with a sister's legitimate child, that is, a child belonging to a different patriclan from its mother.

Uxorilateral relationships

The relationships established at marriage between the agnatic kin of the bride and the agnatic kin of the groom are marked by a certain degree of conflict over the transfer of rights in the woman and the counter-transfer of goods and services. But the hostility lessens with each subsequent transfer of wealth to the woman's kin, payments which turn on the birth of children. For these children not only preserve and strengthen the patriclan of their father; their relationships with the patriclan of their mother serve also to break down the exclusiveness of the discrete agnatic descent groups. And these consanguineal relationships established between the offspring of a conjugal pair and the members of the descent group traced through residual filiation are in marked contrast to those "contractual" affinal relationships established by the act of marriage itself.

In a patrilineal society, therefore, the relationship between sister's son and mother's brother must be viewed within the context of the system of unilineal descent groups. It is in order to emphasize this that I refer to it as a uxorilateral relationship, one that is traced through the mother or the sister, the spouse or sibling, on the non-descent side. From ego's point of view there are two aspects, (i) his relationship with the members of his mother's descent group, (ii) his relationship with the offspring of his "sisters".

Ego's rôles as sister's son or as mother's brother are not unitary, although all are comprised under one and the same kinship term *madeb*, the literal translation of which is "mother male". Within the class of people indicated by this word, four distinct categories may be distinguished, not terminologically but analytically, in terms of the structure of descent groups and customary actions. These are:

> mother's brother (*madeb*) 1. The (eldest) full brother of ego's mother;
> mother's brother (*madeb*) 2. Any male member of ego's mother's patri-
> lineage of the same generation as *madeb* 1;
> mother's brother (*madeb*) 3. Any male member of one's mother's patri-
> clan;

mother's brother (*madeb*) 4. A senior member of ego's (and therefore his
mother's) matriclan.

Similarly, the reciprocal term, sister's child (*arbile*), is used, without distinction of sex, in a number of different ways.

    (i) *arbile* 1. Ego's (eldest) full sister's (eldest male) child;

    (ii) *arbile* 2. The child of any "sister" of ego's patrilineage;

    (iii) *arbile* 3. The child of any female member of ego's patriclan;

    (iv) *arbile* 4 (plural only). The members of an adjacent patrilineage of
        different patriclan whose founding ancestor is said to be a sister's
        son of the founder of ego's patrilineage;

    (v) *arbile* 5. Any junior member of ego's matriclan.

I want to defer consideration of *madeb* 4 and *arbile* 5 until we deal with the
system of matriclans. In any case, these usages are rare. A fellow matriclansman
is normally referred to as *yeb* ("brother", or more exactly, sibling of the same sex)
when a kinship term is appropriate; the alternatives given above are used only
when ego wishes to emphasize his age in relation to that of alter.

When analysing these various relationships, it is essential to do so in the
context of the descent groups to which the individuals belong. This is what the
LoWiili do. They view kinship relations in terms of descent groups; the limits for
the application of a particular kinship term are the boundaries of the descent
group. And descent groups are thought of in terms of kinship ties. "Those are my
mother's brothers", a man may exclaim when the name of such and such a clan
is mentioned.

To ego, the whole of his mother's patriclan are in certain contexts his "mother's
brothers", for generation differences are not usually recognized outside the
mother's natal homestead and never outside her patrilineage. In other situations,
the categories *madeb* 1, 2 and 3 may be differentiated in ways which will shortly
be mentioned. But the narrower and wider usages of the term—I wish to avoid
the concept of extension—all refer to the members of one descent group. With the
reciprocal "sister's child" the wider usage refers to a descent group only in the
somewhat specialized case, *arbile* 4, where it generalizes the supposed kinship
relationship between the founding ancestors of two lineages to the present status
of the two groups. It assumes a junior, dependent, status for those spoken of as
"sister's children". They are visualized only as bride-receivers, although in fact,
where preferred, patrilateral cross-cousin marriage actually occurs, and indeed
without this, there will be a more or less equal give and take between the two
groups concerned. Although the overt reference is to the receipt of rights over
women, the implied reference is to the receipt of land. The lineage of the sister's
son is said to have arrived in the area after the mother's brothers' group.
They had therefore to beg land from the latter, rights which they were granted by
virtue of the residual claim which women possess on the property of their
patriclan. This has been more thoroughly discussed in the section on land
tenure.[1]

In the other and more usual case, the plural usage of the term *arbile* (3) refers
not to a descent group but to a category of kin distributed among a number of
different descent groups. Nevertheless, there are, as we shall see, a number of
occasions on which these kin play a collective rôle. The point I wish to emphasize
is this, in the case of both *arbile* 2 and 3 and *madeb* 2 and 3, these wider classificatory usages of the term centre upon the mother's patriclan; the classifications

---

[1] p.35.

are made with reference to that clan. A man's mother's brothers, in the agnatic framework, fall in one descent group, his sisters' sons in many. This is bound to be the case, unless all marriages occur between two exogamous moieties. Ego's descent group will therefore have a relationship as a group with all the children of its "sisters", which it does not have with all the brothers of its "mothers". There are therefore two aspects to the uxorilateral relationship, the matrilateral or avuncular and the nepotic; from the standpoint of ego's clan, the former individuates members of the sibling group, the latter emphasizes the unity of the clan in relation to the offspring of those members who are excluded from transmitting membership and therefore from transmitting the property of the corporate group.

All the various relationships of ego with his "mother's brothers" and with his "sister's children" must therefore be viewed within the context of the system of descent groups. It is in my opinion wrong to regard the rights and duties of a sister's son to his mother's brother as an extension of the sentiments developed in the maternal bond between mother and son. This is what Radcliffe-Brown attempts to do in a well-known essay which is still employed as the basis for interpreting these relationships.[1] Similar customs to those which Radcliffe-Brown extracted from Junod's account of the BaThonga are to be found among the LoWiili and among neighbouring peoples. But these privileges of the sister's son in his mother's patriclan seem better explained as deriving from the submerged claims of a female to the property of the descent group of which she is by birth a member. These submerged claims cannot be exercised by her as a female but they are transmitted to her male offspring as a residual claim on the group's property. The advantage of such an approach is that it substitutes a structural analysis for Radcliffe-Brown's 'psychological' explanation.

In his early years, a child sees his *madeb* 1 fairly often during his mother's visits to her natal home. Gradually, as the marriage endures, these visits grow less frequent but the children, especially boys, will later call by themselves. Soon he knows fairly well most of the members of his mother's patrilineage. The particular compound which his mother visits always remains an alternative home for him should he run into difficulties with his own agnates, or should his parents' marriage end through death, separation or divorce.[2] Although this is a matter notoriously difficult to assess, with or without the aid of psychological tests, I would like to record the impression that it is the more intractable characters who are likely to have lived some time with their mother's brothers, otherwise than through the dissolution of the parents' marriage, the same sort of person, in fact, that tends to migrate to new farming land or to go south to seek wage employment.

At the age of nine or ten a boy can go to the compound of his mother's full brother and ask for a hen to look after (*no gwöl*); if he successfully rears chicks, one is given to him as his own. He may then be given a goat, later a sheep and finally a cow, to look after on the same basis. The foundation of his personal wealth is laid not by his own, but by his mother's agnates. When he has his first quiver (*lɔʻ*) he goes again and asks for arrows, but not to the members of the same patrilineage (*madeb* 2); his mother's brother (*madeb* 1) gives him one and then directs him to the other lineages (s. *di, diu*, room), who make up the local sector

---

[1] A. R. Radcliffe-Brown, "The Mother's Brother in South Africa", 1924, reprinted in "Structure and Function in Primitive Societies", London, 1952. For recent interpretations based on his approach, see G. Homans, "The Human Group", London, 1951; G. Lienhardt, "Nilotic Kings and their Mothers' Kin", Africa, 1955.

[2] See p.53 *et seq.*

of his mother's clan (*madeb* 3). From these he begs until he has sufficient to fill the quiver. It is from these same lineages that he is entitled to snatch (*ara*) the left front leg of any sacrificial animal. Although a sister's son (*arbile*) refers to the whole of his mother's clan as his *arzie*, the place where he can snatch, the elders would prevent him seizing from his mother's own patrilineage. "We and you", they would say, "share (*puon*), we all eat together. If we have a funeral, you also come and cry; if you come and play the xylophone there, you cannot take home the cowries the mourners throw to you. No. You cannot snatch from us." Sharing precludes snatching. The relationship with the members of the mother's lineage is so strong that I have heard a man say of them "we are all housepeople" (*ti zaa in yidem*); only those linked by agnatic descent would normally describe themselves in this way. In other words, a sister's child is so closely associated with his mother's patrilineage that he is almost a member of it. He cannot snatch from them, only from the other lineages of the same clan.

Snatching is a somewhat disrespectful procedure, a violent affirmation of doubtful claim. It is precisely with those members of the mother's clan from whom one can snatch that one can also joke and play. It would be inconceivable to play with one's mother's full brother; he is too closely identified with the parental generation in whom domestic authority is vested. This applies in a less categorical way to the members of the same patrilineage. Joking occurs only with those members of the mother's patriclan outside her own lineage.

There are a number of types of joking behaviour. That between in-laws of the same generation is different from that between "sister's child" and *madeb* 3 and this again has to be distinguished from the friendly relations existing between members of alternate generations. These joking relationships of person to person are analytically separable from the joking partnerships between descent and other groups. I will discuss these in detail later; here I want to make the point that this distinction is one recognised by the LoWiili themselves. The term *lonluore* applies specifically to such group partnerships. I have occasionally also heard it used to describe the relationship between *arbile* 3 and *madeb* 3, but never for any of the other joking relationships mentioned above.

The reason for this lies in the structure of the uxorilateral relationship in patrilineal societies. The privileges of a sister's son in his mother's agnatic clan (*m ma sãã yidem*, my mother's father's housepeople) involve certain obligations. At a sacrifice to the ancestors over a particularly serious matter (*bun tuo*), a "sister's son" may be asked to kill a preliminary offering known as *bun puru*, a "greeting thing", which cannot be eaten by the clansmen themselves. As an offspring of a female member of the clan, he stands sufficiently close to perform this service and yet sufficiently removed to be able to eat their 'dirt' (*be diora*), that is, the flesh of the animal killed as a preliminary expiation for the wrong done, so that the clansmen may be in a position to sacrifice effectively to their ancestors. The services he performs are analogous to the reciprocal help characterizing group joking partnerships (s. *lonluore*, a joking partner) which exist between patrilineal and between matrilineal clans (*yir* and *bel lonluore*), which function in critical sacrifices to the Earth shrine (*tengaan lonluore*) and which appear in connection with the Bɔɔre ceremonies (*bo lonluore*). There is always a cathartic element in these group relationships. This appears to be why the term *lonluore* can also be applied to the "mother's brother—sister's son" relationship. For the offspring of the female members of a clan stand to that clan in much the same position as the joking partners. They also can make "hot things cold", or, to use an associated metaphor, can "throw ashes" (*loba tampello*). The LoWiili seek assistance in grave

59

ritual situations at the point where direct involvement ceases. A "sister's son" is the closest available person in terms of ancestor worship, for the bond of patriliny has not been completely extinguished by transmission through a female.

The fourth way in which the term *madeb* can be used is to address or refer to a member of one's matriclan of senior generation. There is a more usual alternative in *yeb*, sibling of the same sex, but one would never, I think, use this with reference to the mother's full brother, nor to a member of her patrilineage. However, it must be borne in mind that, in a system of dual clanship, the mother's full brother and the full sister's child both belong to the same matriclan and this affects their mutual relations. Among the LoWiili this fact is of importance in the matter of widow inheritance.

Mother's brother and sister's son call each other's wives "my wife" (*n pɔɔ*). This form of address contrasts markedly with the others recorded by Rattray[1] in the Northern Territories; he states that in Dagbane, Kusal, Nankane, Nabte, Bulea and Wale the terminology corresponds to "mother" and "child". Some LoWiili explain these terms by maintaining that each can inherit the other's wife without making any bridewealth payment to the patrilineal kin concerned; as a man might one day marry his mother's brother's widow, the children call him "father" (*sãã*) and he reciprocates with "child" (*biɛ*). The terminology from their point of view anticipates a possible marital situation.

The LoWiili live at the point at which the matrilineal and patrilineal systems of inheriting movable property meet. It is only possible to understand the emphasis they place on the two systems of descent group within this context, as will be apparent when the ramifications of matriclanship are examined. Most of the inhabitants of Birifu claim to have migrated from a settlement some dozen miles away, one in which members of some of the same clans are still to be found, belonging to the group I have called DagaaWiili. Among these people there is no institution of matriclanship, although culturally they are otherwise very similar to the LoWiili. The possibilities inherent in the situation of such a group coming into regular contact with peoples who transmit wealth along the uterine line can be illustrated from another frontier region to the north. The sector of the *Berewiele* patriclan living at Gwo, near Nandom, changed from the patrilineal to the matrilineal system of inheriting wealth in the following manner. A member of the patriclan married a wife from a sector of a different patriclan that inherited matrilineally. The child of this union therefore became entitled to the wealth left both by his father and by his mother's brother. The latter died first and anyhow was the richer of the two; as the heir was unable to resist this temptation, the way was opened for similar claims at his own death.

The LoWiili regard enquiries on the question of matrilineal inheritance with extreme suspicion; they are now attached to the patrilineal system but evidence has emerged in accounts of former redistributions of wealth that a move was made in the other direction. This process was arrested by the late chief of Birifu who, having amassed considerable property, was anxious it should remain with his immediate patrikin. In societies which inherit wealth in the uterine line although the local group is based upon the patriline, the development of large differences in wealth appears to have the effect of introducing modifications in favour of the patrilineal system of transmission.[2] When the chief died, however,

---

[1] 1932, Vol. I, pp.22-3.

[2] See Forde on the Yakö in "African Systems of Kinship and Marriage", Oxford, 1950, p.309. This appears to be a preliminary stage, found in dual descent societies, in the break-up of the lineage system and the emphasis on the conjugal family which the introduction of wage labour and cash crops involves.

and his final funeral rites were performed, two widows ran to "sisters' children" who now maintain they can take these women as wives without any bridewealth payment. It is not contested that the dead man would be the *pater* of the children of such a union. The claim is strongly resisted by the late chief's inheritor. In this particular case the principal inheritor of the wealth under both systems would be the full brother of the deceased. In Birifu the sons stand next to the full brothers in the line of inheritance except in regard to the widows. According to the majority view, widows can be married without further payment only by a lineage member of the same generation as the dead man, or of alternate generations.

The forms of address used by mother's brothers and sisters' sons to each other's wives are linked to the reciprocal rights to widows which characterize the matrilineal inheritance of wealth.[1] The terms are identically applied among the Birifor and LoWilisi,[2] who both practise this system. The usage highlights the conflict between uterine and agnatic descent, particularly marked in societies on the frontier between the two systems of inheritance. The marriages by two widows of the late chief to his sister's sons is seen by the inhabitants within this wider ethnographic context. In discussion, they betray confusion about the system they follow; the range of actual solutions shows the distribution of wealth or widows in any particular instance to be the resultant of opposing forces, the strength of which vary at different periods and in different situations.

In this discussion of uxorilateral relationships I have been concerned only with those of the first level, those traced by ego through one female only. An individual can also snatch from the patrilineage of both his father's mother's and mother's mother's patriclans, although the chances of him actually succeeding are not very great.

I have also dealt primarily with males, with "sisters' sons". It is they who beg for fowls and arrows, and who act in ritual capacities. For females, the relationship is rather different, because the mother's sister is in some way the counterpart of the mother's brother for the male. She is a person's nearest kinswoman outside her own patriclan, However, her mother's agnates do assist a woman, at her marriage, for example, when they give her domestic utensils to start her kitchen. As with a man, these patriclansmen have a large part to play if a shrine has to be erected on her behalf to the hill and water sprites (*kontome*). Towards her mother's full brother, a woman has to show even more respect than her male sibling; there is little "familiarity" at this level. In the first place, the cross sexual relationship makes for added social distance between close kin whom one is forbidden to marry; and the mother's brother comes within the prohibited degrees because of his identification through siblinghood with his sister; they are both *mamine*, mothers. As a member of the same patrilineage, he also falls within the range of exogamy. In the second place, by a matrilateral cross-cousin marriage, her mother's brother becomes her husband's father and the restraint which is usual between in-laws of different generations operates here too. It is true that the same identification occurs for the male by a matrilateral cross-cousin marriage, but this is much less common.

I have been concerned to place the mother's brother—sister's son relationship in the context of agnatic groups. In dual descent societies, there is a further aspect to be considered, for both individuals are members of the same matrilineal

---

[1] Wealth and movable property are used interchangeably to refer to the classes of object which pass matrilineally. The specific items differ slightly among different LoDagaba communities.

[2] Labouret, 1931, p.251.

descent group. I have deliberately ignored this among the LoWiili. It is true that they have a dual descent system in the strict sense; an individual belongs both to a patriclan and to a matriclan. But the matriclan is not a property-holding group. They do not have double inheritance. All male property is transmitted patri-lineally. It is therefore between agnates that the holder-heir situation falls. A man has only residual claims on the property of his mother's brother.

Quite a different situation exists among the LoDagaba. While they also inherit immovables agnatically, movable property is vested in the matriclan. The holder-heir situation is therefore split and falls principally on the mother's brother—sister's son rather than the father—son relationship. In both com-munities the kinship terms are the same, but the tone of the relationships differs considerably. Among the LoWiili the mother's brother has to be respected as a member of the mother's generation, but the relationship is in general relaxed. Among the LoDagaba, the conflicts which surround the transmission of property centre around the figure of the mother's brother and there is a good deal of hostility towards him. The relationship closely resembles that characteristic of matrilineal societies.[1]

I have stressed the point that the general tone and many of the specific customs which characterize the relationship of the mother's brother and sister's son in patrilineal societies derive from the fact that the individuals concerned, while bound by close kinship ties, are the members of different property-holding groups; they are the nearest extra-clan kin. From this point of view, the counter-part in matrilineal societies is to be found in some aspects of the father—son relationship. For here too the son is excluded from membership of his father's descent group , but through him has certain residual claims on the property of that group. This is recognised by the institutionalized alienation of the property of the matriclan to sons of members in the form of gifts *inter vivos*, a feature which is particularly characteristic of matrilineal societies with virilocal residence.

This situation does not arise among the LoWiili, for although they have double clanship, they do not have double inheritance. Among their neighbours the LoDagaba, the main weight of the holder-heir situation is thrown upon the mother's brother—sister's son relationship which is therefore much more similar to that found in matrilineal societies. The relationship among the LoWiili is basically the same as in patrilineal societies.

Two points of general application have emerged from this discussion. Firstly, the mother's brother—sister's son relationship should not be considered in terms of an "extension of sentiment" from the mother to her brother but rather in the context of the system of agnatic descent groups and the contradiction in the position of their male and female members vis-à-vis the property vested in the groups. Secondly, in classifying dual descent systems, emphasis should be placed upon double inheritance rather than double clanship; for it is the presence of the former which is correlated with significant changes in the nuclear kinship situations and in the total social system.[2]

Housechildren and the concept of legitimacy

The category "sister's sons" (*yepule biir*) includes the illegitimate (*yirbie*, housechild) as well as the legitimate offspring (*arbile*) of a female of the lineage. When a woman is rejected by her husband, the children of this annulled marriage

---

[1] See, for example, Fortes on the Ashanti, in "African System of Kinship and Marriage", 1950.

[2] The literal but loose classification adopted by Murdock, Herskovits, Mead and others makes for a lack of precision in comparative analyses.

become attached to their mother's lineage as housechildren. During the second of the series of *Bɔɔre* ceremonies, the beginning of the initiation itself, the candidates are placed under the special guardianship of the ancestors (*siura*; LoDagaba, *sigra*, tutelary or guardian spirit).

On this occasion the housechild takes his place among his mother's clansmen. The identical status is held by the child of an unmarried girl who has conceived before the bridewealth cowries have been sent to her father's agnatic kin. Although it is theoretically possible for a housechild to marry his mother's clanswoman from a different lineage, I have no record of this having happened in Birifu. The children of an illegitimate son possess full lineage membership and the housechild himself has the rights and duties of a full member in nearly all respects. *Miiri*, a headman of Naayili, lived with his mother's brother's son *Zukono*, a man much older than himself, for his mother had been rejected by her husband. *Zukono* called him "father", as he would a legitimate offspring of his father's sister. Such a man can play an important rôle in the ritual affairs of his lineage and of the community as a whole. He does not appear to have full status in sacrifices to the ancestors but on this subject I encountered conflicting opinions. *Doɛri*, a *Naayiili* housechild from the chief's compound, possessed a greater knowledge of ritual than any other man in Birifu, being the instructor (*bo nɛtuuri*) for his clan sector in *Bɔɔrɛ* initiations and "speaker" at the main Earth shrine during the present interregnum between the death of one custodian and the appointment of another. He addressed all the shrines in the homestead when a sacrifice had to be made, except if the animal was killed to a specific ancestor in the agnatic line, such as the late chief. Nevertheless, *Doɛri* was entitled to a hind leg, the "father's leg" (*sãã gbɛr*), of any sacrifice made in the compound, for the late chief addressed him as "father". The reason for the use of this kinship term is explained later.

Illegitimacy incurs no other disabilities; indeed it is always affirmed that such a child "owns the house" (*so a yir*), although neither in terms of the inheritance of wealth nor of the guardianship of the compound or the shrines within it is this literally true. The axiom holds good only in ritual where the housechild can offer effective assistance to the occupants. Among the LoDagaba living a mile or two away, a housechild and a sister's son inherit jointly in the absence of a full brother; a good proportion of the property would therefore remain in the deceased's compound. Such a child is welcomed as a means of preventing the dispersal of a man's goods and chattels at his death. In Birifu too I have heard men express a desire that a daughter should conceive before marriage so that the continuity of the lineage might be assured. The second generation is completely assimilated and has full status in the lineage.

Kinship terminology identifies an illegitimate child with the generation of his mother; the diagram on page 64 illustrates this.

In terms of lineage structure, a housechild takes his mother's place and the link through a female disappears from the genealogy. In this way *Maalo* and *Dʒato*[1] of Tʃaa now trace their descent through males to the founding ancestor of the lineage. Kinship terms applied throughout matriclans reinforce this mechanism; the child of the father's full sister belongs to the same matriclan as a man's father and the same term (*n sãã*) can be used to address him. Any member of one's father's matriclan can say "I bore you; you are my 'child'". The illegitimate child of the father's sister belongs to both the matriclan and patriclan of the father himself; he is a "father" both in virtue of uterine clanship and by skipping

---

¹See p.56.

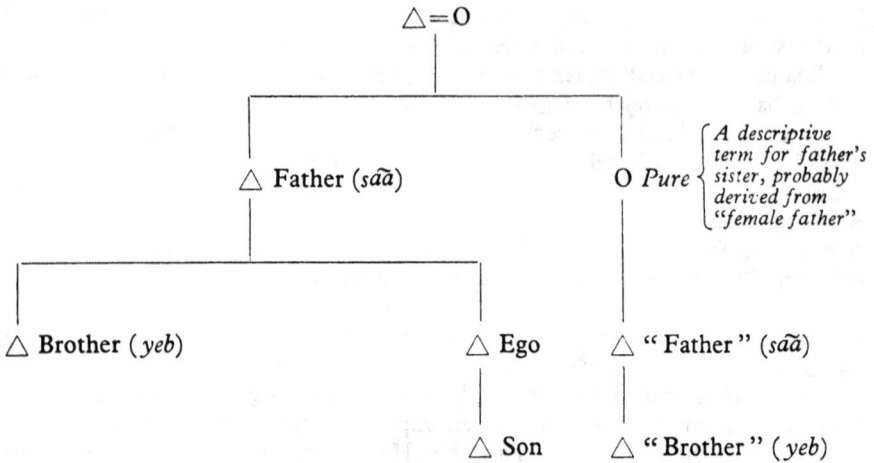

```
                              △＝O
                               │
        ┌──────────────────────┴───────────────────┐
        │                                           │
     △ Father (sẫã)                              O Pure  ⎰ A descriptive
        │                                                ⎱ term for father's
  ┌─────┴──────────────┐                                   sister, probably
  │                    │                                    derived from
△ Brother (yeb)     △ Ego    △ "Father" (sẫã)              "female father"
                       │           │
                    △ Son     △ "Brother" (yeb)
```

a generation within the structure of the patrilineage.

As the offspring of a housechild take on full lineage status, they are no longer "sisters' children". The system of classificatory kinship which extends the referents of kinship terms through both patriclan and matriclan makes it possible to assimilate them completely into the lineage organisation. The operating principle can be stated as "the child belongs to the man who paid the bridewealth" (*libie sob, o la so a bie*). The bridewealth payments for the wife of an illegitimate child are made by his mother's lineage, to which the children therefore belong. A slave was integrated into the lineage by the same mechanism, adopting the matrilineal and patrilineal clan affiliations of his purchaser. The existence of this procedure may be held to account for the absence of attached or assimilated lineages such as are found among the Tallensi.[1]i.

See Fortes, 1945, p.51.

1. Boys Looking After Cattle

2. A New Compound: An elementary family have just moved to their new homestead. The granary has been finished but the long room has yet to be roofed and the wall of the courtyard to be built. Against the wall leans a forked branch; this is a ladder which will later be the only entrance to the compound.

3. COOKING FOOD: A young wife prepares food in her mother-in-law's court-yard. In the farms beyond, mounds have been made in readiness for sowing.

4. REPAIRING A COMPOUND: A man and his sons are replacing some rafters. Behind, a prospective son-in-law and a few of his agnatic kinsmen are repairing another section of the roof.

5. POISONING ARROWS: Members of a patrilineage poison their arrows together and lay them in the sun to dry.

6. FUNERAL OF AN OLD MAN: The dancing reaches a climax when burial is about to take place. Women from the widow's clan sect dance round her as she sits on the ground. In the rear, men from a neighbouring clan section dance *dagaa wobo*, the "dagarti leap".

7. BATHING AN INFANT: The young girl, who is a full sister of the infant's mother, is staying with her to look after the child. The mother is then free to carry on with her many other tasks. The infant is being bathed in an infusion peculiar to the matrilineal sub-clan.

8. CLEARING NEW LAND: A man has brought the other members of his in-law farming group to hoe his father-in-law's land. This particular farm has lain fallow for a number of years and lies on the outskirts of the area under continuous cultivation.

Chapter 4

Descent Groups

The patrilineage

The elders of Birifu point to ancestors two to four generations removed who migrated from their previous home (*teŋkuori*, old country) to settle the land they now hoe. The present descendants of such a founding ancestor inhabit between five and ten homesteads. Within the major ritual area or parish of Birifu, and usually in close proximity, live two or more similar groups of whom they say vaguely that the founding ancestors were "brothers". Of the thirty-one compounds in Tʃaa, two were owned by sisters' sons and three more by members of the adjacent Ŋmanbil Maale sector whose special relationship to the ritual area has already been mentioned. The remaining twenty-six compounds are owned by the patrilineal descendants of three founding ancestors, *Kontʃol*, *Napolo* and *Zaagbwõ*, three generations removed from the present elders. These groups consist of an average of 34 adult males.

The group of agnatic descendants of one man, relatively undifferentiated in corporate action, is known as a "room" (*di*), a 'lineage' as the term is used in analyses of West African societies.[1] Fortes defines a maximal lineage[2] as "all the descendants in the male line of the remotest common patrilineal ancestor known to the members of the lineage". The use of a genealogical structure as a basis for social action is certainly less developed than among the Tallensi where segments of a maximal lineage of eight to eleven generations emerge as groups in particular situations. The LoWiili, while placing considerable emphasis on common descent, do not normally set this within a genealogical framework beyond the "room". I take this genealogical framework to be the critical feature of the lineage as a descent group.[3]

In certain societies in North-East Africa[4] the elaboration of these structures provides a scaffolding for organizing the relationships of territorially distinct groups. The lineage system Evans-Pritchard describes as a "system of agnatic groups",[5] the starting point of which is the minimal lineage of four or five generations; in the case of the dominant clan of the tribe, this unit provides the agnatic core of the village to which the other residents are attached by affinal and cognatic ties. A further criterion is involved in this use of the phrase "lineage system". Evans-Pritchard defines the lineage as "an agnatic group the members of which are genealogically linked",[6] but the smallest such group he recognizes is the *thok dwiel*, which "has a time-depth of from three to five generations from

---

[1] See Forde, 1938, p.311.
[2] 1945, p.30.
[3] See "Notes and Queries on Anthropology", 6th Edition, London, 1951, p.88; Evans-Pritchard, 1940, p.192.
[4] See E. E. Evans-Pritchard, 1940, and 1951.
[5] 1940, p.194.
[6] 1940, p.192.

living persons" and in the case of the dominant clan forms the agnatic core of a village. As the village is the "political unit" of Nuerland, this is the smallest descent group to emerge as a "political segment". The lineage system of "dispersed groups" begins at the point where the genealogical framework organizes the relations between territorially distinct units.

This additional criterion has not been introduced into analyses of West African societies; lineage has here been used in the wider sense of "the descendants in one line of a particular person . . . ".[1] A lineage system of dispersed groups is peculiarly adapted to a pastoral people of low population density. Among the more densely populated agricultural peoples of West Africa, on the other hand, specific genealogical ties are usually traced only within the local community. In the absence of territorial contiguity, the link between agnatic kin becomes generalized to the level of clanship, where common unilineal descent is not traced through particular ancestors but recognized in certain prohibitions, terms of address, a common name, and in a number of other ways. Dispersion may lead to the eventual cancellation of existing descent ties, as among the Konkomba[2] and to some extent the Tallensi; it may lead to their generalization to the level of clanship as in the case of the Ashanti. In an overall, inclusive genealogical system such as we find among the Tiv, it may result in constant changes in the charter which reflects the changing territorial distribution.

The difference in usage emerges in the accounts of the Tallensi and Nuer. In the former the word lineage is used to translate "the children (biis) of so-and-so" or "the house (yir) or people of the house (yidεm) of so-and-so", and in the case of the Nuer, to render into English the phrase thok dwiel. The maximal lineage of the Tallensi consists basically of a localized group living in close proximity; neither in the sense of political structure used by Radcliffe-Brown,[3] nor in the sense used by Evans-Pritchard when he speaks of villages as the "political units of Nuerland",[4] can it be said that the segmentary lineage system of the Tallensi "primarily regulates political relations between territorial segments" unless the unit in these relations is taken to be the inhabitants of an individual homestead. The occupants of one homestead (yidεm, housepeople) are indeed the unit of the Tallensi concept of a lineage, constituting what Fortes designates the "morphological minimal lineage"; as all the male members of a maximal lineage generally live together, there can be no segment which can be called the starting point of territorial or political relations in any other sense.

Evans-Pritchard, following the Nuer, regards the lineage as beginning at the same point as political relations, that is, territorial separation. Fortes following the Tallensi concepts sees a continuous system of groups based upon ties of unilineal descent stretching from the agnatic core of a dwelling group to the maximal lineage.

The Tiv, who have an all-inclusive genealogical structure of shifting agriculture, make a distinction between segments of higher and lower order. "The second great area of genealogical dispute refers to those genealogies explaining

---

[1] "Notes and Queries", p.88.

[2] D. Tait, "The Political System of the Konkomba", Africa, July, 1953.

[3] v. Fortes and Evans-Pritchard, "African Political Systems", Oxford, 1940, p.xviii. "In seeking to define the political structure in a simple society, we have to look for a territorial community which is united by the rule of law", the criterion of legal sanctions being "physical force".

[4] "African Political Systems", p.275. The tribe is defined as a political unit in terms of the rule of law; the village emerges as a unit in the system of territorially distinct groups.

relationships between lineage segments and is associated with vacillation in political loyalties or with discrepancies of size and depth. Genealogies referring to lineage segments ratify relationships between large groups of people for political purposes".[1] The dividing line occurs between three and six generations from living people and is associated with a territorial division, the minimal *tar*, which does not further segment. But the lineage itself segments below this level, like the Tallensi, and the Tiv use the same general name (*uipaven*) for all segments although those of lower order, that is beneath the area of genealogical dispute referred to above, must be called "segments-within-the-hut" (*uipaven ken iyou*) or some other such phrase which serves to distinguish themselves from "segments proper." "Such segments-within-the-hut are primarily of domestic rather than political significance" (p.301). In these studies of the Tiv, the term lineage refers to any group emerging on the basis of genealogical segmentation, no matter what depth. This corresponds to the use of the term in the analysis of the Tallensi. But a qualitative distinction is made between segments which emerge in political contexts and those which do not, a distinction which relates to that made by the Nuer. The anthropologists concerned have each defined their concepts in the light of those employed by the actors themselves and one can see how these are consistent with the structures of the particular societies with which they are dealing. One needs some more general concept for comparative purpose. I therefore adopt the limited definition of the lineage as "an agnatic (or uterine) group, the members of which are genealogically linked". For Evans-Pritchard's addition of a political criterion seems applicable mainly to scattered nomadic societies. Although the Bohannans' distinction between domestic and political lineages among the Tiv recognizes this point, I cannot see that it has any general validity outside the Tiv context because of the vagueness of the criteria of political relationships.

The *thok dwiel*, the *yir* and the *uipaven* are unilineal descent groups whose members are linked through specific genealogical ties, and I have used the term lineage in this way. The LoWiili have no developed "lineage system" in Evans-Pritchard's sense, as the lineage is a contiguous not a dispersed group. Nor do they possess the localized, internally differentiated lineage of the Tallensi. There is a sense in which any genealogical system can be regarded as internally differentiated and, in a society who sacrifice to the shrines of dead ancestors, individuals and groups obviously differentiate themselves in ritual contexts in relation to their common ancestors. The fission of residential and farming groups also occurs with reference to points of differentiation in the genealogical system. I prefer, however, to describe the lineage as undifferentiated. With the above exceptions, no segment necessarily emerges as an action group on the basis of descent from any other than the founding ancestor. Certain situations of group action might appear to contradict this, but in fact comparison with similar groups shows contiguity, not descent, to be the main organizing principle of the action concerned; this is often disguised because the lineage is normally represented by a compact local group, consisting mainly of males, with agnatic ties becoming closer as distance decreases. The lack of differentiation is largely an inevitable consequence of the limited order of genealogical depth. To call the "room" a maximal lineage suggests a series of smaller action groups whose members define themselves in relation to common ancestors within a genealogical structure. I shall therefore use the term "patrilineage" (or "patrilineal group") to indicate

---

[1] L. Bohannan, "A Genealogical Charter, Africa," October, 1952, p.313.

this genealogically defined descent group.[1] If it is necessary to distinguish the living members from the total patrilineage, these can be referred to as the "patrilineage group", while those who constitute the agnatic core of a locality, who live in the lineage home, can be called the "local patrilineage group".

Even within the "room" the LoWiili are vague about genealogies. Confusion arises because of the wide range of classificatory kinship terms which a system of double clanship offers. All patriclansmen senior in generation to the speaker are called "father" (*sāā*), and all the father's father's generation are "grandfathers" (*s.sāākum*). On the principle of the association of alternate generations, these latter are also known as "brothers" (*s.yebe*). Of any "father" one can say "he bore me" (*o dɔɔ ma*). Thus any elder may give a list of "fathers" whom he knew in his youth, but he is likely to say of the majority that his own father's father bore them. Collateral branches more than one generation removed tend to become telescoped into the descent line of the senior member of the patrilineage, unless specific factors, such as the distribution of compounds, which always retain the name of the builder, intervene to maintain their separate identity. The members of a lineage do not define their kinship relations in terms 'of specific genealogical connections; two people, whose fathers called themselves "brothers", will use the same terminology towards each other. As a man's paternal "great grandfather" (FaFaFa) is identified with his "father", he can say of each "my grandfather (FaFa) bore him". There is in any case no accepted kinship term to distinguish any ancestor beyond the father's father. All earlier ancestors are "grandfathers" (*sāākum*, pl. *sāākum mine*) and "grandfather" is a generic term for ancestors. Consequently, discussion of ancestors beyond a man's grandfather (FaFa) tends to be highly confused, even in regard to his direct lineal ascent to the founding ancestor. The LoWiili think of specific genealogical links in the context of inheritance in discussing the dispersion of the lineage compounds from the house of the founder and in making sacrifices to the ancestors. It suffices for these purposes that a man should know the founding ancestor of his lineage, the intervening names which may be called in addressing the shrines and the names of the compounds builders. The LoWiili tend to trace ties of descent only in straight lines; I know very few men who could correctly name the members of collateral branches within their own lineage even to the limited depth of three generations.

The original compound of the founding ancestor is the "senior house" (*yikpɛ̃ɛ̃*) of the lineage and resting place of his ancestor shrine. If the occupants die out, the senior member of the group will transfer the shrines to his own byre. During the Harvest Festival (*Bomaaldāā*) the compound heads of the *Tʃaale* patrilineal group descended from *Napolo* go to the senior house and kill fowl at his shrine. On the other hand, in *Kontʃol's* lineage, each compound head kills at the ancestor shrines in his own byre but calls the name of the founding ancestor. This sacrifice expresses ritually the belief that only in virtue of the toil and initiative of the founding ancestor was the area discovered, cleared and made to grow crops. Death does not extinguish a man's concern in the fertility of the land he farmed, nor in the acts of the children he bore; his social personality survives death. The founding ancestor's interest in the lineage members emerges in the sacrifice of the bull received in the second payment of bridewealth (*doɛ̃*). Two fowl accompany the cattle; one is killed to the girl's nearest patrilineal ancestor, the other to the begetter of the lineage. The bull itself is sacrificed to the founder,

---

[1] As descent is reckoned in both lines it is necessary to employ the clumsy terms "patrilineage" and "matrilineage".

either at his own shrine or at the shrine of the immediate ancestor who will then be asked to give the animal to his forefather. The distribution of meat takes place within the lineage, although small portions may be given to the other house-holders in the clan sector with whom a reciprocal arrangement operates.

We have already seen how the local patrilineage emerges in connection with land tenure, in agricultural sacrifices to the ancestor who first farmed the land, in the consumption of the agricultural produce and in the accumulation and alienation of wealth acquired by selling the surplus. The lineage also possesses rights over and duties towards its widows arising from a common interest in the bridewealth accumulated through farming, as well as in its own continuity as a social group. The lineage holds joint rights over certain types of property; debts between members for example are cancelled by death.

The members of two lineages of the same patriclan are said to have "different eating-places" (dibzɛ dindime). Although the concept of one eating-place arises in other situations, it has particularly strong associations in the context of lineage affairs. In addition to rights over agricultural produce and the flesh of certain sacrifices, the lineage has claims on wild animals killed by a member, his dog or his wife.[1] The hunting shrine of the patriclan is established at the compound of the first lineage member to kill a wild animal; in most cases the compound belonged to the founding ancestor but this is not always so.[2] The animal is brought here to be cooked; it is eaten mixed together with the patriclan's special hunting medicine (wɛ tĩ). All the patrilineages belonging to the dispersed clan are assumed to have the same hunting medicine; the eating of this medicine by an outsider creates a bond of quasi-kinship with the clan. The secrets of the arrow poison, and a special hunting call to increase its effectiveness, are also the possessions of the whole clan; but the actual poisoning of arrows is carried out by the local lineage.

Another aspect of the lineage as a group with joint rights over food appeared in the discussion of the relationship between the sister's son and the mother's brother. A man can never seize the left front leg of an animal sacrificed by a member of his mother's patrilineage; he shares with them. With her lineage he has this very close bond, amounting almost to membership. Outside the range of her genealogically defined agnatic ties, a more formal joking relationship exists and he can seize whenever he is able.

The lineage acts jointly at funerals of its members. A larger contribution towards expenses has to be made for a lineage member than for other clansmen. The lineage cannot bury its own dead, nor take the meat of the cow of the hoe handle (kukuur naab), killed to the dead man's father, except for that meat allocated for special purposes. When a married female dies, members cannot eat the animal given them by the husband's lineage (vaar daar dun, the animal of farm tidying) in appreciation of the agricultural work the woman has done. "We cannot eat our own dirt" they maintain. Another group must take the meat on a reciprocal basis. Such exchanges of food and services do not necessarily take place between patrilineages, but they never do so within them. At funerals, close agnatic descent involves the fulfilment of certain duties and the avoidance of other acts; but the distribution of these tasks within the society as a whole is not organized on the basis of agnatic descent alone. However, the meat forbidden to the patrilineage can be consumed by other members of the patriclan. A clansman from a distant settlement could successfully lay claim to a portion,

[1]See p.51.
[2]See Fig. 7.

although the meat is actually taken by the lineage or group of lineages acting in reciprocal partnership with the similar group of which the deceased was a member. These are referred to as complementary funeral groups, and the services are always performed between agnates. Burial must be considered separately. The burial group may be of another clan; it is recruited on the basis of contiguity. But in both cases, these services cannot be performed by a member of the same patrilineage. The structural basis of these complementary groups is complex and will be considered more fully in connection with the local organization. The distribution of food apart, it would be misleading to over-emphasize the rôle of the patrilineage in the exchange of services at funerals, for although these functions are often attached to lineages they are not exclusively linked to them. The tie of contiguity, which is concealed where the lineage is also the core of the local group, constitutes an equally powerful factor in organizing these cultural requirements.

The patriclan sector

The clan, as a dispersed group of people claiming common descent, is represented in a particular parish by a clan sector which comprises several patrilineages. In Tʃaa the three lineages descended from *Kontʃol, Napolo* and *Zaagbwǒ* live somewhat intermingled. In most other cases in Birifu the dwellings of a lineage are grouped together and spatially separated from similar units; the pull of contiguity reinforces the bond of agnatic kinship. There are five main clan sectors in Birifu, *Tʃaale, Ɖmanbili, 'Yoŋyuole, Naayili* and *Baaperi*, which share equally the meat of animals sacrificed at the main Earth shrine on behalf of the community inhabiting the major ritual area. The LoWiili think of these five sectors as constituting the whole population of Birifu although in fact there are a number of compounds owned by members of other clans whose presence is said to be due to their founding ancestor having come to live with his mother's brother. These subsidiary patrilineages do not act independently in the main ritual situations; no representative need be present at sacrifices at the main Earth shrine (*teŋgaankpɛ̃*), nor do the lineages as such enter into the complex exchange of ritual services organized round the *Bɔɔre* initiatory ceremonials. Of the one hundred and sixty-nine homesteads in Birifu[1] only ten are occupied by members of other clans and one by a complete stranger, a Mossi leather worker.

The members of a local clan sector speak of themselves as belonging to the same house (*yir*) or the same clan (*dɔɔro*); the ties between the constituent patrilineages are the same ties of clanship that operate between similar sectors in different parishes. These clanship ties grow weaker as the spatial distance between the sectors increases. The local sectors appear to the observer as the focus of clanship, the group within which these bonds are continually affirmed in the situations of daily life. This is intensified by the participation of the sector as a unit in the most important rites of the parish, the sacrifices to the main Earth shrine. For worship at the same Earth shrine creates the bonds which make Birifu a political community as distinct from a casual aggregate of independent clan sectors; within the ritual area centred on this shrine the shedding of blood is a sin, only to be expiated by payment of shell money and the sacrifice of animals.

This unity of the clan sector as a segment of the patriclan emerges at funeral performances. During a man's lifetime the horns (*iile*) of a "dangerous" wild animal he has killed are hung on a pole forming part of the lineage hunting

---

[1]This figure is taken from the 1948 Census Report and includes Biro.

shrine, which in theory is the same throughout the clan. At his death the horns are placed amongst those belonging to the ancestors of the whole clan sector. These horns are ceremonially brought before the dead man to the accompaniment of whistling, shouting and a hunting mime, and are placed in his byre until the next funeral of a member of the section. A similar rite is performed at the death of a man who has killed another human being (*ziẽsob*); a slat of the wood representing the slain man is tied in the bundle of similar sticks (*ziẽ tender*) belonging to the sector's ancestors. A number of other services arising at the various funeral ceremonies are perfomed on a reciprocal basis by the lineages which constitute a clan sector. The formation of these complementary groupings will be considered in the discussion of the influence of contiguity within the local community.

The patriclan

Among the western group of Mossi-speaking peoples living between Wa and Diébougou, the same clan names continually reappear in widely separated villages. None of the scattered patrilineages counts agnatic ascendants for more than five generations; but all who share a name have a tradition of common descent and stories of migration which usually lead back to the Wa district. The word for clan (*dɔɔro*) itself is etymologically connected with *dɔɔ*, meaning "to procreate". The concept of clan, the membership of one "house" (*yir*) is, in native eyes, incompatible with marrying-in. From the observer's point of view exogamy is not invariably associated with the groups whose members describe themselves as "people of one house".

Zinkãã, immediately opposite Birifu on the right bank of the Volta, comprises six compounds; the heads of four of these belong to the *Kpiele* clan and trace their descent three generations back to a common ancestor, *Bii*, who left Ŋmanbil Maale in Birifu to settle there. The members of this patrilineal group claim that *Bii* and the founders of the three Tʃaa lineages were "brothers", that one ancestor (*sããkum*, grandfather) "bore" them all. As classificatory kinship terms are applied throughout the clan, any man of these four groups stands in the position of "son", "brother" or "father" to all other male members; "grandfathers" and "grandchildren" are equally "brothers". The clan constitutes the limit of the recognition of agnatic kinship which normally defines the exogamous group. In this particular case, the three Tʃaa lineages, who acknowledge their membership of the *Kpiele* clan, marry women from Zinkãã and any other section of the *Kpiele* clan outside Tʃaa. This situation, explained as resulting from the lack of available brides, is quite atypical; members of adjacent clans accuse the inhabitants of Tʃaa of cohabiting with their own "sisters", a charge which they reluctantly admit. The fission of the exogamous unit involves the differentiation of nomenclature. The break-away lineages rarely refer to themselves as *Kpiele* but rather as *Tʃaale*. The name of the locality from which this derives is said to have originated in an incident in the following manner. Their present habitat was first discovered by an ancestor who was out hunting wild animals. A duiker he had wounded took refuge in a hollow baobab tree; setting light to a bunch of dried grasses, he illumined the dark interior and seized his prey. The present place name they say is derived from the word to light up with a torch (*tʃaalena*). Adjacent clans do not accept this account. Instead they point to a similar root meaning "to do wrong". Enquiries in this area not infrequently reveal quite irreconcilable "etymologies" for clan and place names; the instance quoted demonstrates how two such different explanations arise out of a particular sociological situation.

71

A further stage in the fission of a patriclan may be seen in the parish of Biro, adjacent to Birifu itself. The two main clans inhabiting this ritual area, *Kusiele* and *Bire*, intermarry; I was told that at one time they belonged to the same clan but "divided because of marriage". One has again adopted a place name to differentiate itself. Three other clans in Birifu itself, *Baaperi* (*Samale*), *Dmanbili* and '*Yoŋyuole* claim that they were formerly "housepeople" (*yidem*) living in one vast homestead which became so large that some of the many inhabitants might be gaily dancing to the xylophone without realizing that a funeral had taken place in another courtyard. So they split.

These traditions of the common origin of certain clans are also current among the LoDagaba. They there form a basis for the grouping of small sectors of different clans which perform for each other the same reciprocal services as are carried out among the LoWiili between complementary groupings within one clan sector. At Tom, in the Nandom Division, the two local sectors of the *Nambeŋle* and *Tiedeme* (or *Nayili*)[1] patriclans co-operate in many of the same situations as the three *Tʃaale* lineages of Birifu. At a funeral of a member of one group, the others will share the meat, the cow of the hoe handle at the death of a man, the beast of farm-tidying in the case of a married female member of the lineage. The co-operation of these sectors of different clans has a counterpart in the histories of common origin, of the same nature as that which exists between the *Baaperi*, *Dmanbili* and '*Yoŋyuole* clans of Birifu. Indeed I have heard exactly the same story told to account for their relationship. I speak of these as linked clans.

The *Kpiele* and *Kusiele* patriclans also have traditions of common origin. Sectors of this clan are found in both Tom and Birifu. A comparison emphasizes certain structural differences. In Birifu, the elders of the two clans are certainly aware of the tradition of their common origin. It is retold during the esoteric rites of *Bɔɔre* initiation when great emphasis is laid on remembering such stories for their own sakes.[2] But in none of the relationships between groups within Birifu does this idea of common origin have any importance whatsoever. In Tom, on the other hand, the bond is acknowledged in inter-sector affairs; a man whose mother was *Kusiele* will snatch meat from *Kpiele* and share with *Kusiele*. Identical services of a reciprocal nature which in Birifu are performed by the patrilineages within the same clan sector here emerge as the functions of sectors of different but linked clans. The linkage between clans is given varying weight in the two contexts. It is true that the *Kpiele* or *Tʃaale* in Birifu say that the *Yipiele* near Lawra are "housepeople" (*yidem*). In Tom, however, an elder expressed the relationship between the *Natʃiele* and its linked clans in much stronger terms; "All patriclans have three branches (*per*); we are all housepeople but we inter-marry".

Fission of a patriclan creates two linked clans which co-operate in certain situations. Some evidence suggests that intermarriage between the local sectors of closely linked clans may be forbidden when numbers grow small; this is said to have happened both in Tom and Metɔ to the *Tozili* and *Kăzili*.

---

[1]This is not the same as the *Naayili* clan of Birifu.

[2]In certain contexts of primitive as of civilized life, the exact memory of details is encouraged for its own sake; it is not surprising that this should be so in the *Bɔɔre* initiations where the necessity for retaining the knowledge of long and complicated ceremonials in one's head from one year to the next makes those in charge (*bo netuuri*, "he whose mouth is followed") particularly concerned to repeat precisely what was done and said on the previous occasion. The continued success of any ritual which has proved of assistance in human difficulties is believed to depend upon the exact repetition of the original performance.

The somewhat confused situation arises from the wide dispersion of these clans which consist of a chain of local sectors. The position of these in a local community and in relation to other sectors of the same and linked clans alters according to the numerical strength and the balance of clanship within the ritual area and the surrounding neighbourhood. The concept of membership of one "house", of common descent, extends beyond the designated agnatic group or patriclan (dɔɔro) to include linked clans. The designated descent groups themselves are basically exogamous. The three lineages in Tʃaa rarely call themselves Kpiele; a new clan name based upon the locality is emerging now that the exogamous unit has divided. Indeed, the origin of most clan names is traced to the moment of fission. The Kpiele, Kusiele and Puriyele clans tell how they lived in one house which grew so large that a funeral would take place in one courtyard while others would be dancing. So the Kusiele went to build a house by a rock (kusir), the Puriyele constructed another house by a tree (puri, tamarindus indica) and the others remained in the old house (kpiele, to be near). In certain contexts the members of such clans are all "housepeople" (yidem), a term which implies exogamy. When the matter is raised in conversation, the speaker feels obliged to add an explanation of why linked clans recognizing common descent now intermarry. Ideas of common ancestry and of exogamy are inextricably involved; both centre around the designated agnatic descent group (dɔɔro).

These patriclans, of which Rattray gives a fairly comprehensive list,[1] are distributed throughout the peoples in the north-west. Rattray records the clans in DagaaWiili settlements[2] under their totems or taboos; the names actually used are those given in the account of the "Lober" (i.e. LoSaala). The same clans are found among the Dagaba[3] where they may be known in some areas by the name of the totem. The Birifor certainly have designated patrilineal descent groups; of the few I have noted, some bear names which occur in Rattray's list, while others, known by a locality name, recognize their common origin with such a clan. Labouret's book, "Les Tribus du Rameau Lobi", is perhaps the most comprehensive study of a Voltaic people, apart from the works of Fortes on the Tallensi and those of Griaule and his associates on the Dogon. Labouret, however, describes all these tribes except the Dyan as if they recognized only matrilineal descent. The system of inheriting wealth through uterine kin and land through agnates suggests a double system of clanship. The correlation of these two factors among the Yakö, Tullishi and Nyaro, analysed by Daryll Forde and S. F. Nadel[4], confirms the data from this area. The evidence from the LoDagaba and the Wiili indicates that inheritance down both descent lines requires a double system of descent groups. The "Lobi" peoples described by Labouret have, with the exception of the Dyan, a double system of inheritance similar to the LoDagaba; it would be surprising if designated groups of agnates did not exist. Certainly, among the Birifor, Labouret overlooked this aspect of social organization.

These clans extend across cultural boundaries. The Babile (DagaaWiili) sector of the Kusiele clan inherit patrilineally, whereas the representatives of the clan living in Kwõnyũkwõ (LoDagaba) transmit wealth through uterine kin. DagaaWiili members of the 'Yoŋyuole clan abuse their clan "brothers" at

[1]1932, p.426.
[2]See the chapter on the Dagaba, 1932, p.407, under Gyiraba or Jirapa.
[3]"The Political Organization of the Ulu Division", no author, no date, Second Lawra Record Book.
[4]"African Systems of Kinship and Marriage", edited by A. R. Radcliffe-Brown and Daryll Forde, London, 1950.

Jirapa (Dagaba) as wild beasts (*wɛdun*) because they marry their fathers' widows, other than their own mothers. Clanship also stretches across linguistic boundaries. Many Sisala clans claim to have migrated from Dagaba territory and recognize sectors of their clans still living in their original homes; yet the two languages are mutually unintelligible. At Pina near Lambussie, the process of cultural differentiation can be seen at work; members of the *Berewiele* clan who left Gwo for reasons of land shortage now speak Sisala among themselves and are adopting Sisala patterns of behaviour.[1]

Clans dispersed over so wide and densely populated an area, linking peoples differing in language, in systems of inheritance and other ways, are not corporate groups in the sense that members or representatives of the constituent clan sector ever act conjointly for any purpose. The unity of the clan arises from the idea of common descent, the prohibition against marrying-in and a common name, avoidances and shrines; but on no occasion do the clansmen co-operate as a whole or through delegates. The effective unit of co-operation above the clan sector consists of those sectors living within a radius of a few miles. The principal situations in which these adjacent sectors join together are fighting and funerals. In theory, any patrilineage can call on all other sectors of the clan to assist in fighting. In practice, few elders know of the existence of all the sectors of their clan even within a radius of ten miles. Moreover, these fights apparently began suddenly and ended quickly. Accounts by elders bring to light the haphazard nature of these conflicts. It is doubtful whether a clan sector would come to the assistance of another unless they could hear the noise of the war xylophone (*gbin*; LoSaala *gũ*, an instrument used by the LoWiili, the LoSaala, the Birifor and LoWilisi); only prompt help could be effective in wars such as these.

The area within which a man feels an obligation to attend the funeral of any patrikinsman or member of his domestic family is also roughly defined by the distance one can hear the sound of the xylophone, in this case, the funeral xylophone (Birifu, *lo gil kpɛ̃*, the big *lo* xylophone). Nowadays if a well-known chief or elder dies, messengers are dispatched to acquaintances and relatives living much further away. Incorporation into a more extensive political system has greatly increased the range of social intercourse. Within the clan, every compound head should contribute the sum of twenty cowries, known as byre money (*zɔ lizer*, the byre twenty) to the expenses of a fellow clansman's funeral. If he does not belong to the same complementary group as the deceased, which unites in the performance of certain reciprocal funeral services, he is entitled by this payment to a share of the cow of the hoe handle.[2] The *Kpiele* living in Zinkãã and Kumansaal (Kwõnyũkwõ) regularly attend funerals of their kinsmen at Tʃaa; although they marry *Tʃaale* daughters, they still are entitled to a share of this meat. More *Kpiele* live on the further side of Tanchera, some five miles away; they do not normally come, but if they did so they could claim a portion of the cow. The question of attending funerals of fellow clansmen or of rendering them assistance in fighting is decided mainly by spatial distance between the local clan sectors. Social distance and spatial distance are not entirely coincidental; representatives from patrilineal groups which have recently budded off continue to attend funerals at the parent village however great the distance involved.

The clan can therefore be viewed as a linked series of effective areas of co-operation or neighbourhood groupings. The operative range of clanship ties

---

[1]For details of clan movements, see Armstrong 1933.

[2]See p.69. These complementary funeral groups consist of one or more lineages of the same clan.

differs for each local sector. The clan sectors are thus joined in wider communities. The clan constitutes a political community, in that definite sanctions operate against the killing of another member irrespective of the ritual community to which he belongs. The killing of a clansman is not resolved by violent retaliation as is the case with a member of another clan. It is a sin which cannot be expiated. The murderer is purified in a general way by eating the clan homicide medicine (*ziɛ tii*) given to anyone who kills another human being, but he can never again consume a portion of any sacrifice to the ancestors. He is excluded from this ritual congregation of the ancestor cult. To kill a man who had murdered his fellow clansman would reduce still further the strength of the descent group. The corollary of these sanctions against homicide is assistance in fighting, and attendance at funerals. The death of any clansman concerns all the other members for it weakens the descent group as a whole; the force of this attitude is vividly experienced in listening to the mourning songs sung to the *dagaa* xylophone (*daga gil*) during the three days of the burial ceremony. I have seen tears well up to the eyes of youths and elders when the singer cries that the clan has come to an end as all its members are dying one by one.

The patrilineal descent of the clan members is recognized not by specific genealogical ties but through a name and prohibition held in common. The clan name often refers to the event by which the clan was differentiated from similar groups; or it may indicate the settlement where fission occurred. The avoidance likewise serves as an index of the clan's distinctiveness from other descent groups. Some of these taboos relate to animals, and are therefore of the type described as totemic in accounts of other West African peoples. The animals forbidden are of little importance as a source of food, a fact which stresses the difference between the cosmological totemism of Australia and the totemic observances of West Africa which serve mainly as emblems. Occasionally an elder recounts how the animal assisted an ancestor (*ti sáàkum*, our grandfather) in a critical situation. The consanguinity of clansman and animal may be recognized in some clans; "It's me he's eating!" a man who forbade squirrel once exclaimed to me on seeing a non-clansman roasting this animal. But typically no reason is given for observing the taboo other than that final explanation of all customary behaviour, "our grandfathers did so". It is not necessary that the avoidance should be a species of animal. The *Kpiele* do not eat porridge out of a basket; this all *Kpiele* avoid, it was explained (*pie puo saab—Kpiele zaa tfiiru*). Other taboos not concerned with animals or with prohibitions on food at all are equally trivial. The important function of the clan avoidance is only disguised by the word totemism. The taboo provides a point of reference for clan members, defining the descent group by emphasizing its exclusiveness. All these avoidances are called *tfiiru*. The forbidden animal, known also as *duma*, is regarded in a general way as a guardian of the clan. But its help cannot be solicited on any specific occasion, for no shrine is built and no sacrifices performed.[1]

There is no greater correlation between prohibition and clan name than between designated and exogamous descent groups. The *Kusiele* of Babile who

---

[1] Fortes observes that the Tallensi totemic animals are usually 'teeth-bearers'. "They symbolize, in particular, the potential aggressiveness of the ancestors as the supreme sanction of Tale cultural values" (1945, p.145).

The LoWiili totems have no such symbolic unity. Although it is perhaps presumptuous to argue on the basis of one negative instance, such a procedure is an essential check upon interpretations of symbolic meanings which are not demonstrably explicit to the actor. The LoWilli material does not support Fortes' assumption.

neither eat nor kill the crocodile, expressed surprise on learning that their clansmen in Lawra forbade only the cobra; they explained the situation by maintaining that the people of Lawra had changed to *lo* ways, forgetting the customs of their forefathers. Linked clans sometimes have the same avoidance. Conversely, it would be generally assumed that any two groups with a common taboo were originally descended from one man. Complications arise from the many other similar avoidances associated with medicine shrines (*tiib*, pl. *tibe*). An individual who eats the "medicine" connected with a shrine derives the benefits it confers only by observing certain prohibitions. If he actually acquires a shrine for himself in exchange for animals and cowries, his children will be given the "medicine" and have to observe the same taboos. Prohibitions attached to shrines, which are inherited patrilineally even among the LoDagaba and Birifor, become associated with agnatic descent groups and may be confused with a clan avoidance by all except the most knowledgeable elders; even they are occasionally unclear, for no linguistic distinction is normally made between the two types. Further confusion arises through dispersion; for example, a man in Tom near Nandom whose father had died when he was very young was brought up by his mother who tried, as mothers do, to make the child observe her own clan avoidance. The boy did so until eventually he realized that this was not his own clan taboo. When I met him he claimed he did not know what his own prohibition was owing to his father's early death; his nearest agnatic kinsmen lived several miles away.

Difficulties of a similar kind arise with clan shrines (s. *dɔɔro tiib*). In view of the complexity of these shrines and their association in some areas with the clan tutelary (*siura*), a feature little emphasized among the LoWiili, only one variant will be considered. A clan is thought of as having one hunting "medicine", associated with a certain method of poisoning arrows and with the hunting shrine. The name of the clan's poison (*dɔɔro lɔ' yuor*) is shouted as the arrow strikes the victim in order to increase the efficacy of the poison. The *Naayili* of Birifu shout "*Tuo, tuo*", and the *Tʃaale* "*Gantʃe, Gantʃe*". The former is the name of the section's tutelary (*siura*), a baobab tree, and the latter of the lineage hunting shrines (*piɔra*). In Tʃaa each of the houses at which the three patrilineal groups cook the meat of wild animals killed by the members possesses a hunting shrine called *Gantʃe*. A child raised by his mother's agnates may eat their hunting "medicine" and shout their hunting cry; on return to his lineage home his clansmen would teach him their call, and he would follow this with the cry of his mother's clan. Knowledge of the ingredients of arrow poisons may also pass to the male children of females of the clan; the prohibitions associated with them become distributed throughout the community.

The discussion of patriclans has not been restricted to the LoWiili alone, for the field of clanship extends beyond the boundaries of relative cultural homogeneity. Its function in social relations over the whole of the north-west corner of the Gold Coast will be reconsidered in connection with the territorial organization.

The matriclan

The complementary rôles of male and female in the procreation of children, clearly recognized in the physiological concepts of the LoWiili, offer alternative lines through which unilineal descent may be traced for particular social purposes. Fortes[1] has shown the significance of the uterine line in the strongly patrilineal

---

[1]1949, p.30.

society of the Tallensi. Dual descent has recently been analysed in two societies in the Eastern Sudan and among the Yakö in South-Eastern Nigeria.[1] Double filiation in itself is a physiological fact and gives rise to the bilateral extension of kinship ties in all societies; in these societies, however, there is a recognition not only of bilateral kinship but also of two lines of unilineal descent. The distinguishing feature of these societies and, along the middle reaches of the Black Volta, of the LoWiili and the various peoples inheriting wealth matrilineally, is what Forde calls a "double unilineal kin group system". In a system of double clanship the individual belongs to two descent groups of maximum extent, an agnatic group traced through males, a uterine group traced through females; a balance is held between agnatic and uterine descent.

Physiological ideas acknowledge the necessity for a proper intermingling of sexual fluids. The male (*dakala*) and female (*pakala*) fluids must "catch together" (*nyɔɔn ta*) for conception successfully to follow intercourse; their mere conjunction does not suffice. From the mother, the child inherits its skin (*yangan*). By extension, the members of one matriclan claim to have "one skin" (*yangan bein*).

I have discussed two aspects of the relationships traced through females in a patrilineal society. The rôle of maternal filiation in the domestic family and in the fission of agnatic kin groups was examined in an earlier chapter. Considerable attention was also given to the second aspect, that of uxorilateral relations, the relationships between ego and the agnatic groups of females married to his ascendant patrikin, and also between ego and the offspring of clanswomen who have married out. The third aspect is complementary descent, on the basis of which a strictly uterine group is formed. Among the Tallensi is found one type of complementary descent group; this has a technical term (*soog*) but is undesignated. The LoWiili have a technical term (*belo*) and a name. Although these are descent groups, I prefer to describe the LoWiili as a patrilineal society with complementary descent, rather than as a dual descent system. I reserve the latter term for societies in which not only are there named groups based on both the alternative methods of reckoning unilineal descent, but in which both these groups are also corporate in the sense that property is vested in them and therefore transmitted between their members. The LoDagaba are an example of such a system, for there double clanship is accompanied by "double inheritance".

The uterine descent group of greatest extent is the matriclan (*belo*), of which there are only four, *Some, Da, Hienbe* and *Kambire*. Common descent is expressed in the concept of "one skin"; the members claim to be the "children of one mother" (*ma biir*). When a traveller unexpectedly hears the noise of a funeral, he may run in front of the stand in which the dead body has been propped, crying "Alas, mother's child, alas!" (*m ma biir, wei; m ma biir, wei*). The net of matriclanship stretches so widely that this is the most likely kinship category into which a stranger would fall. Even persons outside the zone of matriclanship can be included in the scheme, for there is an external physical sign which characterises all members. By an extension of the idea of "one skin" matriclan affiliation is believed to be shown on the palm of the left hand, and the matriclan of a man's father by the lines on the right hand. As in many African societies, the right is associated with the male, the left with the female. Once his identity has been established by this means, a stranger is entitled to the hospitality and protection of his fellow matriclansmen.

---

[1] See the accounts by S. F. Nadel and Daryll Forde in "African Systems of Kinship and Marriage", ed. A. R. Radcliffe Brown and Daryll Forde, London, 1950.

The same kinship terms are employed in both uterine and agnatic systems of clanship. Any member of one's own matriclan can be referred to either as "brother" (*yebe*, a term also used between female siblings) or as "sister" (*yepule*; lit. female "brother"); when it is desired to emphasize a difference in age or in generation, the matriclansman is addressed as "mother" (*ma*) or "mother's brother" (*madeb*). If he is ego's junior, the term *arbile*, "sister's child", may be used. Putative matrilineal descent provides an immense field for the application of kinship terminology. Any member of one's father's matriclan can be called "father" (*sãã*); "he bore me" (*o dɔɔ ma*), the speaker will explain. Equally a member of one's paternal grandfather's matriclan is a "grandfather" (*sããkum*). This intricate network of kinship ties within a system of double clanship "binds the house together", a phrase also employed to describe the use of sibling terminology between grandfather and grandson; how it does so has been suggested in the examination of the status of an illegitimate child. It can also be a source of great confusion to the investigator, who may be unaware of the descent context with reference to which the speaker is employing the terminology. Confusion is not limited to the outsider. A respected and intelligent man was talking to his neighbour of the *Natfiele* patriclan in the latter's compound in Kwŏnyŭkwŏ, some six hundred yards from his own house. He addressed him as "mother's brother", which I queried, knowing the speaker's mother was of the *Kpiele* patriclan. He went into a long explanation of how *Kpiele* and *Natfiele* were linked patriclans, which everybody appeared to accept. Curious about this story, I asked for more details. Finally the *Natfiele* elder spoke. "*Some* (the name of one of the four main matriclans) bore me, *Some* bore your mother, therefore she and I are 'siblings'. You are my 'sister's child' and therefore call me 'mother's brother' ".

There are few individuals in his own or neighbouring settlements with whom a man cannot establish ties of this nature, for there are only four main matriclans. Rattray[1] gives thirty-two designated patrilineal descent groups for the "Lober"; his list is not exhaustive and there are in fact over forty patriclans. According to the 1948 Census Report, the combined population of the Lawra and Nandom Divisions is 44,702, giving an average patriclan strength within this area of roughly one thousand persons. Some patriclans are much larger than others and possibly twice this number of members are living in the Ivory Coast and among other "tribal" groups; it is therefore difficult to give an accurate estimate. But they are considerably smaller units than the matriclans of which there are only four main ones, existing under slightly different but recognizably similar names, despite linguistic frontiers, among the Birifor, LoWilisi, Dyan, Gan, Dorossié and Téguessié, another 150,000 people in all.[2] Of these peoples, only the LoWiili do not inherit wealth through the matriclan.[3] I shall be concerned only with the system of matriclanship as it operates in Birifu. However, some reference must be made to the institution as it exists among the neighbouring peoples for it is by this means that individuals in different cultural groups are linked together. The matriclan, the uterine descent group of widest extent, defines a field of application for certain kinship terms; otherwise these groups function mainly in opposition to one another, paired in a joking partnership. The significance of the

---

[1]1932, p.426.

[2]See Labouret, 1931, pp.51 and 222; it should be added that among the Dyan, the descent groups with these names are agnatically defined.

[3]The Dagaba of Jirapa and Wa use a word similar to *belo* (matriclan) to refer to a patriclan but the names and the organization are quite different.

matriclan joking partnership can be more readily understood after similar forms of patterned behaviour have been examined.

The joking partnership

Reference has already been made to the joking which takes place between a woman and her "brother's" wives, and between an individual and a certain category of his "mother's brothers" (*madeb* 3). These relationships are both ones of extra-clan kinship, resulting from the transfer of rights over women between exogamous descent groups.

It is also possible to observe the characteristic elements of verbal play in the behaviour of grandparents and grandchildren towards each other; this occurs both within and without the agnatic descent groups. As in all societies, the relatively relaxed relationship between members of alternate generations stands in strong contrast to the tensions which exist between adjacent generations; for it is the immediately senior generation that provides the main agents in the socializing process. Grandson (*yoŋ*) and grandfather (*sāākum*) can call each other brother (*yeb*). They can refer to each other's wives as "my wife" (*n pɔɔ*) and may inherit them on their "brother's" death. This at least is the position as often stated. In fact, a lineal descendant never inherits rights of sexual access to his grandfather's widow, although it is conceivable that she might become a member of his household. This is not only a matter of disparate ages. The inheritance of the wife of one's own father's father would conflict too greatly with the authority structure of the joint agnatic household. The statement can and does apply to the widows of classificatory paternal grandfathers. But as customarily employed it indicates in a general way the identification of alternate generations and the amity which manifests itself in claims to each other's spouses.

The joking between "mother's brothers" and "sisters' sons" has a similar component, but it is more generalized and often more abusive. The same is true of the relationship between women and their "brothers'" wives. In this case, there is no overt claim to the sexuality of each other's spouses for they are ego's "siblings". The joking however centres around the fact that if the "sisters" had been male members of the clan, they would have been entitled to make such a claim. Hence women refer to their "brothers'" wives as "our wives".

This joking is clearly a type of amity. I have seen similar behaviour between men and their married sisters, although not institutionalized to the same extent. Drinking beer one day at a compound where his paternal half-sister had married, a man threw down the price of the pot saying "Take this and push it in your vagina". The categories of relationship mentioned so far are thought of as "siblinghood" in a classificatory sense; by various mechanisms all are considered kinsmen of the same generation. The LoWiili explain this behaviour axiomatically —"you can abuse your equals" (*fu na tuna fu taaba*). This form of address contrasts forcibly with the restraint which exists between members of adjacent generations. Joking arises in intercourse between equals, that is, between members of the same generation.

The LoWiili speak of this sort of behaviour as "play", *dieno*. They say, for example, that in-laws of the same generation (*dakye*) play, in-laws of adjacent generations (*diem*) don't. I call inter-personal kinship ties of this nature joking relationships. They are often confused in anthropological accounts, as well as in theoretical analyses, with the joking partnerships which exist between the members of different descent or "tribal" groups as members of these groups.[1]

---

[1]See for example, Radcliffe-Brown's discussion of joking relationships, 1952, p.90.

The LoWiili refer to joking partners as *lonluore*. The forms of behaviour are in some ways similar; the element of joking is present in both cases. Abuse of a standardized nature characterizes the social intercourse between members of descent groups as well as persons standing in certain kinship relationships. Significantly, the abuse takes the form of allusion to stories vaunting the superiority of one group or telling of the stupidity of the other, whereas the comparable kinship behaviour centres on insults of a personal nature. A further general feature of this partnership, and most important to the people themselves, is the exchange of ritual services. It was this that Griaule had in mind when he proposed the phrase "l'alliance cathartique".[1] This suggestion draws attention to an essential aspect both of the joking partnership and of the "sister's son"—"mother's brother" relationship, the reciprocal assistance given in grave difficulties. It has already been said that the LoWiili occasionally use the term *lonluore* in speaking of this latter relationship. It is not the element of joking which is here singled out as the common feature, for that also exists in the other kinship relations we have mentioned. It is the ritual assistance which "sister's son" and "mother's brother" may offer one another that makes the relationship in some situations analogous to the "cathartic alliance" or joking partnership.

Each patriclan or group of linked patriclans stands in joking partnership with another clan. In Birifu, all clans except the *Tʃaale* have as their partners the *Tiere* or *Tiedeme*. The nearest representatives of this clan are the *dagaa* (Dagaa-Wiili) inhabitants of the neighbouring ritual area of Kol'ɔra. The *Tʃaale* and the *Kpiele* of Zinkãã have a partnership with the *Gbaane* clan, none of whom live within several miles; I have never seen or heard of this partnership in operation. Because of their partnership with the clan in which the custodianship of the Birifu Earth shrine is vested, the *Tiere* act as allies in certain rituals of the parish. Their position is ratified in a story which relates that *Tiere* arrived in their present abode before the present inhabitants of Birifu. Their clan is said to own the rain (*be la so a saa*) because of its powerful rain medicine, and, when drought begins to spoil the growing crops and all other expedients have failed, the *Tiedeme* will be called in to assist. These services are performed on behalf of the whole parish. A man from any other ritual area can go to the *Tiere* to acquire a house rain shrine, but in Birifu their power over rain also serves the ritual area as a whole.

The nature of their rôle can be seen from the fact that if a diviner traces any death to the Earth shrine, the expiatory sacrifices for the offence have to begin with the *Tiere* "sweeping" the shrine (*pir*, sweep) by killing a dog, which can be eaten by no other clan except themselves.[2] Apart from their rôle as ritual partners to the parish (*teŋgaan lonluore*), the *Tiere* also act as joking partners (*yir lonluore*) to the patriclans mentioned above. In this latter capacity they are able to remove the power of an oath to the ancestors or a curse put on another member of the clan. If a father has cursed his son and wishes to cancel his words, the partner will be called to throw ashes and give him water to drink. The duties of the joking partner are balanced by certain privileges. Theoretically, the ally can snatch the left front leg of any sacrificial animal, the *lonluore bɔ*, the meat to which sisters' sons are also entitled. In practice they seize little; the killing of the cow of the hoe handle after the body has been buried is usually postponed

---

[1] *Africa*, Vol. XVIII, 1948, p.242.

[2] The metaphor "shaving the Earth shrine's head" or "cutting its hair" is also used in this context.

until the partners have departed home. The only occasion I observed meat actually seized by them occurred directly as the result of my enquiries.

Finally it is said that in any fighting the joking partners of either combatant could bring the fight to a standstill by "throwing ashes" (*loba tampelo*), a phrase, often used metaphorically, which invokes the essential features of the relationship, the power to make "hot things cold", to restore equilibrium in situations where the group or individual has lost control. The situation was clearly put to me at a DagaaWiili village established not long since—"Our clan came here by themselves; that was not good. So we called our joking partners to come and settle here too".

Compared with some of the neighbouring peoples, this partnership between patriclans (*yir lonluore*) receives little emphasis among the LoWiili. Within this region of considerable cultural similarity, the same traditional requirements may appear as the functions of groups organized on different principles. This has already been suggested as one of the implications of double clanship in a comparatively mobile society, mobile that is, in a spatial sense. A particular case arises in the study of joking partnerships. The LoDagaba as a whole place greater emphasis on this than the LoWiili. In Toma, a LoDagaba village near Birifu, I heard some *Bimbili* teasing one of their joking partners, a *Bekuone* man: "The only reason we don't shoot you", they said, "is that one day we may need your help". Historical factors may have influenced the attitude of the LoWiili; with the *Gbaane* living at such a distance they and the *Tʃaale* can offer each other little effective assistance. Matriclan partnerships play a correspondingly greater rôle. Birifu is a more self-contained community than any of the surrounding settlements, depending less upon inter-clan linkages and ties of patriclanship outside the local clan sector.

The joking partnership between matriclans (*bel lonluore*: ally of the matriclan) comes to the fore during the funeral celebrations of a senior man or woman. On the day after the death itself the joking partners solicit cowries from members of the deceased's matriclan, often resorting to sharp words and grotesque acts ridiculing the grief displayed by the bereaved. This behaviour fits the LoWiili conception of the "people of the ash" (*tampelodem*), for these actions tend to restore the community to its normal state.

The joking partners can seize the left front leg of the animals killed during the funeral. This leg is the customary compensation for ritual assistance. The one belonging to the cow of the hoe-handle is seized either by the patriclan ally (*yir lonluore*) or by the "sisters' sons", while the patriclansmen themselves divide the remainder of the animal. It is important to note that they have to seize the leg and are not presented with it. This emphasizes their structural position. They are not members of the group offering the sacrifice and therefore cannot "share" (*puon*) in the distribution of the meat. They have forcibly to assert the claim, arising from their ritual assistance, by seizure.

Another cow is killed at most funerals, the roof or matriclan cow (*gaar naab, bel naab*), the meat of which is distributed according to matrilineal ties. The legs of this animal like the cow of the hoe-handle are distributed among the joking partners, "fathers", "brothers" and "children", but in this case the categories are reckoned in the context of matriclanship. The "fathers'" leg of the cow of the matriclan is divided amongst those who belong to the matriclan of the dead man's father, the "brothers'" leg amongst those of the deceased's own matriclan (*o bel taaba*) who have contributed towards the funeral expenses, the "children's" leg amongst those whose fathers are of the same matriclan as the deceased and who are also members of the same patriclan. Finally, the ally's leg (*lonluore bɔ*) is regularly taken by the joking partners of the deceased's matriclan. The distribution of the matriclan cow thus parallels the distribution of the cow of the hoe-handle within the patriclan. In Birifu little of the meat of the matriclan cow is in fact consumed outside the dead man's patrilineage, for the killing of the animal is usually postponed until the majority of the mourners have dispersed.

The matrilineal descent groups which are linked in joking partnerships are the units of widest extent, the four main matriclans. The pattern of the alliances is:

Some and *Da*

Hienbe and *Kambire*

These partnerships have a wider frame of reference than funerals alone. As with the similar patriclan partnership, the ally can be called upon to cancel an oath or a curse. Because of this, somebody is always close at hand, usually within the compound itself, to remove the injudicious oath and to intervene at the required moment. In sacrifices to the matriclan shrine (*bel tiib*) the joking partners have a similar cathartic rôle which also has patriclan parallels. This will be considered in the next section.

We have seen that the two aspects of these relationships, joking and ritual assistance, linked as they are, do not completely overlap. Verbal play characterizes intercourse between individuals of equal status; in group behaviour, particularly in stress situations, it indicates social distance. Joking partners can imitate the wailing of the mourners because their clan stands sufficiently close to offer assistance in distress and yet is not directly involved in the death; by their behaviour, a state of normality is restored. During the three days of the burial performances, these allies have an important part in the process by which acceptance of misfortune supercedes intense personal grief. If a man's father dies, it is a joking partner who is sent to tell him the news; for he can help to calm the bereaved and minimize his loss. At this point the cathartic alliance and joking partnership coincide. A sister's son can intervene effectively in difficult sacrifices to the ancestor shrines because he is excluded from the community of worshippers and bears no responsibility. The identical service may in certain cases be rendered by members of other lineages of the patriclan, for they also sacrifice to a different founding ancestor. These groups between which no joking partnership exists act reciprocally in the distribution of funeral meat; their structure will be examined in connection with the influence of contiguity in the formation of social groups.

Cathartic assistance is sought from the nearest non-participants; in moments of crisis, only those not directly involved can indulge in joking. Cathartic assistance and joking behaviour are therefore often found in conjunction. Both are important elements in intergroup relationships above the clan level; in the absence of centralized organization, these partnerships integrate descent groups into a wider framework. They offer an alternative between open hostility and the obligations of amity created by common descent.

The differentiation of the matriclan

I have explained that the left front leg of the matriclan cow (*bel naab*) is seized by the joking partners of the deceased's matriclan and that the "fathers'" leg is divided among the matriclan of the dead man's father. But in this second case, the group referred to as *belo* is only a segment of the descent group of widest extent. It is a named section and may be called a matrilineal sub-clan. The application of kinship terms is normally limited to this more restricted field.

It is necessary to bear in mind that among the LoDagaba exogamy obtains only within the matrilineal sub-clan and marriage is permitted with members of attached sub-clans said to be descended from women purchased as slaves. Although the common descent of the whole clan is accepted, a man might be in a position through such a marriage to refer to a member of the same matriclan but a different sub-group as "my father". The use of kinship terminology tends therefore to be restricted to the exogamous group.

The division of the matriclan into sub-clans varies according to the locality, as an examination of Table 12 will show. According to Labouret's evidence, a much greater degree of fragmentation exists among the LoWilisi and the Birifor.[1]

Table 12

MATRICLANS AND THEIR SUBDIVISIONS

	Birifu		Lawra	
Matriclans	Sub-clans	Attached sub-clans	Sub-clans	Attached sub-clans
1. Some . .	Bãã	Topior Monyuur	Palesi	
2. Da . . .	SomDa Sɔɔla Dabire KorenDa MeDa	SomDa Ziɔ	=KpoDa[2]	
3. Kambire . .			Kambire Sɔɔla	Kambire Ziɔ
4. Hienbe . .			Hienbe Dabi Hien	

As all the sub-clans listed under Birifu are also present in Lawra, I have only shown the additional groups under the latter heading.

The clans are often said by the LoDagaba to have divided in order to make marriage possible. Matrilineal inheritance of wealth normally takes place only within the exogamous group. Attached sub-clans present a special case. Two clans and one sub-clan are split into a black (*sɔɔla*) and a red (*ziɔ*) segment. The latter are said to be descendants of women slaves. A *SomDa* for example is said to have purchased a woman in the market. As usual, the slave then belonged to the patriclan and matriclan of the owner, but the group descended from her is stigmatized "red" to indicate its origin. Intermarriage is permitted between full and attached segments of the same sub-clan but inheritance of each other's property is prohibited.

In Birifu, neither the matriclans nor the sub-clans are exogamous groups; the attached sub-clans, whose functions among the LoDagaba centre upon marriage and inheritance, are only occasionally acknowledged even in discourse. In fact, of all the sub-clans, only those of the *Da* matriclan function in action situations. Throughout the region, these represent a further degree of differentiation when compared with the sub-divisions of the remaining clans. Rattray's list of "blood groups" confirms this point; he records ten *belo*, the four main clans, together with the sub-divisions of *Da*.[2] The groups descended from

[1] 1931, p.223.
[2] 1932, p.428. *Kpoda* and *Korenda* are identical; the *Kpole* given in his list might refer to *Palesi*, a *Some* sub-clan.

slaves are attached directly to the matriclan in all cases except that of *Da* where they form segments of the sub-clans. Sub-clans other than those of *Da* merge in most situations; it is only *Da* sub-clans which have separate shrines. In Birifu they receive but little emphasis, for the sub-clans and attached groups do not define areas of exogamy and property rights and are therefore virtually without function. In a society inheriting wealth patrilineally it matters little whether a man is *Bãã Some* or *Monyuuri Some*. However, in order fully to appreciate the LoWiili position, some further reference must be made to the rôle of the sub-clan among the LoDagaba.

When the final funeral of a LoDagaba has been performed the members of his sub-clan living within the neighbourhood gather at his compound to discuss the redistribution of the movable property, if there is no claimant among the close uterine kin. The matriclansmen of the neighbourhood constitute an effective unit of co-operation within the matriclan, as in the case of the patriclan;[1] the factors defining the range of participation are similar and its extent cannot therefore be defined outside a particular situation. When these local members of the matrilineal sub-clan meet to decide upon the heir, emphasis is laid upon the fact that the property belongs to the sub-clan as a whole, the chosen individual acting as custodian on its behalf. If no close kinsman exists, the property may be allocated to a matriclansman who can trace no genealogical connection with the deceased. These rights carry correlative duties. If a man died at some distance from his natal settlement, the members of his sub-clan living in the community where he died would be responsible for the burial ceremonies and could claim any property he had in his possession. The corollary of common ownership is responsibility for debt. Even in Birifu it was acknowledged that formerly the property of a fellow matriclansman of the debtor might be seized in repayment of a debt. Nowadays such an act would no longer be permitted.

Although seizure of the cattle of a fellow matriclansman of the debtor was formerly allowed, the normal procedure in Birifu was to seize those of a fellow patriclansman of his. For here wealth appears in the past to have been inherited along both descent lines. The conception of a man's herd belonging in part to the uterine kin, in part to the patrikin (*Ma per bume ma mine so*, things from the mother's branch, "mothers" own; *kur bumé a yir so*, things' of the hoe, the house owns), authorized this double procedure whereby seizure for debt took place with reference to both sets of clans. In this interstitial community complications arise not only from the distribution of certain functions between groups organized on different descent lines as in Yakö society. In some social situations the same functions may be attached to both uterine and agnatic groups. This form of double clanship offers the individual or group alternative frames of action. However, this special situation no longer exists in Birifu as far as the settlement of debt is concerned. A man can be held directly responsible only for the members of his farming group which is agnatically defined; within this group no debt (*san*) can be created. Within the patrilineage, the possessors of "one hoe", an individual can borrow (*pion*) from another, but after the death of the creditor no claim would be pressed. In contrast to the LoDagaba, the matrilineal sub-clan does not now constitute a unit with common rights over wealth.

The matrilineal sub-clans are exogamous groups among the LoDagaba, and I have heard old women in Birifu, too, say that you cannot marry into your own sub-clan. They maintain that if a man weds his uterine "sister" he will spoil her

---

[1]See p.74.

powers of childbearing (*o na sɔɔna dobo*). The danger of sterility can be avoided only by a formal cleaving of the line of descent. The husband stands inside the byre grasping the forelegs of a sheep and the wife outside holds the hind legs; a member of the matriclan with whom a cathartic alliance exists then cuts the beast in half. Once again the axioms of the LoWiili differ considerably from their observed behaviour. The incidence of marriage within the sub-clan testifies to the lack of concern on the part of young and old alike at failure to conform to this ideal pattern of exogamy. I know of no case where a sheep was killed at the doorway, although the procedure was spoken of as a cure for sterility.

Marriage, however, is not permitted with matrilateral parallel cousins; neither the offspring of one's mother's full sister to the second generation nor the children of close matrilineal kin are considered as possible mates. These restrictions are rooted in the strictly uterine tie, not in the bond between agnatic groups established by marriage. It is unlikely that strong disapproval would be offered to a marriage with the children of one's mother's half-sister or classificatory "sisters", that is, daughters of the same patrilineage or clan as one's mother. These relatives belong to the mother's patrilineage, but not to her matriclan.

"Close uterine kin" are the offspring of one grandmother, genealogical links being traced for two generations. This matrilineal group can be referred to as *m ma per*, my mother's root.[1] The precise extent of the group denoted by this phrase depends upon the context; a *Bãã Some* and a *Monyuuri Some* could claim that they were members of one *belo* but that their *ma per* were different, meaning they belonged to different sub-clans. The phrase may denote any sub-division of the matriclan. *Sãã per* has a similar range of meanings in the case of the patriclan. In the expression "we are all of one patriclan (*dɔɔro*) but of different *sãã per*", it is the patrilineage which is indicated. Lower orders of genealogical segmentation could be described in the same way. However, in the case of both uterine and agnatic groups the main referent is the group tracing descent through precise genealogical steps.

This group is structurally similar to the *soog* of the Tallensi. It is known by a technical term but has no specific name. It conforms to none of the usual criteria of a corporate group. It is non-localized. It is not a property-holding group. Its members never meet together, nor do representatives of segments, and it is therefore not an assembling group. And the authority structure outside the mother-child relationship is minimal; younger members show a general respect to their seniors but in most situations the emphasis is on equality of status within the matriclan. Though limited in its functions and vague in its conceptualization, it nevertheless constitutes a social group in the accepted sociological sense.[2] The existence of a technical term itself indicates a consciousness of unity, and its function is explicitly to regulate marriage on the non-corporate side. Although in a previous account I used the term matrilineal group, I prefer "matrilineage" as the group is defined genealogically and therefore conforms to Radcliffe-Brown's definition.[3] But I would emphasize that it is not corporate in any of the four senses mentioned above, nor does it form part of an extended lineage system. It is indeed the limiting case.

---

[1] I have not translated the metaphor literally; *per* may signify the rectum, the foot of a tree or the base of a shrine.

[2] "Any collection of social beings who enter into distinctive social relationships with one another", R M. MacIver, "Sociology", 1937, p.13.

[3] Radcliffe-Brown and Forde, 1950, p.14.

In Birifu the matrilineage only emerges in the context of strict exogamy. Among the LoDagaba wealth normally passes to a fellow member of this group; and the group as a whole might on occasion be called together for sacrifice at a sacred locality associated with the grandmother. The distinction made by the LoDagaba between *ma per bagre* (a sacrifice concerning one's matrilineage) and *ma yir bagre* (a sacrifice concerning one's mother's patrilineage) exactly corresponds to the difference between uterine and matrilateral relationships in a dual descent system to which attention has been drawn.

The wide extent of matriclanship makes comparative discussion of the institution in neighbouring communities essential to an adequate interpretation of the data offered by any one community. Only in this wider context can a satisfactory approach be made to the ritual functions of the matriclan.

Each matriclan and each *Da* sub-clan possesses its own shrine (*bel tiib*) within the Lawra District. These are thought of as shrines for the whole matriclan, but in view of its wide territorial distribution, similar shrines certainly exist in the Ivory Coast. Sacrifices are made to the shrines when mystical trouble is diagnosed to be connected with the matriclan (*bel bɔɔre*). The principal reason given for such performances is fear of the matrilineal descent group dying out (*dɔɔb bɔɔre*, procreation sacrifice). The neighbouring LoDagaba maintain that, if a man inherits property which rightfully belongs to another matriclan, the clan's shrine will kill him. Two of these altars, hidden in sacred groves, are found among the LoWiili: the shrine of the *Some* at Bãã in Birifu itself and the *SomDa* shrine at Kõ, Zinkãã, in the Ivory Coast.[1] The *Hienbe* and *Kambire* shrines are situated near Lawra among the LoDagaba. The location of these shrines corresponds to concentrations of clan members. The great majority of the inhabitants of Birifu are either *Some* or *SomDa*. Bãã, the *Some* grove, thickly covers the laterite scarp at a point where water flows perpetually from beneath the rocks; the spring provides a dry-season supply for many compounds and keeps certain areas of Tʃaa moist enough to allow two, or even three, crops a year. Appropriately enough, as their shrine is associated with a most unusual and valuable source, *Some* are said to "own the rain" and hence all water everywhere. Sacrifices at Bãã may be made to procure the well-being of the whole parish and not merely of the descent group alone. Three types of sacrifice occur there, each made at different altar stones:

i. Sacrifices arising out of personal trouble. For example, a man from outside Birifu, whose wife was *Some* had begotten no child; he went to Bãã and swore a conditional oath (*o kuon o nuɔr*). A child was born and after his death the animals he had promised were killed at the shrine.

ii. Rain sacrifices. These are made on behalf of the community as a whole and in the presence of the parish elders (*teŋgaandem*).

iii. Matriclan sacrifices, made inside the grove itself.

It is the last which possess the greatest interest from the point of view of interaction of descent groups. The members of a matriclan cannot themselves perform the sacrifice at their own shrine nor even enter their sacred grove. The animals must be killed by the joking partners who also consume the meat of the slaughtered beasts while the clansmen sit at some distance from the grove they are forbidden to approach. These sacrifices occur only at long intervals and their significance should not be overestimated. But frequent reference to the reciprocal ritual services and to the exchange of meat on such an occasion extends the

---

[1] See Fig. 6.

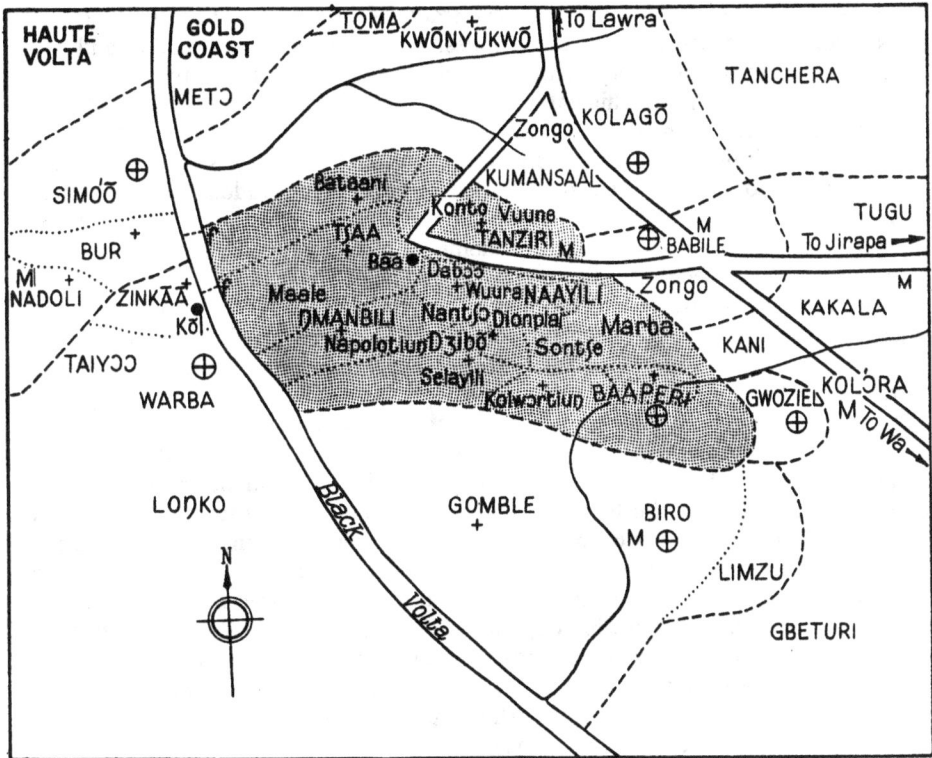

FIG.6. THE SETTLEMENT OF BIRIFU

- - - - Boundary of main ritual area   + Minor Earth shrine

▓ Birifu ritual area   ● Matrician shrine

.... Boundary of minor ritual area   f Ferry

⊕ Main Earth shrine   M Market

effects on the society over the intervening years and emphasizes the principle that the community must be organized around at least two descent groups linked in "joking partnership", the presence of both being essential to the survival of either. An account, given many years later, of a sacrifice at Kŏ, the *SomDa* shrine, will demonstrate more clearly the rôle of the matriclans on these occasions.

Two inhabitants of Nadoli, *Dapla* and *Kunla*, members of the local sector of the *Bire* patriclan which had migrated across the river from Biro, both belonged to the *SomDa* matrilineal sub-clan. *Dapla's* son regularly passed by *Kunla's* house when he was out herding his father's flock. One day, the boy stole a goat and in the fight which ensued between the two compounds, he mortally wounded *Kunla* with an arrow. A child of a *SomDa* had killed his "father". To prevent all *SomDa* from dying out, the crime had to be expiated at their shrine. *Gandaa*, the chief of Birifu, and himself a *SomDa*, called upon the inheritors of another child of a *SomDa* father, dead over four years, to provide the

87

sacrificial cow and informed matriclansmen of his as far away as Batʃɛ and Nandom, a distance of some thirty miles. A great concourse attended and saw *Some* perform the expiatory sacrifice on behalf of their joking partners.

The evidence is insufficient to permit a statement of the precise rôle of matriclan sacrifices in bringing individuals together over a wide area. Accounts of local conditions in pre-European times emphasize the dangers that befell those who ventured outside their own parish. The dangers undoubtedly inhibited travel though they might be mitigated by the mobilization of uxorilateral and uterine ties, as these linked together members of diverse local clan sectors. More recently such a special sacrifice might be the result of the desire of an ambitious chief to make his name widely known. Old men whose matriclan shrines were not in their own neighbourhood sometimes appeared hardly aware of their existence. It would therefore be unwise to exaggerate the integrating function of these sacrifices.

The matriclan, or sub-clan in the case of the *Da*, plays a significant rôle in the final funeral ceremony (*ko dãã 'baaro*, cool funeral beer). This takes place after the guinea-corn has been cut, unless postponed until a subsequent harvest through lack of supplies. On the fourth day of the ceremony the dead man is formally admitted to the company of the ancestor spirits when his shrine (*sãã daa*, father's stick, or *kpiin daa*, spirit's stick), carved nominally by his senior son but in fact by a member of the complementary funeral group, is placed in the byre of his own compound. The following day, in the *Biipol* ritual, the children are sat upon a wooden pole in order of the seniority of their mothers as wives of the dead man. Meanwhile the members of the father's matriclan from the patrilineage, the clan sector, the parish and the neighbourhood gather in front of them. An individual from the group who carved the ancestor shrine takes a cock given him by the oldest member (*zusob*) of the deceased's matriclan present at the ceremony and, cutting its throat, encircles the children in a ring of blood. Pointing to the group before them, he cries "See your 'fathers'; know those that sit there". Porridge made from the dead man's guinea-corn is then eaten and the cock divided between the "fathers" and the children. The rôle of the dead man as father is redistributed between the uterine and agnatic lines of descent. Even when a full brother of the dead man survives to inherit the entire estate, the children will be shown their "fathers" outside the patriclan (*mwo puo sããmine*, lit. "fathers" in the bush, a member of the father's matriclan) as well as their "father" (*yir sãã*, house father) within the patriclan. In this the LoWiili place less emphasis on matriclanship than the LoDagaba; among the latter the matriclan "father" is entitled to the two hind-legs (*sãã gbɛɛ*) of any wild animal killed by his "child". The LoWiili speak of such a person as a possible stand-by in trouble; it is said that disobedience to his commands would bring supernatural retribution. These central aspects of the social relationships of parents and their offspring are recognised by the sharing of the fowl and the contribution of twenty cowries made by each matriclansman of the deceased. These are later divided between the "fathers", that is, themselves, and the children. The difference in emphasis on the rôle of matriclan "fathers" is directly related to the different systems of inheritance. Among the LoDagaba a few items of movable property, including axes and hoes, invariably pass in the agnatic line. The quiver, hidden until the final funeral ceremony by the complementary funeral group, is brought forward on the fourth day of the ceremony. An arrow is withdrawn by members of this complementary funeral group whose matriclan stand in certain relationships to that of the deceased. In this way mystical dangers are removed and the remaining arrows are made "cool" enough for the proper recipients to touch. Like the basket (*duɣ*) containing cloth and trousers, the quiver, arrows and bow are normally returned by an extra-lineage inheritor (*gbandire*) to the sons in order that they may protect the house (*gun a yir*). The LoSaala distinguish the "cool" quiver (*lɔɣ 'baaro*) which the inheritor can take and present to the sons, and the "hot" quiver (*lɔɣ tuo*) which is claimed only by members of the closest sub-clan of the same matriclan. The LoWiili are not now involved in the complications of matrilineal inheritance and their method of dealing with the quiver cannot be precisely formulated. The "cooling" of the arrows still takes place at the final funeral ceremony, but the conflict between patrilineal and matrilineal inheritance of wealth makes it doubtful whether the quivers now hanging in the rooms where their owners died will ever be taken down by the senior matriclansman (*zusob*) of the neighbourhood for transmission to a uterine kinsman. Such a procedure smacks too strongly of *gbandiru*, the inheritance of wealth within the matriclan. In the past this was done; the quiver belonging to the father of the late chief of Birifu was sent to a close uterine kinsman living some thirty miles away in the Ivory Coast, when the local members of his matriclan, *KorenDa*, had met together, killed a cow (*lɔɔ naab*, cow of the quiver) and with the aid of a diviner, decided upon the recipient. After a lengthy journey, the quiver was finally restored to an illegitimate child of the deceased's lineage, *Doɛri*, whose position has already been discussed. *Doɛri*, being a son of one of the dead man's full sisters, belonged to the same matriclan. The quiver was returned by the "father" outside the patriclan (*mʷo puo sãã*) to the lineage "father" (*yir sãã*), that is, by a member of the deceased's matriclan in a different patriclan (*mwo puo belo*) to another member within his lineage. The late chief called *Doɛri* "father" and allotted him the appropriate legs of the domestic animals he sacrificed and the wild ones he shot. By the mechanics of the kinship terminology the sister's son is promoted a generation in the lineage structure. In a system of double clanship the sister's son belongs to the same matriclan as the father and is in some contexts a classificatory "father".

The interaction between the groups organized on the alternative lines of descent often constitutes a basic structural feature of societies in this area; the situation remains static neither in a temporal nor a spatial sense. Only by a lengthy examination of the rôle of the matriclan and its sub-groups has it been possible to suggest this dynamic process, an examination which is prompted by the obscurity present in the existing ethnographic material on this area.

Three main levels of uterine descent group have been distinguished:

i.   The matriclan, the descent group of maximum extent, operating in the context of the joking partnership.

ii. The sub-clan and the attached sub-clan.

iii. The matrilineage within which genealogical ties are traced.

In discourse the four main clans are differentiated by well-known stories of a trivial nature, usually recounted by a joking partner to raise a laugh among the audience. Other distinguishing features are absent. Although the *Some*, like the *Tiedeme* patriclan, claim to "own" the rain, the remaining matriclans are not vested with specialized duties to be performed on behalf of the community as a whole and no symbiotic structure is therefore built up. A few of the matrilineal sub-clans avoid certain animals and all these groups prescribe a certain leaf (*vaa suɔr*) to be soaked in the water with which an infant is bathed.

On no occasion do representatives of the same matriclan act jointly; no mechanism for such action exists, for there is no constituted authority system, leadership being vested temporarily in the oldest member in a neighbourhood for the purposes of a particular ceremony. Otherwise there is no differentiation among members; the joking partner who kills the fowl (*nokora*) at the clan shrine holds no position of authority either in his own clan or in that of his allies.

Among the LoDagaba it is said that the matrilineage sometimes sacrifices together. But they never act as a whole in opposition to similar groups; social relations within the sub-clan are not the result of membership of a group of lower order but arise directly from membership of the larger unit. This feature distinguishes the position of the matrilineage within the sub-clan from that of the patrilineage within the clan sector.

Both matrilineages and patrilineages represent the field of recognized genealogical ties within the system of descent groups. The limited emphasis on remembered genealogies characterizes the descent groups of the LoWiili in contrast to the extended lineages of the Nuer and the Tallensi, societies which also lack centralized political organizations. The essential feature of these extended lineage systems is that groups of a lower level combine together for a particular social purpose at the next order of segmentation. "Small units of a particular form are, like cells, associated together into larger units of the same general form, and these again associated into still larger units of analogous or identical form, and so on up to the limits of the system."[1] These particular systems are built around the framework provided by the genealogy. In the social organization of the LoWiili this process is partial, never continuous. In a limited sense, the patriclan operates on this principle of association up to the level of the clan sector, but the matriclan not at all. At other levels the segments are not associated in the organized manner which characterizes extended lineage systems. Matrilineages do not stand in distinct opposition one to another and do not therefore merge at the next structural level in the way described by Fortes. From ego's point of view, membership of the various orders of sub-divisions within a matriclan is given simultaneously at birth and does not appear to arise from membership of a sub-group of the next lower order as would be the case in an extended lineage system.

Apart from the mother and her children living in one room, the cell of the polygynous family, the only body of matrikinsmen that acts conjointly consists of those members regularly attending each other's funerals. This neighbourhood grouping is the active field of clanship. Both the matriclan and the patriclan may in fact be viewed as an overlapping series of such groupings of neighbouring clansmen maintaining active, face-to-face, relationships.

---

[1]Fortes, 1945, p.232.

Chapter 5
The Territorial System

Ritual areas

The LoWiili have no nucleated villages in the western European sense. In populous districts homesteads stretch continuously over the farmland, fifty, a hundred, two hundred yards apart. A cartographer can select no convenient land-mark to pin-point a settlement on his map. There are no public buildings such as men's meeting houses and the only distinctive feature to catch the eye is the closely packed strangers' quarter in the villages along the trade route. But behind this apparent lack of differentiation there is an intricate system of territorial organization.

The basic territorial division of the land in this region is the "parish", the ritual area associated with a particular Earth shrine. Both shrine and parish are known by the name *teŋgaan*, a word which is etymologically connected with *tiuŋ*, the country and *tene*, the soil. The main Birifu shrine is situated in a sacred grove and consists of a circular ring of stones roofed with dead branches. Nearby are buried pots containing the cowries paid as fines to the Earth.

Every stretch of country has its appropriate altar, which was either shown to the first settler by the previous inhabitants or discovered by the founding ancestor himself. No land exists which does not "belong" to a shrine. The shrine's particular jurisdiction lies in the most important sector of human life for an agricultural community, the interaction between man and the land he farms. Hills and streams are inhabited by bearded dwarfs (*kontome*). In marshes and the banks of streams are buried those whom the Earth shrine rejects as having broken its fundamental taboos. The bush (*wio*) has its own shrines and prohibitions similar to the Earth's which come into force during the hunting season. The Earth shrine owns all these places and yet its particular sphere of effective participation lies in those human activities directly connected with the soil.

When a new house is being constructed, a sprig of a tree associated with the *teŋgaan* forms part of the shrine guarding the unfinished building. On the completion of the house and before occupation, three stones from the Earth shrine are laid in the doorway of the byre and covered in the faeces of children and of the various species of domestic animal which will live there and require protection.

Money made in pot-making, an activity directly concerned with the "Earth shrine's soil" (*teŋgaan tene*), can be used only for buying food and clothes; if used for bridewealth, the children of the marriage would "belong" to the *teŋgaan*. Another craft, smithing, has strong associations with the *teŋgaan*. The iron, formerly smelted from laterite rocks dug out of the local earth, provides the raw material for the hoes which cultivate the land and the arrows which protect its produce. The furnace itself is likened to the Earth shrine and the smith shares certain of the functions of the *teŋgaansob* or custodian of the Earth shrine. The striking of the earth with the smith's hammer (*zer*) has the same effect upon an armed conflict within the parish as the throwing of ashes by the custodian himself; any person continuing to take part automatically incurs supernatural retribution.

The annual sacrifice at the Earth shrine arises directly out of man's basic task, the production of food. In April, shortly before the seed is due to be sown, all compounds within the ritual area bring guinea-corn flour, and the five main clan sectors contribute fowl. The parish elders (*tiuŋdem* or *teŋgaandem*) mix a little of the flour from each compound and, placing some on the various altars which comprise the shrine,[1] cut the fowl's throat so that the blood drips over flour and altar alike. Beer is offered at the same time, and the remainder of this and of the guinea-corn are then consumed by those present. This sacrifice (*teŋgaan dãã*) is the most important of the annual agricultural ceremonies of the LoWiili. The corresponding offerings to the house and farm shrines (*bomaal dãã*), held at different times clan by clan, either before the harvest or in the middle of the dry season, may be omitted in any one year because of a bad harvest or the shortage of fowl, but the sacrifices to the Earth shrine must of necessity be performed for the sake of the continued well-being of the community. Rain, in whose power the harvest lies, can be withheld by the Earth shrine if its displeasure has been incurred. When drought threatens the crops, the LoWiili search incessantly in an attempt to find the reason. The diviner's diagnosis usually points to the *teŋgaan*, who has kept back the rain not because of any malice towards human beings but because members of the ritual community have disregarded its taboos. At this time, past failures to observe these avoidances are dragged to the surface in an attempt to rectify the situation. During the wet season of 1951 the remains of an old man recently dead were dug from the grave in the courtyard of his house and reburied on the edge of a stream. He had once been sold in slavery and on his return to his natal community his kinsmen had not made the required payment to the shrine. He was not entitled to a full burial and the diviner discovered that the Earth was angry because he had been given one. His decaying flesh was disinterred therefore from the patio of the house he had built and put in a trench dug in the bank of a stream, so that when the rains came the impurity would be taken outside the parish itself. In another instance a man had farmed on the day of no hoeing (*takuɔr daa*), the day of the week set aside for beginning the building of houses and for other activities associated with the shrine. The *teŋgaan's* anger caused the rain to stop. The threat of drought forms a powerful sanction to the shrine's taboos.

The prohibitions and performances so far discussed link the community in its joint exploitation of an area of farm land. The shrine has equally important functions in guarding and protecting those who dwell within this area, in securing a reasonably stable framework for the prosecution of agricultural tasks. The Earth shrine likes humanity (*o nona nibe*). I was told that in the old days, before medicine shrines (*tibe*) were known, only the *teŋgaan* and the hill and water sprites (*kontome*) were there to guard children against the many dangers which encompass them. When an infant had attained three months, or four in the case of a girl,[2] soil was rubbed on the gums to secure the shrine's protection. An

---

[1]The ancestor shrines of former custodians of the Earth shrine are addressed first. It has been explained that a man's medicine shrines will be transmitted patrilineally on his death; his descendants must first sacrifice to his ancestor shrine before the medicine shrine can be approached. The ancestor shrines of former ritual leaders are conceptually, not physically, a part of the shrine; lodged in the care of their agnatic descendants, they are worshipped by the whole parish. Only in this case does the cult community in ancestor worship extend beyond the limits of genealogical ties.

[2]This patterned insistence on three for a male and four for a female runs throughout West Africa. The rôles of male and female are thus differentiated at an early age.

unweaned child whose mother dies is taken by a uterine kinswoman and placed under the guardianship of the local Earth shrine (*teŋgaanblɛ*). In the same way a stranger can make himself safe from murder by putting a small quantity of soil in his mouth; his subsequent death would cause the destruction of the whole lineage of the slayer. A stray woman also belongs to the shrine and her children are *teŋgaan biir*; her daughters have to be redeemed from the shrine before marrying as is the case with all female children placed under its protection.

Although shrines are universal, ritual communities are independent. A particular shrine is effective only for the inhabitants of the ritual area, and for strangers who have eaten the soil or drunk the water. By its taboos, the shrine unites a territorial area and its inhabitants.

The most important prohibition of the Earth, one which defines the major field of social control, is that which forbids the shedding of human blood (*zũ tʃiir*) within the main ritual area. Before it is possible to examine its detailed operation in Birifu and in the neighbouring settlements, further attention must be given to the structure of the ritual area itself. These contiguous areas, which I have called parishes, vary in extent. The Birifu *teŋgaan* covers some five square miles and is inhabited by approximately two thousand people. The neighbouring parish of Babile embraces some seven hundred. The elders point to rocks, trees or gulleys as marking the limits of an area. As I have previously mentioned, although these boundaries are defined, they are undoubtedly also influenced by considerations of patriclanship.

The close association of shrine and inhabitants is reflected in the claim the Earth has on human property without an owner. Stray persons, unclaimed domestic animals and objects of iron, especially hoe blades, belong to the shrine. I have taken the critical feature of a main *teŋgaan* area to be the ownership of stray cattle found within its boundaries. This corresponds to the local usage of the word *teŋgaankpɛ̃ɛ̃*, for where one ritual area is regarded as a segment of a larger, cattle found there are offered to the major shrine.

The necessity for such a limited criterion arises from the dynamic structure of ritual areas. These are not laid out in a final unchanging pattern but alter in the face of social pressures. As in the case of clanship, the investigator is confronted with a process of continuous fission as the population increases. Ritual areas are found at all stages in this process, linked in various segmentary series.

The parish of Birifu is divided into ten smaller areas associated with minor Earth shrines (*teŋgaanblɛ*). These shrines consist of an altar stone surrounded by a sacred grove, smaller but marked by the same type of tree (*kyie*, pl. *kyiir*, Celtis integrifolia) as the grove of the major Earth shrine. During the dry season of 1950–1 the whole district suffered a particularly bad fowl pest which reduced the killing of fowl to a minimum; no sacrifices at these smaller shrines were performed during that period and I am therefore unable to present evidence derived from observation. In normal years, it is said, beer and flour are first offered here before they are offered to the major shrine, that is, shortly before the rains. Stray goats belong to the minor, stray sheep and cattle to the major shrine.

The area associated with a minor Earth shrine tends to correspond with the home-farms of a lineage; the actual position in Birifu itself is analysed in Table 13.

The three patrilineages in Tʃaa are largely intermingled but the descendants of *Napolo* are still known as the Bataan people (*Bataandem*) from the location of their ancestral home.[1] *Vuune biir*, a *Ɖmanbili* lineage, joined the 'Yoŋyuole

Table 13
THE DISTRIBUTION OF PATRILINEAGES IN RELATION TO MINOR EARTH SHRINES

1. Clan	2. Clan Sector	3. Patrilineage	4. Locality Name	5. Minor Earth Shrines
A. Kpiele	Tʃaa	i. Kontʃol ii. Napolo iii. Zaagbwŏ ⎱	Intermingled; though ii are known as Bataandem ⎱	1 for Bataan, 1 for remainder of Tʃaa and Maale (E. iv)
B. Naayili		i. Wuura ii. Dabɔɔ iii. Nantʃɔ iv. Sontʃe v. Marba		⎱ + ⎰ +
c. Samale	Baaperi	i. ii.	Baaper Kolwɔrtiuŋ and Kolagŏ	+ +
D. 'Yoŋyuole		i. ii. Konto iii. at Biro	Selayir Tanziri	+ with E.v. with Biro
E. Bimbili	Ŋmanbili	i. Dionpla ii. Dʒibŏ iii. Napolo iv. Maale v. Vuune	Gɔrpuo „ „ and Selayir Tʃaa Tanziri	⎱ + + with A. with D.ii

Column 3 gives the names of the founding ancestors by which the lineages are known.
Lineage and locality name are derived one from another unless otherwise stated.
+ indicates minor Earth Shrines.

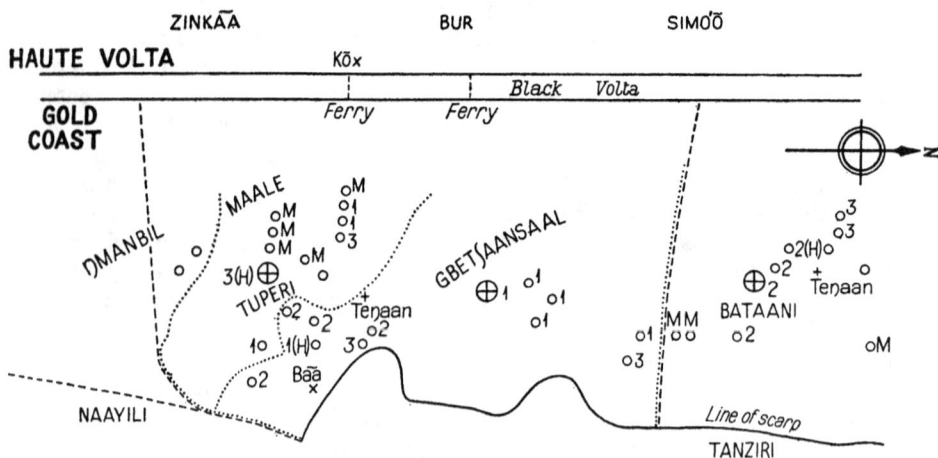

FIG.7. THE DISTRIBUTION OF COMPOUNDS, TʃAA, BIRIFU
.........Area within which reciprocal interment takes place
_ _ _ _Boundary of minor ritual area
1= Kontʃol's lineage   2= Napolo's lineage   3=Zaagbwŏ's lineage
(H) Compound where the meat of wild animals is prepared
⊕ Compound containing founder's shrine
M Ŋmanbil Maale compound

94

group in Tanziri and both sacrifice at the same shrine. *Ɔmanbil Maale* kill fowl at the Tʃaa shrine for reasons which have already been explained.[1] Otherwise lineages or combinations of lineages belonging to the five main clans have their own altars. In the three cases where lineages sacrifice together, they are considered to have closer ties with each other than with any other lineage of the clan. This is not expressed in a genealogical idiom, for the patrilineage by definition represents the limits of precise agnatic reckoning. An elder once suggested a closer bond of descent existed between the members of the *Naayili* rooms of *Wuura*, *Dabɔɔ* and *Nantʃɔ* who sacrifice together at one Earth shrine, but normally the founders of the five lineages which constitute the Birifu sector of the *Naayili* clan are said to be children of one man by different mothers. These two groups of lineages perform important reciprocal services at each other's funerals; this in itself indicates the greater social distance the offspring of *Wuura* stand from *Marba* and *Sontʃe* than from the lineages with which they sacrifice at the same shrine.

The stone which acts as the altar of a minor Earth shrine is said to have been taken from the major shrine, and the inhabitants regard the lesser ritual area as a segment of the whole parish. Local traditions claim that the main shrine was established by the first settler, the founding ancestor of the *Selayili* lineage of the 'Yoɲyuole clan. The origin of the smaller altars is attributed to dissension on the part of the forefathers (*ti saakum mine ziɔra*, our ancestors quarrelled, or fought). By the transfer of a stone from the main shrine, an independent point of communication with the Earth was made available to the local descent groups involved. The segmentation of ritual areas therefore tends to follow the main lines of cleavage in the social structure of the parish, firstly between clan sectors and then between patrilineages. Although subsequent movement has obscured the situation in Tʃaa, the establishment of the *Bataani* shrine is visualized in terms of a disagreement between the offspring of *Napolo* and the other two lineages.

The present function of these shrines centres on agriculture; the minor ritual community tends to be a patrilineage having certain joint rights and obligations to farmland, of which the most prized areas, the home farms, lie within its boundaries. The association between descent groups and minor ritual areas has already been noted in the analysis of the dissolution of a domestic family through the death of the wife.[2] A child still feeding at the breast is taken by one of the mother's uterine kinswomen and, by eating the earth and the produce of the land, is placed in a special relationship to the shrine to which she owes allegiance. The infant becomes a "child of the Earth shrine" whom his agnatic kinsmen must redeem with certain offerings for the shrine if he is again to become a full member of their clan. These same payments have to be made by the future husband of a girl borne by a stray woman or of a female child who has been presented to the shrine to cure a sickness.

The establishment of a separate altar can be seen as a stage in the fission of a ritual area. On the eastern edge of Birifu, a *Zoɣe* section moved from the adjoining DagaaWiili region into Guoziel which formerly lay within the boundary of the main ritual area. Stray animals found in Guoziel theoretically belong to the Birifu shrine. But now when a sacrifice is performed, one cow will be killed at the main altar and a second at the local shrine. This shrine has taken over other functions too. Hoes and metal objects are no longer sent to Birifu, while the annual offering and rain sacrifices are made locally instead of at the main shrine.

---

[1] See p.54.
[2] See p.53.

95

Fission has occurred along the line of cultural differentiation, for the inhabitants of Guoziel reckon themselves as DagaaWiili and strongly disapprove of the LoWiili use of matriclans. The joint occupation of the Birifu *teŋgaan* makes violence between the two groups subject to supernatural sanctions. On the other hand the inhabitants of Guoziel would on no account assist Birifu in its struggles with the DagaaWiili of Tugu, among whom many of their patriclansmen are to be found. The conflicting pull between ritual duties and the obligations of patriclanship is illustrated in a well-known incident. Some thirty years ago, the chief of Tugu appointed a headman at Guoziel who, according to the inhabitants, made them do more than their share of the labour formerly required by the Administration. The people hated this individual and laid a curse of the Earth shrine upon him. His death was attributed to this curse but no concluding sacrifice was offered (*be be iira nε*, lit. they didn't take away the mouth). Years later a suicide was committed in Guoziel and the inhabitants wanted to perform the expiatory sacrifice at the main Birifu shrine. The parish elders, however, decided not to allow them to do so in view of their failure to conclude the previous affair. This incident was critical in the transfer of important functions to the Guoziel shrine.

The settlement of Biro, to the south of Birifu, illustrates a further stage in this process of separation. The altar is said to have originated in Birifu but stray animals are now no longer sent there. Sacrifices concerned with the well-being of the community take place at the Biro shrine which is spoken of as *teŋgaankpɛ̃ɛ̃*, a major Earth shrine. None the less, the ritual areas of Biro and Birifu are one (*teŋgaan boyen*) in a most important sense—the killing of a member of one settlement by a member of the other requires a joint expiatory sacrifice at the shrine whose taboo was broken by the shedding of blood. This function of the Earth shrine, the maintenance of sanctions against bloodshed, particularly between the clan sectors living within the area, makes peaceful co-existence possible; it creates the community of law and order. This community is founded on ritual sanctions. No delegation of powers existed outside the lineage until the introduction of chiefship (*nalo*) by the Administration. The only type of authority beyond the lineage level was the ritual leadership of the custodian of the Earth shrine. I shall briefly outline his duties before examining the integration of parishes into wider groups.

The office of *teŋgaansob* is normally vested in the lineage who first discovered the area. The *Selayili* patrilineage of the 'Yoŋyuole clan are recognized to have been the first to arrive in Birifu. When their founding ancestor came from their previous home at Sier, the *Tiedeme* had already established themselves in Kol'ɔra, a neighbouring ritual area of the DagaaWiili. The *Tiedeme* and 'Yoŋyuole are joking partners and the *Tiedeme* consequently have a special rôle to play in the most serious sacrifices at the Birifu Earth shrine. The complementary activities of these two clans with regard to each other's parish are reflected in the sexual differences ascribed to shrines, *Tfiire*, the Kol'ɔra shrine, being male and the Birifu shrine, *Ulu*, female. If the inhabitants of either parish offend their respective shrines, rain will cease over the whole countryside.

Within the Wiili area the ritual leader is normally selected from the patri-lineage descended from the original custodian, the first man to arrive in the area. Such is the case with the neighbouring *Kusiele* of Babile. But in this respect, as in so many others, the system of double clanship offers alternative groups in which rights and obligations may be vested. The last three custodians of the Kwõnyũkwõ *teŋgaan* at Kumansaal each belonged to a different patriclan in the area; here the office is vested in the matriclan, not in the patriclan, of the first arrival. "The sister's son takes over (*dina*, lit. eats) the office". Although the inhabitants of Kumansaal now inherit all property patrilineally, matrilineal clanship provides an alternative framework for certain institutions. Among the LoDagaba the office is invariably vested in the matriclan and not infrequently in the patriclan of the first settler. At Gbiiri, for example, the custodian must be a member of the *Binale* patriclan and the *MeDa* matriclan. A similar situation exists at Biro; only a member of the *Biro* patriclan who is also a *Dabire* can succeed to the office. The explanation of the specific matriclan is given in kinship terms. The Birifu custodian, who must be *SomDa*, gave part of the ritual area for another sub-division of the *Da* matriclan to look after. In Birifu itself, although it is said that '*Yoŋyuole* were the first sector to arrive and therefore "own the land", the office is no longer vested in that patrilineage but only in the matrilineal sub-clan of the original custodian. The tale which explains how this occurred emphasizes the fluidity given to the social structure by the system of double clanship.

When a former custodian, *Gbagber*, died, he left in his house his wives and his full sister, *Biertono*, a widow who had been married at Baaperi and had returned to live in her natal home. The dead man's patrikinsmen were anxious to marry his widows but not to look after their own "sister". She was angry at this and said she would keep her brother's widows herself. One of these women reported to the husband's kin that *Biertono* was preventing her from remarrying and suggested that they should murder her. *Biertono*, however, was forewarned. One night her "brothers" came to the house and, finding three sleeping forms on the roof of Biertono's room, shot an arrow in the centre of the group. But *Biertono* and two of the widows had arranged bundles of faggots under a mat in their usual sleeping place and lay safely in a hut nearby. The next morning she called everyone to come to her house and told them how her kinsmen had tried to kill her. "I am a *SomDa*", she said, "my brother's things are mine, the Earth shrine included. Henceforth only *SomDa* can own the shrine." Subsequently the office passed to a "sister's son" in Baaperi and then to the late chief of Birifu, a member of the *Naayili* patriclan.

The actual selection of the new priest is made by a continual recourse to diviners, beginning after the final funeral ceremony. Only *SomDa* are considered and in particular those related through specific uterine ties to a daughter of the *Selayili* patrilineage, the lineage of the first custodian. "The shrine follows the mother's branch" (*a teŋgaan tuura ma per*), like wealth among the LoDagaba. Even within this range of possible custodians the choice is far from depending upon the fall of the diviner's cowries. The whole matter is thrashed out in informal discussion over many months. During my stay in Birifu, the office stood vacant and such discussions were constantly taking place. It was said of the most likely candidate that the late chief, his full brother, had warned others against his bad temper; in a fit of anger he might misuse his powers and destroy the parish. The phrase *soŋa tiuŋ*, spoil the land, which was used of this and indeed any major disaster, expresses the most bitter experiences of human existence.

Although separated by a boundary (*tɔɔra ziɛ*) which can be roughly indicated by those in its immediate vicinity, Biro and Birifu are said to be one ritual area. I have been told that no such division exists between Birifu and Kwõnyũkwõ because the ritual areas are one, but I believe the words must be interpreted in a very limited sense. I have heard the same said of two ritual areas between which certain obligations existed; and yet shortly after another individual pointed out to me certain natural features as the boundary marks of these same two areas. The relationship between the Kwõnyũkwõ and Birifu areas has considerable importance in the analysis of the system of territorial groups. The ritual offices of both communities are vested in the *SomDa* matriclan; while one story tells how the land once belonged to the Birifu Earth shrine. The inhabitants of Birifu also maintain that the settlements of Simo'õ, Metɔ, Dapla and Gbiiri, all lying further to the north in the main line of migration, once formed part of their ritual area which they divided in favour of the newcomers. The *Da* matriclan, they say, still "owns all". Representatives of these parishes do not sacrifice or meet together on any occasion; cattle and other domestic animals are killed at their own major shrines. But an idea is preserved of that fundamental obligation of individuals owing allegiance to a common shrine, expiation for the killing of another member. In present circumstances it is impossible to evaluate the possible effectiveness of this obligation in an actual situation. The evidence suggests that the murderer's kin would have considered it too dangerous to go and greet (*pure*) the kin of the victim and offer the requisite payment to the shrine if they lived in a different parish. It will be seen however that this association of ritual areas into these loose maximal ritual areas was an important factor in the formation of war alliances.

A study of the wider setting of this system of minor, major and maximal ritual areas makes it possible to resume the examination of the parish itself, or major ritual area, as the focal field of social control, the community of "law". The *teŋgaan* "likes people" (*o nona nibe*). It binds together the individuals and descent groups within its boundaries by upholding sanctions against certain types of disruptive behaviour. It "owns" and protects its worshippers. Offences against the shrine include witchcraft, the selling of other members into slavery, suicide and murder. No mourning will take place for anyone the diviners diagnose as a witch until the patrikin have made a payment of animals and cowries to the shrine; indeed, any person who dies on the day consecrated to the shrine is automatically regarded as a witch. The selling of one's children impoverishes the community and weakens the descent group; if it is unexpiated all that lineage will perish (*be na kpiin baar*). Suicide and murder must also be expiated by sacrifices and the heaviest of monetary payments. In all these cases, the joking partners are called in to make the preliminary offering of a dog, the one domestic animal not under the jurisdiction of the shrine; only for the gravest crime of bloodshed (*zũ tfiir*, known also as *teŋgaan pũ*, Earth shrine arrow), is a dog sacrificed to cleanse the Earth shrine. This sacrifice is called "shaving the head of the Earth shrine", an act which is carried out on a human being when an offspring has died.

The members of the ritual community owe allegiance to a particular shrine and are thereby placed in a relationship of dependence upon each other. Within the area, an offence against the shrine may harm the entire parish unless it is expiated. In the event of suicide, for example, the shrine can hold up the rain as well as kill off the remaining members of the dead man's lineage or clan sector. An individual persistently breaking the taboos of the shrine was formerly expelled from the community by the ritual leader driving a wooden stake (*Gaa*, Diospyros mespiliformis) into the ground in front of his compound. Acts such as killing, which are considered praiseworthy outside the ritual area, become a grave offence within it. It is said that the ritual leader might intervene to prevent internal fighting, although accounts of local conflicts do not suggest he was always effective. Even within the area, the killing of a member of another clan would provoke active retaliation. Only subsequently would difficulties related by a diviner to this outbreak of violence cause the parties to make the required expiatory sacrifices. The custodian had little scope to act on his own initiative. He cannot, for example, approach the shrine himself but selects two individuals, sons of *SomDa* matriclansmen, to perform the sacrifices. His rôle is essentially that of an intermediary between the shrine and the ritual community. Decisions are made after discussion among the parish elders, an informal council concerned only with the Earth shrine and its affairs.

Contiguity and the local community

Every person who eats the soil or produce of the soil of a particular ritual area enjoys the rights and duties of a member of that community. Performances at the main shrine, however, are essentially the obligation of the larger patriclans within the parish. In Birifu, there are five main clan sectors. Representatives of other clans living within the confines of Birifu do not normally attend the sacrifices. If such an individual did so, he would not be entitled to a share of the meat, although another clan might cut him a portion (*ŋman ko*, cut and give) as a "sister's son". In sacrifices at the minor shrines the stranger compounds can properly claim a share of the meat which is divided by compounds (*puon a yir*) and not by clan sectors (*puon a dɔɔro*). Residents of Birifu who do not belong to one of the five main clans are dependent to a much greater degree upon their relations with patriclansmen in other parishes. The original five clan sectors are almost independent of outside groups, other than the *Tiedeme*, the joking partners of the 'Yoŋyuolê, the first clan to arrive, and therefore also of their Earth shrine, for the adequate functioning of their social system. In other parishes among the LoDagaba and the DagaaWiili, considerably more emphasis is placed on ties between clans and clan sectors than was the case in Birifu. Normally each clan is associated with a natural feature such as a hill or tree to which first-born children are taken in order to discover their tutelary or guardian spirit (*siura*); a man who migrates to a new area will return for this purpose to his natal village. The *Doyili* patrilineage of the *Zoɣe* clan, who live in Birifu intermingled with the Baaperi sector, their "mothers' brothers", continue to take their children to the "place of the tutelary" (*siura zie*) in the village of Wiili from whence they came. When a lineage multiplies in its new surroundings, a stone may be transferred from the "place of the tutelary" at the original home. The migration histories preserve the memory of previous settlements and in serious difficulties elders may be sent back to consult their "brothers" in the "old country" (*teŋkuori*); as these have the custody of the old ancestor shrines and the "place of the tutelary", they will know the best course of action to recommend.

The LoWiili perform analagous rites during the opening stages of the Bɔɔre initiation; the "places of the tutelary" of the various clans sectors are all situated within the parish itself and they have no knowledge of any such shrine at their ancestral home, Sier. Indeed social intercourse of any sort with this village is negligible although it is no more than ten miles away. I found no one in Birifu who knew its precise location or who had ever made the journey.

The slighter emphasis on patriclanship outside the ritual area may be influenced by historical reasons which now lie beyond recovery. Experience of the settlements in which patriclanship receives greater prominence suggests a sociological factor. LoDagaba communities tend to be composed of a greater number of small sectors of different patriclans; co-operation takes place between

99

clans rather than between the lineages of one local clan sector. The tight network of bonds between descent groups within the ritual area does not appear to have developed so completely in these more fragmentary communities which, in matters of reciprocal ritual services, rely to a greater extent upon outside patri-clansmen.

The complex inter-relationships between these local groups cannot be considered in detail. The most involved are those connected with the Bɔɔre ceremonies whose intricacy requires a lengthier analysis than can be given here. These performances, carried out by different clan sectors or patrilineages every year, are organized on the basis of agnatic descent groups, although the repre-sentatives of the other clan sectors take part in supervising the initiation and in the accompanying festivities. The patterned exchange of ritual services between clan sectors is paralleled by a series of distributions of food and beer embracing the parish as a whole. It should be added that the Bɔɔre ceremonies are performed among the LoDagaba, the DagaaWiili, and the Birifor. There are two varieties, the Bɔ Kã or Oil Bagre and the Bɔ Pla or White Bagre. A member of the "secret society" can attend performances in other settlements providing it is the same type. This dichotomy and the general opposition between initiated (s. bɔɔ) and non-initiated (s. dakume) form another possibility of alignment in individual and group relations. The latter succeed in cutting across the lines of intersection between ritual areas and descent groups.

Stranger lineages are dependent on their patrikinsmen outside the parish for the performance of the Bɔɔre ceremonies. The web of services and privileges embraces only the five major clan sectors of the parish. But there are other action groups in which a stranger participates immediately and which are based primarily on contiguity of habitation. The situations in which these groups emerge are concerned with farming and the disposal of the dead.

The members of farming parties assist each other in carrying out obligations to in-laws and in reciprocal work on their own farms; they consist of between ten and twenty young men. These men are normally agnates because it is the patrilineage which forms the basis of the local groups and the people who assist each other in the fields are those who live near together. A man living at his mother's home works with her patrikinsmen, not with his own; a man farms with his neighbours. The farming parties have to remain roughly equal in strength for reasons of reciprocity. If a man takes a certain number of men to his father-in-law, he expects his son-in-law to bring a party equally large. Tʃaa consists of three farming parties, one in Bataani, one in Gbɛtʃaansaal and one on the southern side.[1] These are determined mainly by contiguity. Tʃaa represents a test case in this respect as the compounds of the different lineages are inter-mingled. Where the dwellings of the lineage remain spatially distinct as in Naayili the operating principle is not so clearly brought out.

Burial of the dead is another reciprocal service performed by groups whose membership is based primarily on propinquity rather than descent. The actual interment cannot be performed by members of the same lineage as the dead man; a reciprocal arrangement is made with another group. These arrangements are constantly in a state of transition; the enquirer is told that "formerly such a lineage buried our dead but now we have changed". The reason given is either carelessness or tardiness in the performance of the task. The formation of burial groups does not necessarily follow the lines of cleavage between descent groups. The first essential is that the service has to be carried out by immediate neigh-

---

[1] See Fig. 7.

bours. In Naayili, *Wuura's* lineage recently changed their burial partners from another lineage of the same clan to a '*Yoɲyuole* patrilineage; this corresponded with a tendency for their compounds to move up the scarp into the Tanziiri minor ritual area which is inhabited mainly by members of the '*Yoɲyuole* clan. The *Tʃaale* homesteads linked together for burial are a little different from those which form farming groups. In Bataani, descendants of *Napolo* bury descendants of *Zaagbwõ*; in Gbɛtʃaansaal and part of the adjoining area of Tuperi, the compounds numbered 1 and 2 in Fig. 7 bury 3, 2 and 3 bury 1, and 3 and 1 bury 2. In the southern area, *Ɗmanbil Maale* bury 1 and 3.

In Tʃaa, when a sacrifice has to be made to the ancestors over a serious matter, it is these same groups which can come to each other's assistance, except that non-clansmen are now excluded; in the southern area 1 and 3 therefore act reciprocally. Assistance is given, for example, when a dead father quarrels with his son (*sãã bɔɔre*); "we call them to come and greet the ancestors when they are angry". In other clans this preliminary offering or reparation gift (*bun puru*, a greeting thing) is killed by a sister's son, but in Tʃaa this is not usually the case. These same groups kill the cow of the hoe-handle at each other's funerals, and are entitled to the whole carcase. If any other clansman not taking part in these reciprocal services were present, he would no doubt be given meat by members of his lineage but this would remain a gift; he would have no right to a share of the cow. It is the representatives of the whole patrilineage, not of these local sub-groupings, who in Tʃaa play the important rôles in the central rituals of the funeral ceremonies. The day following the burial of any member of Group 1, an elder of Groups 2 or 3 performs the rites which introduce the children to their new status as orphans (*kpielo*, orphanhood); at the final funeral ceremony members of the same groups cut the ancestor shrine on behalf of the senior son, withdraw the arrows from the quiver and show the children their matriclan "fathers". These complementary funeral groups are normally patrilineages. The five smaller *Naayili* lineages form two complementary funeral groups which assist each other in these performances. In this case the same groups consume each other's funeral meat; there is no further sub-division as in Tʃaa.

The fission of the *Tʃaale* patrilineages into sub-groups for certain ritual functions can be easily understood as the same process is elsewhere constantly at work. The division into sub-groups occurs in relation to the sharing of meat. The distribution of a sacrifice, particularly at funerals where a large number of people are concerned, leads to lengthy arguments often of a considerable bitterness. An animal may be divided stealthily so that only near neighbours are aware of what is happening; a cow may be killed at one burial and only a sheep at the death of the next member of the complementary funeral group. In both cases a feeling that reciprocity has not been maintained may lead to the fission of the groups which formerly gave each other the meat they were not permitted to eat themselves. In Tʃaa, fission within the patrilineage occurred on the basis of contiguity of habitation. The patrilineages retained their complementary rôles in the important funeral ceremonies but local sub-divisions controlled the distribution of the flesh deemed unclean for the nearest kin. I have heard threats in Naayili that a similar split was about to occur. At the funeral of the late chief, the complementary funeral group consisting of the *Marba* and *Sontʃe* lineages had a whole cow to themselves. When an important man in Marba died a year later, the chief's immediate kin claimed a whole cow in return. Nonetheless only one cow was killed. The chief's lineage refused what was offered and returned home saying that they would in future allow only *Sontʃe* to take their meat. In Naayili another patrilineage can serve as an alternative to the existing arrangement. But in Tʃaa the compounds of the patrilineages are not concentrated together in one area and the lines of fission were strongly influenced by the factor of contiguity.

The interplay between descent and contiguity determines the structure of these action groups. In the graver sacrifices to the ancestors and in the burial of the dead, there are some tasks which cannot be undertaken by the lineage members themselves. In the second case, contiguity plays a greater part in the structuring of such pairs of groups, which may include "sister's sons" as well as agnates. With regard to ritual assistance, it is the lineage which divides along lines of locality. The distinction must be made between groups organized solely on the basis of contiguity and those principally structured on descent but modified by ties of locality.

Armed conflict

Armed conflicts are designated by the word *zioro*, etymologically connected with the verb 'to fight'. When the ancestors display anger towards their descendants, they are also described as fighting (*kpime ziora*).

The three main causes of armed conflict are said to be women (*pobo*), the theft of pots left in the bush for white ants (*kpo laar*) and the stealing of livestock (*dun zuune*).[1]

Such conflicts occasionally arise between clan sectors living in the same parish. The account of a fight between two sectors in Birifu is typical of such incidents. *Dʒipla* of *Kontʃol's* lineage, Tʃaa, and a man from Baaperi were lovers of a woman married at Ŋmanbili. The woman died in childbirth and in the funeral divinations both these men were implicated. Some inhabitants of Baaperi came to Tʃaa and shot a number of arrows without causing any bloodshed. Tʃaa retaliated by climbing on to the roof of a Baaperi house at night and killing one of the occupants who was sleeping there. At a later date, Baaperi returned and killed one of *Dʒipla's* sons. As both the parties inhabited the same major ritual area, expiatory sacrifices had subsequently to be performed at the Earth shrine. No other descent groups within the settlement took part in the fighting.

Debts outside the clan were also settled by self-help. The main alienation of wealth in this society is the bridewealth given by the groom's to the bride's kin during the course of the marriage. The sanction against non-payment is the recall of the woman; and, in the case of the first instalment, the clan affiliation of the offspring is also at stake. There was therefore no need to resort to armed force in order to settle bridewealth debts. Fighting was more likely to break out because of abduction, where other types of debt (*san*) were involved; payments for marital rights, and for their abrogation, could be enforced by other means. However, for the abduction of a wife there was no compensation, other than the eventual return of the bridewealth through the medium of the women's patrikinsmen. In this case, the resort to self-help, immediately or at some future date, was not uncommon. Between clan sectors, the debts which led to violence centred mainly around women. Between more distant groups they were created by the seizure of domestic animals or, less frequently, of other objects kept outside the homestead such as the pots placed in the bush for white ants to build in. Just as killing outside the clan was differentiated from the murder of a clansman, so seizure by force (*faano*) is morally quite distinct from theft (*zuune*). Seizure

---

[1]White ants build inside these pots and are then fed to young chickens during their first few weeks.

led to retaliatory action of the same kind, which might result in armed conflict. Armed conflict was indeed merely the most extreme form of retaliatory procedure, itself the counterpart of reciprocal exchanges of goods and services. It could arise indirectly in the course of the settlement of debts created in the above ways, or directly as the result of a homicide. For such debts can finally be settled only by equivalent retaliatory measures.

Although both are known by one name (*zioro*), there is a differentiation, albeit one of degree, between the type of conflict limited to descent groups and the more extended fighting where the war xylophone is played and whistles blown, the sort of struggle in which Birifu engaged with the *Lo* and the *Dagaa*. On these latter occasions, the ritual area generally co-operated as a whole. In this context I speak of war as distinct from feud; the difference as everywhere is one of degree, feud here being an armed conflict between descent groups and war one between territorial groups. Feud is a form of retaliatory action in which the return is equivalent in kind but not in degree. It merges on the one hand into the less restricted forms of the regulated combat such as war and on the other into the more limited types of regulated vengeance, namely the vendetta or vengeance killing. The incidence of these forms of violence depends upon the structural distance between the individuals and groups involved. A conflict between Tʃaa and their Nadoli neighbours serves as an example of the vendetta. A Nadoli man was killed by a *Tʃaale* as the result of a quarrel over a woman; Nadoli were about to come and fight Tʃaa when the latter sent a message that it would be better if they waited until finding a Tʃaa man about to drink beer with one of their wives at a Bɔɔre ceremony; they could then shoot him and the affair would be closed.

On the other hand, between Birifu and the "Lobi" (Birifor) of Malba (*Ŋmul*) and the *Dagaa* (DagaaWiili) of Tugu there formerly existed a perpetual state of enmity which still lingers in the thoughts of old men. In such struggles the inhabitants of Zinkãã and Nadoli to the west, of Kwõnyũkwõ and Tanchera to the north, and of Biro to the south, tended to assist the inhabitants of Birifu in war and expected aid in return. They "all have one bowstring" (*be zaa tɛra tammyuur boyen*), the inhabitants explain, meaning that in certain circumstances they all fight together. The range of these war alliances does not altogether coincide with the area claimed once to have belonged to one Earth shrine; the inhabitants of Guoziel are culturally DagaaWiili who have no such alliance with Birifu although they live in the same *teŋgaan*. Nor is it co-extensive with areas of cultural homogeneity. The people of Nadoli now largely follow Birifor ways but usually align themselves with the LoWiili. Most of the inhabitants of Kwõnyũkwõ and all those of Tanchera inherit wealth matrilineally; to the LoWiili they are *LoPiel* or white Lo. These two factors, ritual allegiance in the Earth cult and cultural homogeneity, interact to produce a vaguely defined alliance which is none the less the widest territorial grouping within which obligations between all the constituent groups are recognized.

By these alliances Birifu is sealed off from hostile neighbours, with the one exception of the DagaaWiili; even in this case, intermarriage between members of the neighbouring lineages creates a situation which, while they recognize no mutual obligations to assist each other in war, lessens the chance of conflict between them. It is said that Baaperi, whose compounds lie closer to the Dagaa-Wiili than those of any other clan sector in Birifu, at times aided the *Dagaa* of Tugu in war because of affinal ties. The LoWiili do not explain such assistance in this way, for the relationships between in-laws are not characterized by friendliness; it is in terms of the bond between the mother's brother and the sister's child that this co-operation is visualized.

The influence of cognatic ties indicates that these alliances are not permanent. With the people of Babile, whose social institutions represent an intermediate step between those of Birifu and those of Tugu, the LoWiili disclaim any alliance whatsoever. Formerly they claim to have fought together but more recently Babile helped the DagaaWiili; *be kpena Dagaa*, they joined the *Dagaa*. The inhabitants of Babile explain this quite simply, saying "our sisters' sons are in both places". These alliances were probably always much less stable than current accounts suggest for, as the occasion for them has disappeared, local concepts have crystalized around the arrangements which existed at the arrival of the Europeans.

Similar difficulties have been encountered in trying to estimate the actual assistance rendered by descent groups outside the parish. It is doubtful if the accepted obligations of the patriclan were effective beyond the range of the war xylophone; no case to the contrary has come to my notice. Only nearby clan sectors actually came to one another's aid. Matriclans did not aid each other in armed conflicts. It was recognised that the killing of a fellow matriclansman in battle was unfortunate but unavoidable. Even in the areas where matriclans are wealth-holding groups, segments never emerged in the context of fighting; "the arrow does not enter the matriclan" (*pũ be puoi beloe*). The only exception was fights over inheritance (*bel pũ*) and even these subsequently developed into fights between sectors of patriclans and the parishes themselves. The vengeance groups tended to emerge on the basis of the localized patrilineal groups rather than the non-localized matrilineal ones, for the uterine alignment would destroy the solidarity of the central structural units of the society and thus make armed violence impossible, even on a small scale.

Violence was most likely to break out where peoples who normally had no social contact, who were beyond the usual range of affinal ties, assembled together. Markets still form the main meeting place for people of different parishes. The special jurisdiction of the custodian of the Earth shrine over the market place tends to inhibit the outbreak of violence. This market peace has the same function as festival peace, the prohibition on bloodshed established in many societies for the duration of the main periodic ceremonials.

At the same time, these gatherings provided special opportunities for other types of friendly social intercourse besides trade. *Tontol* of Birifu once seized a woman going from Diébougou to her father's house in Tugu. It was arranged by an intermediary that he should meet her brother in Babile market. As the result of this meeting he agreed to send a cow to the woman's kinsfolk. Had *Tontol* gone to Tugu to discuss the matter he would certainly have been shot. This rôle of the market as an interparish meeting place is particularly emphasized at the time when the guinea-corn flowers and the *Kobine* (hoeing dance) is performed there. Among the LoSaala, the Birifor and the LoWiili, teams of dancers from neighbouring parishes come on market day to celebrate the end of hoeing in friendly competition.

Other mechanisms existed for the establishment of peace beside the meeting on sanctified ground. Ritual specialists could also be appealed to. The conciliatory rôles of the custodian of the Earth shrine and the smith in conflicts within the ritual area, and of joking partners in war have already been indicated. Uxori-lateral ties were also important in this respect, the best mediator being an extra-clan kinsman of both disputants. Uxorilateral ties, the ritual sanctions of the

Earth cult and the varied mechanisms for re-establishing peaceful relationships militated against long and extensive fighting. Although arms were frequently employed on a small scale, memories of war centre around the activities of slave raiders and of the European powers.

Chapter 6

The Social System : A Recapitulation

In this final chapter, the social organization of the LoWiili will be recapitulated so that certain problems which have arisen during the course of the analysis may be reconsidered in the light of the system as a whole.

The scattered compounds normally house joint families organized around close agnatic kinsmen. Several of these adjacent homesteads comprise an "extended family" whose male members trace descent by genealogical steps to a founding ancestor two to four generations removed from the oldest living member. When this forefather arrived in Birifu from the previous settlement, he is said to have laid claim to the cultivated land which forms the main farming area of the lineage. I emphasized the point that even among the peoples of this area who inherit movable property matrilineally, farmland and compounds are transmitted in the agnatic line. Certain rights over farmland are vested in patrilineages as a whole; sacrifices connected with farming troubles are made at the shrine of the founding ancestor and the members of the group have obligations to assist each other when food is short. The meat of wild animals killed by members is prepared jointly. The patrilineage is therefore differentiated from similar groups in the production and consumption of food, as well as in the worship of common ancestors. The lineage then is basically a local group; its daughters disperse through marriage but the men are bound together by their interest in a common patrimony, the land inherited from their founding ancestor. Dispersion causes these ties to lapse. The descendants of a lineage member who migrates from his natal settlement will cease to trace genealogical relationships after two generations. As among many agricultural societies of West Africa, the recollection of genealogies, which form the framework of the lineage, is associated with the inheritance and exploitation of farmland; migration leads to the replacement of lineage ties by the more generalized bond of clanship.

Historical reasons were put forward for the upper limit of four generations in reckoning genealogies. The evidence suggests that the previous inhabitants of the region were pushed north-westwards during the latter half of the eighteenth century. It has been maintained by previous writers[1] that this was connected with the north-westerly movement of the Mossi-speaking peoples from Dagomba which established them in Wa. This receives some confirmation from the fact that the inhabitants of the Lawra district claim to have migrated from the Wa area. It is worth while recalling, however, that other societies with a double system of unilineal descent groups, such as the Yakö, the Tullishi and the Nyaro, do not reckon genealogical connections beyond this limit. Forde in his paper on "Fission and Accretion in the Patrilineal Clans of a Semi-Bantu Community in Southern Nigeria"[2] analyses fissive tendencies in a Yakö lineage and concludes: "The disposition towards fission is associated with, and is likely to be in part a consequence of the abnormal size of this group. In conditions of increasing

---

[1]Eyre-Smith, 1933 and Labouret, 1931.
[2]1938.

population the lineages are likely to exist as stable and integrated groups for only four or five generations. The lineage is thus a small group of kinsmen with their adopted adherents, the internal coherence of which lasts only so long as the group remains small and intimate" (p.325). The Yakö lineages are segments of a localized patriclan. Their functions include the "provision of food at funeral rites", "inheritance of membership of secret societies", "mutual aid in farmwork and patrilineal rights and obligations of inheritance". In view of the depth to which other West African societies such as the Tallensi trace genealogical descent, the question arises as to why fission of the patrilineage should occur at this point. What particular function of the lineage requires a "small and intimate" group with an average "effective" strength of twenty adult males and a genealogical depth of "three to five generations?"

The patrilineage of the LoWiili, like the nuclear lineage of the Tallensi, has "common interest in, and joint rights of inheritance to particular patrimonial farmlands".[1] The genealogical depth is not as great. Fortes states that the founding ancestor of the nuclear lineage, which forms the basis of the expanded family, may be placed from four to six generations back. The functions however are similar. The LoWiili patrilineage has common rights over land derived from its founding ancestor and in addition recognises joint obligations in the distribution of food. In each case this basic lineage serves as an inheritance group defining the range of likely heirs and as the group which organizes the distribution of food among its members on certain ritual occasions. The fission of these lineages tends to occur in the context of the latter function rather than the former. For with regard to inheritance the members of the group, other than the primary heir, tend merely to have reversionary rights, whereas in the distribution of food each has an equivalent right on every occasion and the question of numbers therefore becomes of crucial importance.

This is certainly the case among the LoWiili, among whom the fission of descent groups centres basically upon the exchange of rights over women, and over food. The breakdown of clan exogamy leads to formation of two linked clans. The failure to observe reciprocity in the distribution of food leads to the establishment of distinct lineages. It is the sharing of animal sacrifices in particular which requires a "small and intimate" group and leads to fission under the pressure of an increasing population. A large lineage tends to split into two groups for this purpose and results in the emergence of a pair of lineages of two to three generations depth which no longer traces agnatic kinship through specific, named ancestors.

The nuclear lineage of the Tallensi is of course one of a series of more inclusive lineages, whereas the corresponding lineage among the LoWiili and the Yakö represents the limit of genealogical reckoning and is associated with similar units only by the concept of clanship, by non-specific bonds of agnatic descent. Among the LoWiili, it is possible that historical factors may have placed limitations on the length of settlement and therefore on the development of genealogies. On structural grounds, however, it seems doubtful whether prolonged settlement would increase the depth to which genealogical ties are recognized in the organization of descent groups. This conclusion is strengthened by a comparison with similar societies. A system of double clanship greatly extends an individual's membership of kin groups and his possible kinship ties. For a LoWiili, the range of these systems is immense; everyone he meets can be placed in some kinship category. The greater specificity of genealogical relations is not required by the political system; spatial separation dissolves the genealogical

[1] Fortes, 1949, p.9.

ties and substitutes the generalized bond of clanship. There is then a possibility of a continuous telescoping of the genealogy to a depth of three to four generations. Instances were found of elders being unable to name the owners of certain of the most ancient compound sites and ancestor shrines of their own lineage. This provides no definite evidence of the elimination of steps in the direct line of genealogical descent as both shrines and compounds may have belonged to collateral branches whose members are all dead. But it seems more probably an indication of telescoping.

Neighbouring patrilineages co-operate together as a clan sector in important funeral performances. In Birifu the sector as a whole participates in Bɔɔre initiation ceremonies and in sacrifices at the main Earth shrine. Widely separated clan sectors are bound together by membership of one patriclan, which involves exogamy and assistance in war. The patriclan, the widest agnatic descent group, consists of a chain of groups separated by allegiance to different Earth shrines, and displaying considerable cultural and even linguistic diversity.

The LoWiili are atypical of the peoples in this region in recognizing both agnatic and uterine lines in the formation of descent groups and yet transmitting all property patrilineally. The evidence from this and other areas suggests that double clanship is essentially associated with the transmission of property along both descent lines. The neighbouring LoDagaba, like the peoples analysed by Daryll Forde and S. F. Nadel, inherit land, compounds, shrines, hoes and growing crops patrilineally, and wives, domestic animals, money and harvested crops matrilineally. The basic productive requirements of an agricultural society remain within the agnatic line; the wealth, the surplus of production over consumption, essential in bridewealth transactions, is distributed among the uterine kin. Rights over property required in the production of food remain in the patriline, rights over the property required in the reproduction of children remain in the matriline.[1] The LoWiili recognize the matriclan but its functions are severely limited in comparison. Like their easterly neighbours, the DagaaWiili, they inherit wealth patrilineally. The inhabitants of Birifu claim to have migrated from what is now a DagaaWiili village. It seems likely that, coming into contact with the LoDagaba and the Birifor, they adopted the matriclans and had made a move towards the matrilineal inheritance of wealth by the time of the British arrival. As the process can be observed in similar situations today, it is possible to indicate how this could have happened.

The peoples of this region show little aversion to marrying a woman from a different cultural group, providing the bridewealth is no heavier and the services to her kinsmen no more onerous than in their own community. The inhabitants tend to choose the nearest available brides not excluded by ties of uterine and agnatic descent, and cultural diversity has little inhibiting effect on their selection. The son of a man who has married a woman from a group inheriting wealth matrilineally will be taught the rights and obligations of matriclan membership by his mother; on the death of her brother, he may have a claim on the movable property. Whether or not the child actually aquires this wealth depends upon a complex of factors which determine the relative strengths of uterine and agnatic groups in the society at a particular time. But it would seem to be the case in such a situation that increased emphasis on the matriline is generally due to the

---

[1]Bridewealth payments are a restricting factor in marriage; a young man whose father is poor will have difficulty when he wishes to take a second wife. Leguminous crops are often sold and the money used in marriage transactions. In this district there are rarely any surplus cereal crops left for this purpose; they provide the basis of the diet and constantly enter into ceremonial exchange.

agency of a member who, brought up by his mother's kinsmen to accept the matrilineal inheritance of wealth, later returns to his natal settlement. A man would often reside for a time with his mother's kinsfolk if he had quarrelled with his own or if one of his parents had died. Clearly both these situations would tend to highlight the benefits of this system of transmission. The ramifications of matriclanship spread then through inter-marriage; in this situation of culture contact the recognition of matriclans precedes succession to the wealth of a uterine kinsman and predisposes the society to accept such an institution.

While it is true that within these interstitial communities situations arise in which an individual may elect to inherit wealth matrilineally rather than patrilineally, it is also true that there are pressures operating in the contrary direction. The junior generation tends to favour complete patrilineal inheritance. The conflicting factors at work can best be seen by examining two cases from the neighbouring LoDagaba among whom the matrilineal inheritance of wealth prevails. In Kumansaal, part of the settlement of Kwŏnyŭkwŏ, the *Kpiele* and *Puriyele*, whose ancestors had moved from Tanchera, adopted the patrilineal scheme when they came into contact with the inhabitants of Babile and Birifu. On the other hand the forefathers of the *Kusiele* lineage a few hundred yards to the north had moved from Babile and changed from the LoWiili pattern to the inheritance of wealth along the uterine line. The members of these lineages recognize these changes quite openly. *Baaluon*, a *Kusiele* elder of Kwŏnyŭkwŏ, admitted that his "grandfather" had "eaten and spoilt" (*ti saakum di soŋ, boŋzu ti dina gbandiru*) that is, taken his mother's brother's possessions contrary to former practice. But he argued that a further change would again anger the ancestors. He repeated the story of a *Kusiele* lad in Babile, a member of his own lineage who although those remaining in Babile inherit patrilineally, collected seven of his mother's brother's cows after his funeral; this branch of the lineage died out completely as a consequence, destroyed by the dead ancestors. *Baaluon's* sons were openly hostile to his wealth leaving the compound, for he was a comparatively rich man. But their father refused to give them his support for fear of the ancestors. Despite the pressure from below the matrilineal system remained, reinforced as it was by ritual sanctions. Economic as well as ritual factors tend to inhibit change. The conflict was particularly intense in the case of my cook who came from Nandom, in the LoDagaba area. He regarded the matrilineal inheritance of wealth with great distaste for he had worked with "patrilineal" Europeans for a long period and had also had the experience of his father's movable property being taken by a member of another patriclan. Nevertheless, he violently opposed any suggestion of change as he would thereby lose his own mother's brother's possessions. The matrilineal system of transmitting wealth tends therefore to be economically self-perpetuating, quite apart from the ritual sanctions against change. But among the LoWiili there has developed a definite resistance to the dual system of inheritance. Reports indicate that in the past it was practised at least by some members of the community who had uxorilateral kin among the LoDagaba. Now it is practised by none. And among the LoDagaba the system is often criticised, though it continues to operate for the reasons mentioned above. Why this move away from the matrilineal system?

The same general trend away from matrilineal inheritance has been noted by Forde among the Yakö[1]; Fortes detects a similar shift in emphasis among the Ashanti.[2] It is often assumed that this tendency is the result of a direct adoption

[1]Forde and Radcliffe-Brown, 1950, p.309.
[2]ibid, p.271.

of European institutions. While it is true that the institutions of the dominant group are invested with a degree of prestige, particularly among the educated members of the community, this explanation fails to do justice to the complexities of the situation. The increased significance of the elementary family as a domestic and economic unit, and therefore as an inheritance group is to a considerable degree a result of the introduction of wage labour. The larger kingroups have consequently a less crucial rôle to play in the productive tasks of the community and this has led to an overall diminution in their importance. The emphasis on the family leads to a preference for direct (that is, patrilineal between males) rather than indirect (that is, matrilineal between males) transmission of rights and duties.

These factors may be held to account for the changes taking place in the matrilineal and dual descent peoples of the coastal areas of West Africa where there has been much contact with Europeans and where wage labour is an established institution. But the Northern Territories of the Gold Coast have certainly not reached this point. The less radical changes which have taken place there require a different explanation..

Both in dual descent societies and in matrilineal systems where the elementary family constitutes a dwelling group, a situation of possible conflict is bound to exist by virtue of the fact that wealth passes outside the elementary family and outside the co-residential group. This does not mean that such societies are "unstable". There are some conflict situations which such systems resolve to a much greater extent than others. On the other hand in this type of community there always tend to be institutionalized, or partly institutionalized, methods of retaining at least a portion of the wealth within the compound, arrangements whereby it passes between father and son. The passage of wealth between the discrete, local patriclan sectors solves certain conflicts and creates others. Of its positive functions the most important are in giving a material correlative to uxorilateral and uterine kinship ties and in reducing tension in the father—son relationship. It works satisfactorily, however, only in an economically egalitarian society where exclusive rights are not concentrated in the hands of a small number of individuals. In such conditions the system operates in a reasonably reciprocal manner. If ego's mother's brother is as well-off as his father, it does not matter much from the point of view of profit or loss how he inherits. But with a greater degree of economic differentiation, it does. Among the LoDagaba opposition to wealth leaving the compound comes principally from those who possess, or are about to possess, a greater than the average share of the resources of the community. There has undoubtedly been a considerable increase in such economic differentiation in recent years. This has not been primarily the result of the development of wage-labour, for here the economic rewards have been spread fairly evenly over the community. It is rather the consequence of introductions of certain changes in the political system. Both Rattray and Eyre-Smith called attention to the exaction of "a not inconsiderable amount of tribute" by European-appointed chiefs.[1] The much greater differentiation of wealth created by the new dispensation, and its increased importance in the lives of educated clerks for whom the land no longer remains the basic means of gaining a livelihood, militate against such an egalitarian institution and in favour of the direct system which maintains concentrations of property within the living-together family group.

---

[1] Eyre-Smith, 1933, p.40.

One point of historical and ethnological interest arises out of this discussion of dual descent. In the preface to his account of the Northern Territories, Rattray writes:[1] "The tribes speaking Vagale and Tampolem (like the Lobi) appear to be among the last survivors in this northern area of those tribes which still trace inheritance through the sister's son—like the Akan. Evidence, indeed, is not lacking that in the not very remote past—and contrary to all our pre-conceived ideas on this subject—the whole of the Northern Territories was inhabited by peoples inheriting through the female line, the change-over to a patrilineal way of reckoning among other of the tribes being due to the invasion of those outsiders who, in so many localities, today form the ruling class". These immigrant rulers are later described as "in some cases conversant with the rudiments of Mohammedanism and accustomed . . . to a patrilineal manner of reckoning descent" (p.xii). Baumann[2] asserts that the Dagaris, that is, the LoDagaba, whom he wrongly equates with the Dagaba of Rattray, "ont été soumis en partie à l'influence des Mossi et en partie à celle des Akans matri-linéaires" and that among the Lobi "le droit matrilinéaire s'est substitué à l'organisation patriarcale des peuples voltaïques paléonigritiques". These diametrically opposed assumptions about the method of reckoning descent in "palaeonegritic" societies point to the danger of such speculations. Rattray's "Lobi" (i.e. LoDagaba) certainly provide no basis for any such general deduction. As an interstitial group their insistence upon the matriline might well have been due to their settling in the vicinity of other peoples. In the north-west, two systems of inheriting wealth exist side by side; no evidence can be gathered there as to whether one generally preceded the other throughout the whole culture area. Rattray failed to appreciate double clanship except as a stage of transition between systems of kin groups based on a single line of descent. The studies of Forde and Nadel make it necessary to reconsider the whole problem of dual descent as a stable system of social organisation; for this is more common in Africa than has been supposed.

The inhabitants of a ritual area have been described as a political group. Within its confines homicide necessitates the performance of expiatory sacrifices by representatives of the whole community. Outside its boundaries, armed self-help constitutes the main procedure for the settlement of disputes between clans. Local groups which now owe allegiance to different shrines may recognize a diffuse extension of this obligation by virtue of a tradition that the areas were formerly one, but this has little force as a sanction against killing.

The dispersed patriclan also forms a field of social control. The killing of a fellow clansman is a sin which automatically excludes the murderer from participating in the ancestor cult. But whereas the chain of patriclanship links together local clan sectors in different ritual areas, the recognition of obligations within a matriclan forms a thread between individuals rather than between groups and its extra-parish functions are therefore more limited in scope. The basic sanctions behind the cohesion of strictly localized groups more inclusive than the clan sector derive from common allegiance to an Earth shrine, though the ties of patriclanship and uxorilateral relationships are also major factors in limiting the outbreak of armed conflict.

One of the most remarkable features of the political structure, in establishing a community which recognizes certain rights and duties between members and

---

[1] 1932, p.ix.
[2] Baumann and Westermann, 1948, p.405.

provides an alternative to armed conflict in the settlement of disputes, is the extensive development of the joking partnership and the cathartic alliance. The maximum range of these institutions, normally but not necessarily coincidental, is very wide. All "Dagarti" (i.e. Western Mossi-speakers) and all "Farafara" (i.e. Eastern Mossi-speakers) are said to be joking partners. By Farafara the LoWiili apparently mean not only the Nankane[1] but all the other Mossi-speaking peoples in the north of the Protectorate. As the "Dagarti" and "Farafara" are separated by the belt of Grusi-speaking peoples, perhaps one hundred miles in width, the partnership probably arose outside the present "tribal" areas. Both regions are characterized by heavy population density and, probably as a consequence, by a comparatively high percentage of labour migration and it seems possible that the joking partnership arose in the South. It established a relationship neither of complete friendliness nor yet of open hostility between peoples who recognized the affinities of their speech and culture in contrast to the Ashanti among whom they were working. A Farafara man from Bolgatanga once remarked to me: "If I told these people to stop (i.e. quarrelling) they would do so. If I see a Dagarti man in the market with something I want, I will take it. Once it is in my hand he can do nothing, although if he begs I may return it to him". These institutions working at the more inclusive levels of social organization integrate groups between whom no ties of descent exist. Joking partnerships in fact tend to operate where the recognition of unilineal descent ends and before armed conflict begins. However these partnerships are also characterized by the exchange of reciprocal ritual services and therefore partake of the nature of cartharitic alliances. But the exchange of these ritual services may also take place within clans whereas joking partnerships operate only between them. In relation to the Tallensi, these institutions would seem to take the place of "quasi-clanship" and of the greater depth of the patrilineages in promoting integrative ties both within the parish and beyond its confines. Ties of clanship and interclan partnerships are important in creating wider ties than those which exist among the congregation of a ritual area, for by such means the localized descent groups within the parishes are linked with similar groups in other settlements.

In the opening chapter a preliminary attempt was made to define areas of relative cultural homogeneity which had some corresponding unity in the concepts of the inhabitants themselves. The difficulties encountered can now be seen to result from the diffuse political system. The lack of any integration of territorial units outside the ritual area, apart from the loosely articulated war alliance, is paralleled by the absence of any delegated authority outside the lineage, except for the rights and obligations vested in the custodian of the Earth shrine and in the informally constituted body of elders who assist him. Within the lineage, "fathers" are responsible for "sons" and the senior member (nikpɛ̃, important man) who addresses the shrines in all sacrifices to the founding ancestor (saakum bɔɔre) has a similar but less precise responsibility for the whole patrilineage. A man must consult a person of the senior generation before embarking upon marriage payments or acts of similar importance. Any money gained through farming has to be shown to the "father" or nearest lineage member of superior generation; the "father" will take a little—he is entitled to as much as he wishes—and leave the remainder for his "son". The patrilineage, holding generalized rights over land inherited from the founding ancestor,

---

[1]Also known as the Gurense; this Mossi-speaking people should not be confused with Grusi, a term I have employed for the Kasen-Isal group of languages; see Rattray, 1932, p.232 and Fortes, 1945, p.15.

is an economic unit in the process of food production. As in the vast majority of West African agricultural communities the lineage emerges as a localized, land-owning group. Dispersed descent groups are linked not by specific genealogical ties but by clanship. Authority, then, is delegated to the senior living member of the local patrilineage, seniority being defined by age within generation categories. In a less definite form, the senior or most competent head of the constituent patrilineage may dominate certain decisions made by the clan sector as a whole. These situations would be concerned mainly with sacrifices to the Earth shrine. In view of the lack of formality, the absence of jural definition, this decision taking should be spoken of as influence rather than as authority. Above the level of descent groups, there is the custodian of the Earth shrine who performs important functions on behalf of the community as a whole and acts as an intermediary between the occupants of the land and the Earth shrine to which they owe allegiance. The degree to which he actively intervened appears to have depended to some extent upon the individual himself. I was once told by an elder that if a quarrel had arisen between two sectors within the same ritual area and these had later assisted each other in war, the custodian might speak to them in the following manner: "Now you all fight together. Why at other times do you fight among yourselves?" There could be no clearer statement of what is often spoken of as the "segmentary process", whereby opposing groups co-operate together in the face of a general threat.

Apart from the ritual offices connected with the Earth shrine and with the Bɔɔre society, and apart from the positions of authority within the lineage, there was in the past little differentiation in status among the adult members of the community. Authority was rarely delegated to one man even for limited social purposes. Even in war there was a relative absence of formal leadership, a fact which is highly indicative of the nature of warfare among the LoWiili. Any individual who had been successful in previous fights and was known as the *tammyuursob*, or owner of the bowstring, might take the lead in battle by virtue of his skill and achievements with the bow. In the communal hunt, it was a *wiosob*, a possessor of a powerful hunting shrine, who made the ritual and other arrangements for its success. Again, the title of *kukuur na*, or hoe-handle chief, was accorded to a man whose own energies and those of his male offspring had given him wealth and through this, an influence in the settlement of his neighbours' disputes. The number of his sons and possible presence in his compound of an "owner of the bowstring" provided his decisions with a certain sanction of force. The lack of jural backing again characterizes this as influence rather than authority. This evident lack of delegated or imposed authority is counter-balanced by the numerous mechanisms by which normal relations between any two groups in conflict were restored by the intervention of a third party. In addition to the joking partners the rôle of peacemaker could be assumed by certain ritual functionaries such as the custodian of the Earth shrine and the smith, as well as by certain categories of uxorilateral kin.

The diffuseness of the political organization gives rise to the lack of distinct tribal nomenclature. Such designations as exist, however, arise not primarily from a consciousness of unity, which would surely lead to a recognized name within the tribe itself, but from a consciousness of the differences between their own institutions and those of neighbouring peoples. I have described this process as definition by opposition. The LoWiili themselves illustrate this in a particularly vivid manner. The name was given to a small group who inherit property patrilineally and yet possess a system of double clanship. By the neighbouring peoples they may be called *Dagaa* or *Lo* according to the cultural position of the speaker; explanations are usually couched in terms of a greater or lesser emphasis on matriclanship. Within the group itself, no accepted designation exists. It is true that outsiders sometimes include Biro and Zinkãã people in the term Birifuole but in Biro itself this could refer only to those owing direct allegiance to the Birifu Earth shrine. Biro and Birifu indicate their cultural identity by the phrase *ti in ni boyen*, "we are one people". Equally, Kumansaal people say, referring to the inheritance of wealth, "We have the same ways as the Birifuole". Even within the small group I have designated LoWiili, some diversity exists and consciousness of these differentia continually manifests itself. I refer here not specifically to diacritical features of clanship but to the continuous interlocking of culture change across the region, a melting of one area into another.

The interstitial position of the LoWiili, and their cultural eclecticism, are demonstrated by the confusing array of xylophones at their command, a mixture of White LoDagaba (*LoPiel*), DagaaWiili and Birifor "traits". The internal differentiation of the Birifuole is expressed in such remarks as "Biro cannot play the small *Lo* xylophone (*lo gil prumo*); they are only learning". Biro and Babile are in several respects closer to the DagaaWiili, whereas Zinkãã are more like the Birifor, and Kumansaal, the White LoDagaba (*LoPiel*). The institutions of each clan sector display slightly different emphases according to its position.

The LoWiili are as conscious of these cultural differences as of their uniformity. Any unity they possess arises from situations which emphasize the different institutions of neighbouring groups. Even this unity is indirectly visualized. In discussing the DagaaWiili they will associate themselves with the *Lo*; in talking of the Birifor they place themselves among the *Dagaa*. The people I have grouped under the name LoWiili, because of the presence of certain institutions, only recognize this relative homogeneity obliquely, by giving the two terms, *Lo* and *Dagaa*, a common set of referents.

Problems such as these led Labouret to speak of a "particularisme accusé" and Lowie to select "Les Tribus du Rameau Lobi" as the extreme African example of political anarchy. Detailed study modifies this view; it is not sufficient to equate a diffuse political system with anarchy. Despite the lack of constituted authority before the arrival of the Europeans, the society was so organised as to make possible the peaceful co-operation which agriculture demands.

A Bibliography of the LoWiilli

In view of the confusion concerning 'tribal' nomenclature, I have included references to the Lobi as well as the Dagari speaking peoples.

The numbers placed against 'tribal' names in the Bibliography refer to the classification of tribes used in this account, i.e.

1. LoWilisi (Fr. Lobi)
2. White LoDagaba (*LoPiel*; Fr. Dagari)
3. Black LoDagaba (*LoSaala*)
4. DagaaWiili (Fr. Dagari-Wilé or Oule)

5. Dagaba (Angl. Dagarti)
6. Dyan
7. Birifor
8. LoWiili

GENERAL

Census Reports for 1921, 1931, 1948 *and* 1960. Govt. Printer, Accra.

HINDS, J. H. (1947) *A currency problem in the Lawra district: picturesque money customs of the Lobi*[2,3] *and Dagarti*[5] *people of the Gold Coast*, W. Afr. Rev., 1428-32.

(1951) *Agricultural Survey of the Lawra-Wa District*, Monthly News Letter, 4, 5, 6 and 7, Dept. of Agriculture, Accra.

MORRIS, K. R. S. (1946) *The control of trypanosomiasis by entomological means*, Bull. Ent. Res., 37.

(1949) *Planning the control of sleeping sickness*, Trans. Roy. Soc. Trop. Med. and Hygiene, 43.

(1950) *Fighting a Fly*. Public Relations Dept., Accra.

RAEBURN, J. R. (1950) *Report on a Preliminary Economic Survey of the Northern Territories*, Colonial Office, London (mimeo).

THE LOWIILI AND NEIGHBOURS

ANON. (n.d.) *The Political Organization of the Ulu Division*,[5] unpublished MS.

ANON. (1931) *Interim Report on the Peoples of the Nandom*[2] *and Lambussie Divisions of the Lawra District*, unpublished MS.
(I have ascribed this to J. A. Armstrong but Pogucki gives the author as J. Guiness.)

ARMSTRONG, J. A. (1933) *Report on the Peoples of the Lambussie and Nandom*[2] *Divisions of the Lawra-Tumu District*, unpublished MS.

BARGY, M. (1909) *Notes ethnographique sur les Birifous*, Anthropologie, 20.

CAUSSE, J. J., BOUTILLIER, J. L. et autres. (1961) *Une enquête de ménage en pays lobi*[1] (*Haute-Volta*), 1956-1957. Paris: Institut national de la statistique et des études économiques.

CHARLES (1911) *Les Lobi*[1], Rev. Ethnog. et Soc., 2, 202-20.

DELAFOSSE, M. (1900) *Sur des traces probables de civilisation égyptienne et d'hommes de race blanche à la Côte d'Ivoire*, Anthropologie.

(1902) *Les ruines de lobi*[1], Anthropologie.

(1903) *La délimitation de la frontière entre la Côte d'Ivoire et le 2e territoire militaire et la Côte d'Or anglaise*, Afr. franc. 13.

(1908) *Les frontières de la Côte d'Ivoire, de la Côte d'Or et du Soudan*, Paris.

(1911-13) *A propos de constructions en pierres maconnées existant dans le Lobi* (*Bassin de la Volta Noire*). C.R. de l'Institut franc. d'Anthrop., Anthropologie.

(1912) *Haut-Sénégal-Niger*. Paris.

DUNCAN-JOHNSTONE, A. (1927) *Diary of an Overland Journey from Lorha to Dakar*, Gold Coast Rev., 3.

EYRE-SMITH, St. J. (1933) *Comments on the Interim Report on the Peoples of the Nandom and Lambussie Division of the Lawra District*, unpublished MS.

(1933) *A Brief Review of the History and Social Organisation of the Peoples of the Northern Territories of the Gold Coast*. Accra.

GIRAULT, L. (1958) *Concrétisation de l'expression de la douleur chez les Dagara-Wile*. Notes afr., IFAN, 77, 15-16.

(1959) *Essai sur la religion des Dagara*. Bull. IFAN, 21, 329-56.

(1960) *Processions rogatoires au pays dagara*. Notes afr., IFAN, 88, 119-20.

GOODY, J. R. (1954) *The Ethnology of the Northern Territories of the Gold Coast*,

West of the White Volta. Colonial Office, London (mimeo).

(1957) *Fields of Social Control among the LoDagaba*[2], J. R. Anthrop. Inst., 87, 75-104.

(1958) *The Fission of Domestic Groups among the LoDagaba*[2], in *The Developmental Cycle of Domestic Groups* (ed. Goody). Cambridge.

(1959) *The Mother's Brother and the Sister's Son in West Africa*[2,8], J. R. Anthrop. Inst., 89, 61-88.

(1959) *Death and Social Control among the LoDagaa*[2,8], Man., 204.

(1961) *The Classification of Double Descent Systems*[2,8], Current Anthropology, 3-25.

(1962) *Death, Property and the Ancestors*[2,8]. Stanford University Press.

(1962) *LoDagaa Rituals of Death*[2,8], New Society, 18-19.

GRIVOT, R. (1945) *Cognagui, Lobi*[1] *et Somba sont-ils de même origine?* Notes afr., IFAN, 22.

GUINESS, J. M. (1932) *Report on the Origins and Journeys of the People of Tumu*, unpublished MS.

HAUMANT, J. C. (1929) *Les Lobi*[1] *et leurs coutumes*. Paris.

HOLAS, B. (1948) *Le divorce chez les Dagari*[2] (*Haute Volta*), Notes afr., IFAN, 39, 1-2.

(1953) *Et les flèches entrent en jeu* (*schéma d'un combat coutumier en pays lobi*[2]), Notes afr., IFAN, 58, 16-20.

IBOS (1939) *La société Lobi*[1], Rev. Troupes col., 200, 249-67; 258, 54-64.

JULIEN, PAUL (1936) *Door Lobi-Land. Ervaringen tijdens een Expeditie voor bloedonderzoek langs de Zwarte Volta*. T.K. ned. aardrijsk Genoot., 53, 725-48.

LABOURET, H. (1916) *La guerre dans ses rapports avec les croyances religieuses chez les populations du cercle de Gaoua*, Annu. et Mém. Com. Et. hist. et sci. A.O.F., 1916, 298-304.

(1916) *La terre dans ses rapports avec les croyances religieuses chez les populations du cercle de Gaoua*, Annu. et Mém. Com. Et. hist. et sci. A.O.F., 1916, 305-16; 1917, p.496.

(1916) *Legende des premiers hommes* (*Lobi*)[1], Annu. et Mém. Com. Et. hist. et sci. A.O.F.

(1916) *Notes sur les Lobi*[1], Annu. et Mém. Com. Et. hist. et sci. A.O.F.

(1918) *La chasse et la pêche dans leurs rapports avec les croyances religieuses parmi les populations du Lobi*[1], Annu. et Mém. Com. Et. hist. et sci. A.O.F. (1917), 244-276.

(1920) *La mystère des ruines du Lobi*[1], Rev. Ethnog. et Trad. pop., 177-96.

(1920) *Mariage et polyandrie parmi les Dagari*[2] *et les Oulé*[4], Rev. Ethnog., et Trad. pop., 267-83.

(1921) *Mutilations labiales et dentaires parmi la population du Lobi*[1], Anthropologie.

(1922) *La divination en Afrique noire*, Anthropologie.

(1923) *Language tambouriné et sifflé*, Annu. et Mem. Com. Et. hist. et sci. A.O.F.

(1925) *L'Or du Lobi*[1], Afr. franc.

(1925) *La Côte d'Or anglaise et l'A.O.F.*, Geog., 43.

(1925) *Les Bandes de Samori dans la Haute Côte d'Ivoire, la Côte d'Or et le Pays lobi*, Afr. franc., supplement.

(1929) *La parenté à plaisanterie*, Africa, 3.

(1931) *Les tribus du Rameau Lobi* [1,2,6,7]. Paris.

(n.d.) *Monographie du Cercle de Goua*, unpublished MS.

(1958) *Nouvelles notes sur les tribus du rameau lobi: leurs migrations, leurs évolutions, leurs parlers et ceux de leurs voisins* [1,6,7]. Dakar: Mém. IFAN, 54.

LESOURD, J. (1939) *En Afrique occidentale française: Les Dagaris*[2]. Paris.

MANOUKIAN, M. (1951) *Tribes of the Northern Territories of the Gold Coast*. London.

PATERNOT, M. (1953) *Lumière sur la Volta, chez les Dagari*[2]. Paris: Association des Missionaires d'Afrique.

PIAZZINI, G. (1954) *Horizons noirs* (*Dogon et Lobi*[1]). Paris: Ed. de la Toison d'Or.

MARCELLIN, L. (1939) *Une cérémonie funèbre chez les Lobi*[1] *de la Volta Noire*, Sci. et Voyages, Paris.

MARIE LOUISE, H.H. Princess (1926) *Letters from the Gold Coast*. London.

NORTHCOTT, Lt.-Col. H. P. (1899) *Report on the Northern Territories of the Gold Coast:* Intelligence Division, War Office, London.

PALES, L. (1948) *Le Bilan de la Mission Anthropologie de l'A.O.F.* (Jan. 1946—August 1948). Dakar.

POGUCKI, R. J. H. (1950) *Report on Land Tenure in Native Customary Law of the Protectorate of the Northern Territories of the Gold Coast.* Lands Dept., Accra.

RATTRAY, R. S. (1929) *The Tribes of the Ashanti Hinterland.* J.Afr. Soc.

(1929-30) *Report on Anthropological Research in the Northern Territories of the Gold Coast,* unpublished MS.

(1932) *The Tribes of the Ashanti Hinterland* [3,5,7]. Oxford.

RUELLE, Dr. (1904) *Notes sur les populations noires du 2e Territoire militaire,* Anthropologie.

SAVONNET, G. (1962) *La colonisation du pays koulango (Haute Côte d'Ivoire) par les Lobi* [1] *de Haute-Volta.* Cah. d'outre-mer, 15, 25-46.

SHIELDS, C. H. St. B. (1926) *The Western Gonja (Bole) District of the Northern Territories of the Gold Coast,* J.R.Geog. Soc.

SIDIBÉ, MAMBY (1938) *La culte des morts chez les Oulé* [4] *de la subdivision de Diébougou,* Educ. afr., 27, 27-28.

(1939) *Famille, vie sociale et vie religieuse chez les Birifor et les Oulé* [4], 1923-5. Bull. IFAN, I, 697-742.

(1946), *Chez les Dian de Diébougou* Notes afr., IFAN, 13-14.

SMEDDLE, M. (n.d.) *The Lobi Tingani* [3], unpublished MS.

TAMAKLOE, E. F. (1931) *A Brief History of the Dagbamba People.* Accra.

TAUXIER, L. (1912) *Le Noir du Soudan* [2]. Paris.

(1921) *Le Noir de Bondoukou.* Paris.

(1924) *Nouvelles notes sur le Mossi et le Gourensi.* Paris.

(1928) *Un dernier chapitre de l'histoire de Bondoukou,* Rev. d'Ethnog. et Trad. pop.

TRAORE, D. (1949) *Ceremonies de purification chez les Lobi* [1] *(Haute Volta).* Notes afr. IFAN, 43, 82.

VERNEAU, Dr. (1950) *Notes sur quelques cranes du 2e Territoire militaire de l'Afrique occidental française,* Anthropologie.

WATHERSTON, Lt.-Col. A. E. G. (1908) *The Northern Territories of the Gold Coast,* J.Afr. Soc., 7.

WINKOUN, HIENN D. (1956) *La légende du Strophantus hispidus en pays Wilé* [4] *du cercle de Diébougou.* Notes afr., IFAN., 72, 102-6.

WITHERS-GILL, J. (transl.) (1924) *The Moshi Tribe.* Accra.

LANGUAGE

BAUMANN, H. and WESTERMANN, D. (1948) *Les Peuples et les Civilisations de l'Afrique.* Paris.

CLARKE, J. (1848) *Specimens of Dialects: Short Vocabularies of Languages and Notes of Countries and Customs in Africa.* Berwick.

DELAFOSSE, M. (1904) *Vocabulaires comparatifs de plus de 60 langues ou dialectes parlés à la Côte d'Ivoire et dans les régions limitrophes.* Paris.

(1911) *Les Langues Voltaïques.* Mém. Soc. ling. de Paris, 16.

(1924) Chapter in *Les Langues du Monde* (Meillet, A. and Cohen, M. eds.), Paris.

GIRAULT, L. (n.d.) *Notes sur la Langue Dagara,* Documents Linguistiques, I, Université de Dakar, 11.

(1963) *Le verb en dagara et les familles de verbes dérivés,* Actes 2e Colloque int. Ling. négro-afr., Dakar, 173-81.

(1964) *Note sur la particule post-verbale na en dagara,* Buii. IFAN., 26 (B), 499-504.

GREENBERG, J. H. (1949) *Studies in African Linguistic Classification. I. The Niger-Congo Family,* South-Western J. Anthrop., 5.

KENNEDY, J. (1966) *The Phonology of Dagaari.* Collected Language Notes, No. 6, Inst. of African Studies, Legon.

MANESSY, G. (1963) *Rapport sur les langues voltaïques*, Actes 2e Colloque int. Ling. négro-afr., 239-266, Dakar.

MIGEOD, F. W. H. (1911-1913) *The Languages of West Africa*. London.

PROST, A. (1963) *Le verbe dans les langues voltaïques*, Actes 2e Colloque int. Ling. negro-afr., 161-172, Dakar.

WESTERMANN, D. (1911) *Die Sudansprachen, eine sprachvergleichende Studie*. Hamburg.

(1913) *Die Mossi-Sprachengruppe in westlichen Sudan*, Anthropos. 8.

(1927) *Die westlichen Sudansprachen und ihre Beziehungen zum Bantu*. Berlin.

(1935) *Nominalklassen in westafrikanischen Klassensprachen und in Bantusprachen*, Mitt. Seminars oriental. Sprachen, 38.

WESTERMANN, D. and BRYAN, M. A. (1952) *Languages of West Africa*. London.

OTHER REFERENCES

ARMITAGE, C. H. (1924) *The Tribal Markings and Marks of Adornment of the Natives of the Northern Territories of the Gold Coast Colony*. London.

(1913) *Notes on the Northern Territories of the Gold Coast*, United Empire, 4.

BINGER, L. G. (1892) *Du Niger au Golfe de Guinée*. Paris.

BOVILL, E. W. (1933) *Caravans of the Old Sahara*. London.

CARDINALL, A. W. (n.d.) (around 1925) *The Natives of the Northern Territories of the Gold Coast*. London.

(1927) *In Ashanti and Beyond*. London.

(1929) *The State of Our Present Ethnographical Knowledge of the Gold Coast Peoples*, Africa, 2.

(n.d.) *The Gold Coast*, 1931. Accra.

EVANS-PRITCHARD, E. E. (1940) *The Nuer*. Oxford.

(1951) *Kinship and Marriage among the Nuer*. Oxford.

FORDE, D. (1938) *Fission and Acretion in the Patrilineal Clans of a Semi-Bantu Community in Southern Nigeria*, J.R.Anthrop. Inst., 68.

FORDE, D. and RADCLIFFE-BROWN, A. R. (eds.) (1950) *African Systems of Kinship and Marriage*. London.

FORTES, M. (1945) *The Dynamics of Clanship among the Tallensi*. London.

(1949) *The Web of Kinship among the Tallensi*. London.

FORTES, M. and EVANS-PRITCHARD, E. E. (1940) *African Political Systems*. London.

GLUCKMAN, M. (1954) *Rituals of Rebellion*. Manchester.

HENDERSON, F. B. (1898) *West Africa and the Empire*. The Idler.

JONES, W. J. A. (1938) *The Northern Territories of the Gold Coast*. Crown Colonist.

LEACH, E. R. (1954) *Political Systems of Highland Burma*. London.

(1961) *Rethinking Anthropology*. London.

MURDOCK, G. P. (1959) *Africa*. New York.

NADEL, S. F. (1942) *Black Byzantium*. London.

(1947) *The Nuba*. London.

PAULME, D. (1940) *Organisation sociale des Dogon*. Paris.

RADCLIFFE-BROWNE, A. R. (1952) *Structure and Function in Primitive Society*. London.

SOUTHALL, A. (1965) *A Critique of the Typology of States and Political Systems* in *Political Systems and the Distribution of Power*. (A.S.A. Monographs, 2). London.

Abduction of women, 102
Adultery, payments to ancestor shrines, 49, 53, 55
Affinal relations, and house-building, 40; and cooking, 47; and marriage payments, 49f.; and generations, 50f., 61; and war alliance, 103f.
Agnates, 36, 40, 63, 106, 108; and migration, 10f., 32; and slavery, 27; and farming group, 33f.; and joint family, 42, 79; eating together, 43; and bridewealth, 50; and inheritance, 62; as members of a patrilineage, 65ff.; and funerals, 69f.; and ancestor shrines, 92; and farming parties, 100; *See also* Patrilineage, Complementary Funeral Groups
Ancestor cult, and lineage elder, 35; role of sister's son in sacrifices, 60; as sanction, 75, 111
Ancestor, founding, 69, 107; and land of patrilineage, 34, 44, 65, 67, 106; sacrifices to, 51, 68, 112; shrine of, 44, 58; of lineage of ritual leader, 96
Ancestor shrines, 38; sacrifices at, 32, 44, 67f., 82; carving of new shrine, 39, 43, 88, 101; transfer to new house, 40, 44; and duties of senior son, 43, 44, 88, 101; of founding ancestor, 44, 68; and bridewealth, 49; and adultery, 49, 53, 55; of ritual leader, 92n.
Ancestors, and land, 34f., 68; and sister's child, 36; and fertility of women, 49; and bridewealth, 53, 68; and housechild, 63; kinship terms used for, 68; of clan sector, 70; and oath, 80; and segmentation of ritual area, 95; anger of, 102; attitude toward matrilineal inheritance, 109
Ancestral home, 99; *See* Migrations
Arrows, poison, and sister's son, 58f., 61; and clan, 69, 76; in funeral ceremony, 88f., 101
Armed conflict, 36, 99, 102ff., 111; and clan unity, 74; and joking partnership, 81; and smith, 92
Babile, town of, 4, 8, 27, 93, 104, 109, 114
Biipol ritual, 88
Birifor, the, 3, 4, 16, 18, 19, 21, 33, 36, 40, 43, 61, 73, 74, 78, 83, 100, 103, 114
Birifu, village of, 4, 9, 20, 28, 29, 31, 38, 49, 60, 61, 65, 80, 84, 102, 106, 108, 114; population of, 27; clan sectors in, 70, 72, 80, 81; ritual area of, 80, 93, 95ff.; and matriclans, 83, 86; ritual community, 99; enemies of, 103
Biro, settlement of, 20, 72, 114; and Birifu, 27, 103; fission of ritual area of, 96, 97
Bohannan, 67
Bɔɔre ceremonies, 52, 59, 63, 70, 72, 99f., 108, 113
Bridewealth, payments, 49ff., 52, 108, 108n.; and rights over women, 52f.; and ancestors, 53, 68f.; and wife inheritance, 54, 60; and divorce, 55; and rights over children, 55f., 63f.; and illegitimacy, 63; and fighting, 102

British Administration, the, 9, 14, 27, 46, 96
Brothers-in-law, relationship between, 50f.
Burial, of women, 51; groups, 70, 100ff.; and LoDagaba, 84; and sanctions of Earth shrine, 92
Bush farm, 32n., 34
Bush, shrines of, 91
Cathartic alliance, *See* Joking Partnership
Cattle byre, 38, 43, 44, 68, 88, 91
Chiefs, 74, 96; establishment of and authority of, 14; and food supply, 27; wealth of, 30, 110; and polygyny, 41; and inheritance, 60
Childbirth, 38
Children, and breastfeeding, 47; clan membership of, 50, 55f.; descent group affiliation of, 51; care of in polygynous family, 54; motherless, 54; *See also* Siblings of different maternal origin, Siblings
Clan, 33, 58, 90, 106, 108, 113; membership through females, 42; membership of child, 49, 55f.; definition of agnatic group, 66; exogamy, 71f., 73; common origins, 71f.; names of, 73, 75; and fission of, 73f.; unity of, 74; homicide within, 75; totemic taboos of, 75f.; *See also* Patriclan, Matriclan, Interclan Partnerships
Clan sector, 69, 73, 88, 90, 95, 114; generational depth of, 33; and housebuilding, 40; definition and composition of, 70, 108, 111; and ritual, 70, 98, 99, 111; and funeral, 70f., 88, 108; and assistance in armed conflict, 74; and political community, 75; and *Bɔɔre* ceremony, 100; and war alliances, 104, 113; and exogamy, 108
Clan shrines, 76, 99
Clans, linked, definition of, 72; and exogamy, 72f., 107; and totemic taboos, 76; and joking partnership, 80
Clanship, double, 62, 73, 81, 96, 97, 111, 113; and kinship, 68, 89, 107; and sister's son, 60, 76, 89; definition of, 77, 108; and debt, 84
Clitoridectomy, 49
Complementary descent group, 77
Compound, description of, 38ff., 45; and occupants, 41f., 107; and division of food, 43; fission of, 43, 44; head of, 44; establishment of new, 44, 91; and founding ancestor, 68, 69; *See also* Dwelling group, Homestead
Consanguineal relationship, *See* Uxorilateral Relationship
Contiguity, tie of, 69f.; and farming groups, 100; burial groups, 100ff.
Cow, of the hoe-handle, 30, 69, 74, 80, 81, 82, 101; roof or matriclan, 81, 82
Co-wives, 46ff., 54
Cultivation, 30ff., 43; and Earth Shrine, 92; and bridewealth, 108; *See also* Farm land
Dagaa, differentiating term, 17, 19ff., 24 (diagram), 25, 114

DagaaWiili, the, 21, 26, 73, 99, 108, 114; livestock holdings of, 29; and matriclanship, 60; and fission of ritual area, 95, 96; and *Bɔɔre* ceremonies, 100; and war alliances 103, 104

Dagaba, the, 21, 26, 30, 73; language of, 3

Dagari-speaking peoples, 3, 4, 11, 30, 32; map of, 5; migration, 15

Day of no hoeing, 40, 92

Debt, and livestock, 37; between husband and wife, 47; between lineage members, 69; responsibility for, 84; and fighting, 102f.

Descent groups, 58, 59, 60ff., 65ff., 73, 76, 78, 90, 99, 108, 113; and contemporary migrations, 32, 112; and land, 32; segmentation of, 44; and position of child of broken marriage within, 53, 54, 56; and kinship relations, 57; unilineal, 67, and death, 75, 100; and joking partnership, 80, 86f.; and *Bɔɔre* ceremonies, 100; modified by locality, 101f.; and fighting, 102f.; *See also* Dual descent

Diviner, 44, 80, 92, 97, 99

Divorce, 55f., 62

Double unilineal kin group system, *See* Dual descent

Dry season, 1, 7

Dual descent, 60n., 61f., 73, 77, 84f., 106, 110, 111

Dwelling group, fission of, 34, 42, 43; composition of, 41ff.; and cooking, 46

Earth, fertility of, 32; used for house-building, 40

Earth, the, 95; fines paid to, 91; blood prohibition of, 93; claims to stray humans, 93

Earth cult, 35, 103; ritual sanctions of, 98, 104

Earth shrine (*tenggaan*), 7, 9, 59, 63, 91ff., 95, 99, 114; sacrifices to, 32, 40, 70, 80, 92, 102, 108, 113; and land, 35; eating soil of, 36, 93; drinking water of, 36; ritual sanctions against homicide, 36, 93, 96, 98, 102, 111; its day, 40, 92; and ebony, 52; and fostering, 54, 93; and political community, 70; and joking partner, 80; and pot-making, 91; and smith, 91; and rain, 92; as protector, 93; and fission, 96, 98; payments to, 98; *See also* Ritual area, Sacrifice

Earth shrine, custodian of, *See* Ritual leader

Earth shrines, minor, 38, 53, 54, 93ff., 98, 99

Elders, of farming group, 34, 35; of lineage, 35, 44; women, 52; within lineage, 112, 113

Elopement, 48

Europeans, the, 9, 12, 103, 109f.

Evans-Pritchard, E. E., 65ff.

Exogamy, 49, 108; mother's brother and sister's daughter, 61; and patriclan, 71f., 73, 74, 107; and matrilineal sub-clans, 83f., 85; and matrilineage, 86

Family, living arrangements of, 39f.; elementary, 41, 109; joint agnatic, 42f., 47, 77, 106; eating together, 43; cooking groups of, 46, 47, 48; polygynous, 46, 47,

groups of, 46, 47, 48; polygynous, 46, 47, 48; division of food within, 46; fission of polygynous family, 46f.; dissolution through death, 53; dissolution through divorce, 55; conjugal, 60n.; and wage labour, 109

Farafara people, 112

Farm, compound, 33; division of, 34

Farm, home, 33, 93, 95; division of, 34

Farmland, 31, 92; shortage of, 32; rights of wives in, 33; inheritance of, 34; lineage rights in, 34, 107

Farm shrines, 35, 92

Farming group, 30, 31, 33ff.; senior members of, 34, 35; fission of, 34, 43, 44, 46; inheritance within, 38n.; and homestead, 43; and sacrifices at ancestor shrines, 44; and division of food, 46; and debt, 84

Farming parties, *See* Contiguity

Father and son relationship, 39, 43; conflict over land, 34; and bridewealth, 50; begetter as legal father, 55; compared to mother's brother and sister's son, 62; father's matriclan and son, 88; dead father's quarrel with son, 101; in matrilineal system, 110; and ancestor shrine, 39, 43, 88, 101

Feud, 102, 103; *See* Armed conflict

Fission, of farming group, 34, 43, 46, 67; of dwelling group, 34, 42, 43, 67; of polygynous family, 46; of exogamous groups of patriclan, 71f.; and clan names, 73; of ritual areas, 93, 95, 96; of complementary funeral groups, 101f.; of lineages, 106f.

Food, distribution of, 46, 69, 70, 107

Food exchanges, 101; at funerals, 69

Food supply, 27, 28, 36; and hunting, 29; and lineage, 44; wife's personal, 47; women's guinea corn, 47

Forde, Daryll, 73, 106, 108, 109, 111

Fortes, Meyer, 19, 41, 42, 51, 65f., 73, 75n., 76, 77, 90, 109

Fostering, payment, 53; and uterine kin, 53; and Earth shrine, 54, 93

Fruit trees, and land grantor, 36

Funeral, and distribution of meat, 29, 101; of women, 52, 53; sister's son and mother's lineage, 59; and lineage, 69; and patriclan sector, 70f., 108; attendance at, 74; mourning, 75; and joking partnership, 81f., and matriclan, 88

Funeral groups, complementary, 69ff., 74, 88, 95, 101f.

Generations, depth of, 33, 67, 71, 106; and fission of dwelling group, 43; joking between, 59; relationships between, 51, 61, 79

Guardian spirit, 50, 76, 99; *See also* Clan shrines

Guoziel, village of, 96, 103

Harmattan, 1

Harvest Festival (*Bomaaldaa*), 68

Headman, *See* Chief

Hill and water sprites (*Kontome*), shrines to, 38, 55, 61, 91, 92

History, 13, 15

Hoe-blades, 28, 93

Homestead, 40, 43, 45, 46, 106; *See also* Compound, Dwelling group

Homicide, and sanctions of Earth shrine against, 36, 93, 98; and rites at hunting shrine, 71; clan medicine, 75; of fellow clansman 75, 111

Husband and wife, relations between, 39; and debt, 47; and divorce, 55f.

Housechild (*yirbie*), definition of, 42; and illegitimacy, 42, 62; membership in mother's lineage, 42, 55f., 63; and bridewealth payments, 50; and descendents 64

Hunting, 29

Hunting medicine, 69, 76

Hunting shrine, 69, 70f., 76, 113

Illegitimacy, *See* Housechild

Infant betrothal, 41, 48

Inheritance, double, 62, 77, 109

Inheritance, matrilineal, 22, 23, 62, 78, 88, 108; and woman's work, 43; changing from matrilineal to patrilineal, 60f., 109ff.; and matrilineal sub-clans, 83f., 88f.; *See also* LoDagaba

Inheritance, patrilineal, 62, 88, 97, 108; of farmland, 33, 34, 107; and farming group, 38n.; changing from matrilineal to patrilineal, 60f., 109ff.; and matrilineal sub clans, 84, 89

Interclan partnership, 59, 112

Joking (*dieno*), between brothers-in-law, 51; between brothers' wives and husband's sister, 51, 79; within mother's patriclan, 59; between brothers and married sister, 79; between grandfather and grandson, 79

Joking partnership (*lonluore*), 78, 79, 80ff., 87, 88, 90; as cathartic alliance, 51, 59, 80, 82; and mother's brother-sister's son relationship, 80; between patriclans, 80f.; and clan of custodian of Earth shrine, 80, 96; and share of sacrificial animal, 80, 81, 82; and armed conflict, 81, 112; between matriclans, 81f.; and funeral celebrations, 81, 82; and sacrifice at shrine of matriclan, 86ff.; and expiatory sacrifice for suicide or murder, 98f.

Joking relationship, 59, 69, 79; *See* Joking, for specific references

Kinship, and food, 44; terminology, use of, 57, 60, 62, 63, 78, 82, 83, 89, 97; terminology, classificatory, 57, 64, 68, 71; bilateral, 77; and joking, 79, 80; and cognatic ties, 104; and system of double clanship, 107; *See also* Agnates, Matriclan, Patriclan, Patrilineage

Kumansaal, town of, 27, 96f., 109, 114

Kwŏnyŭkwŏ, town of, 4, 27, 96, 97f., 103, 109

Land, shortage of, 32; fertility of, 32, 68; division of, 34; inheritance of, 33f., 35; rights of lineage to, 34f., 106; rights of tillage, 35, 36, 37; selling of, 35; secondary rights to, 35, 36; and rights of sister's son to, 35f., 58; grantor, 35, 36; and population density, 37; ancestors care of, 68; and founding ancestor, 106; *See also* Farmland, *So*

Lawra District, 4, 8, 13, 29, 30, 83, 85, 86,

106; history of, 14f.; population of, 27

Lineage, *See* Patrilineage, Matrilineage

Lineage systems, 60n., 65ff., 90

Livestock, 29f., 37; and bridewealth, 51; and sister's son, 58; and debt, 84; and Earth shrine, 93; and fighting, 102

Lo, differentiating term, 17, 19ff., 24 (diagram), 25, 43, 75, 103, 114

Lobi-speaking peoples, 4, 9, 11, 30, 33

LoDagaba, the, 20, 21, 25, 72, 73, 81, 100, 111, 114; language of, 3; livestock holdings, 29; land holding, 30ff.; patrilineal inheritance, 33, 76, 109; matrilineal inheritance, 33, 43, 62, 84; movable property, 33, 62, 84, 88; bridewealth, 50; mother's brother, 50, 62; matriclan, 62, 83f., 86, 88, 97; housechild, 63; and medicine shrines, 76; dual descent systems, 77, 110; double clanship, 77, 108; double inheritance, 77; matrilineal sub-clans, 83f., 86, 88, 90; shrines of matriclan, 86f.; and ritual leader, 97; and patriclan, 97, 99

LoSaala, the, 21, 73, 74, 89, 103

LoWilisi, the, 20, 21, 61, 74, 77, 83

Madeb, *See* Mother's brother

Male and Female, differentiations, 32, 50, 51, 77, 92, 92n.

Marriage, 47, 48ff., 51, 52ff., 55, 60ff., 108; monogamous, 41; polygynous, 41, 48; arranged, 49; rights transferred at, 52f.; economic services of, 53; remarriage, 54, 55f., 60f.; leviratic, 55; dissolution through divorce, 55; between mother's brother and şister's daughter, 61; annulled, 62f.; prohibitions, 85; *See also* Exogamy, Divorce, Procreation, Widows

Intermarriage, 83, 103, 108; with descendents of sister's son, 36; within patriclans, 71ff.

Markets, local, 6, 6n., 9, 40n., 103

Matriclan, the (*belo*), 57, 58, 62, 76ff., 82ff., 86ff., 108, 109, 111, 114; and joking partnership, 59, 79, 81, 86, 88; and housechild, 63, 64; and kinship ties, 78; names of 82; subdivisions, 83; and debt, 84; and ritual function 86; shrines of, 86; and funeral, 88; and ritual leader, 94; and armed conflict, 104

Matrilateral kin, 10, 11, 36, 48f., 58

Matrilateral cross-cousin marriage, 48, 61

Matrilateral parallel cousins, 85

Matrilineage, 62, 68, 76f., 81, 85, 86, 90, 109

Matrilineal sub-clans, 82ff., 88f., 90; and exogamy, 84; shrines of, 86; role at funeral, 88f., and ritual leader, 97

Medicine shrines (*tibe*) 32, 44, 52, 76, 92, 92n.

Migrations, of Dagari-speaking people, 15; contemporary, 32; and segmentation of descent group, 32, and land shortage, 32; and clan shrine, 99; and clanship, 106

Mother's brother (*madeb*), and sister's son, 56ff., 59ff., 69, 79, 80, 103, 109, 110; and matrilineal inheritance, 60f., 62, 109, 110; and sister's daughter, 61; and joking relationship, 59, 69, 79 lineage of, 36, 57

Mother's patriclan, rights of children in, 36, 42, 58; and mother's brothers, 57; and joking, 59; and matrilineal inheritance, 109

Mother's patrilineage (*ma yir*), and housechild, 50, 63f.; and motherless child, 53f., 76; and mother's brother, 56ff., rights of child in 59, 69; and marriage with, 85; and matrilineal inheritance, 109

Mossi language group, 2, 3, 4, 21, 71, 106, 112

Movable property, 33, 60, 61n., 62, 84

Native Authority, the, 9, 28

Neighbourhood, 90, 100, 101; *See also* Contiguity, Ritual area

Nomenclature, of LoWiili, 17ff., 20ff., 25f.; 113; of clans, 71, 73, 75,

Nuer, the, 66f., 90

Orphans, 101

Parish, *See* Ritual area

Patriclan (*dogro*), 40, 46, 56, 61, 62, 69, 71ff., 74ff.; and migration, 15, 33; and joking partnership, 15, 59, 80f., and villages, 15; definition of, 33; and land, 34; membership through females, 42; and housechild, 63f.; exogamy 71f., fission of, 72f., 96; totemic taboo, 75; number of, 78; boundaries, 93; and ritual leader, 96f; and ritual community, 99; and war alliance, 104; and clan sector, 70, 108; and social control, 111; *See also* Mother's patriclan

Patrilateral cross-cousin marriage, 52, 57

Patrilineage, 33, 35, 38, 44, 52, 57, 59, 61, 65ff., 68ff; 71, 74, 75, 82, 90, 98, 99, 100, 113; and rights in land, 34, 36, 107, 112f.; and inheritance of land, 35, 107; and descendents of sister's son, 36; and illegitimate child, 42, 63; and common ownership of food, 44, 112; and dispersion, 45f.; rights over women, 49, 51, 53; and inheritance of widows, 54, 69; and matrilineal inheritance, 62; and lineage systems, 65ff., definition of, 67f., 106; founding ancestor of, 68, 96, 107, 112; and funerals, 69f., 88, 101, 108; and debt between members of, 84; and minor earth shrines, 94, 95; and ritual leader, 96; fission of 101, 102 *See also* Agnates, Inheritance, patrilineal, Patriclan

Play, *See* Joking

Political community, 70, 75, 111

Political system, 27, 66n., 74, 112

Polygyny, *See* Marriage, Family

Population density, 27, 30f., 32, 37; and land, 32, 37;

Procreation, 47, 50; rights over women's 51f., and conception, 77; and exogamy, 85

Property, *See* Land, Movable property

Radcliffe-Brown, A.R., 49, 58, 66, 79n., 85

Rain, 32, 40, 86; owner of, 80, and Earth shrine, 92, 98

Rainfall, 1, 6

Rain shrines, 32, 80

Ritual area, (*tenggaan*), 35, 37, 52, 91ff., 98ff.; of Birifu, 65, 87, 91, 93, 97f.; and segmentation of 93ff.; and war alliance, 97, 112; and armed conflict, 103; and social control, 98, 111; *See also* Earth shrine

Ritual area, major, *See* Ritual area

Ritual area, minor (*tengaanble*) 93, 94 (diagram), 95f.

Ritual assistance, between sister's son and mother's lineage, 59f.; between housechild and mother's lineage, 63; and joking partnership, 80, 81, 82, 86f., 112; by joking partner of Earth shrine, 80, 99; and funeral, 82, 112; and neighbourhood groups, 100ff.

Ritual community, 35, 36, 37, 75, 93, 96f., 98, 99f.

Ritual leader (*tenggaansob*), and land rights, 35, 36; own descent group, 35; selection and succession to office, 35, 97; joking partner, 80, 96f.; and smith, 91f., and shrines of 92n.; as intermediary between community and Earth shrine, 99, 113; jurisdiction over markets, 103

Sacrifice, and distribution of meat, 29, 69, 70; to ancestor shrines, 49, 59, 63, 67, 68, 100; to guardian spirit, 50; to founding ancestor, 51, 68, 82; and fostering payment, 53; by sister's son for mother's clan, 59, 82; at Earth shrine, 70, 113; expiatory sacrifice to Earth shrine, 81, 98, 99, 102, 111; to shrines of matriclan 86, 88; for rain, 86; annual sacrifice to Earth shrine, 92; and fission of ritual area, 95; *See also* Cow

Seniority, *See* Elders

Settlement, 15, 32, 81

Sexuality, rights over 48f., 52f.; *See* Procreation

Siblings, and division of farm land, 34; unity of group, 51; individualization of and mother's brother's lineage, 58; and joking between, 79

Siblings of different maternal origin, and division of farmland, 34; and division of family, 47

Sister's daughter, and mother's sister, 61; and mother's brother, 61

Sister's son (*arbile*), and migration, 10; and rights to land, 35, 57; intermarriage with descendents of, 36; rights in mother's patriclan, 36, 42, 58, 59; and inheritance of mother's brother's wife, 55, 60, 61; and mother's brother, 56ff., Radcliffe-Brown and, 58; personal wealth from mother's patriclan, 58; and snatching, 59, 69, 81; and joking relationship with mother's brother, 59, 69, 79, 80; and assistance at funerals, 59; and assistance at ancestor shrines, 82, 101; in holder-heir situation, 62

Slavery, 9, 13, 27, 64, 83, 92, 98, 105

Smith, the, and Earth shrine, 91f., and mediation, 104, 113

Snatching, 59, 61, 69, 80, 81

Soil, 31, 32, and eating, 36; and Earth shrine, 91ff.

So, definition of 33, 34; and patriclan, 34; 35; and son of leviratic marriage, 54

Son-in-law, and labour for father-in-law,

50f.
Specialization, 28
Sterility, 52, 85
Suicide, and Earth shrine, 98
Tallensi, the, 19, 28n., 51, 63, 75n., 76, 77, 90, 112; figures on polygyny, 41f., lineages, 65ff., 107; *soog*, 85
Territorial dispersion, 33
Theft, and fighting, 102
Tiv, the, lineages of, 66f.
Totemic taboos, 75, 75n.
Trade goods, European, 9; native, 7, 8
Trade routes, 7, 11
Trading quarter, 4, 7, 11
Trees, rights over, 28, 36
Uterine kin, 33, 67, 88, 93, 104; and fostering, 53, 95; and matrilineal inheritance, 61, 108, 110; and illegitimate child, 63; and descent groups, 77f., 89; and debt, 84; and exogamy, 84f.; definition of, 85; *See also* Double clanship, Matriclan
Uxorilateral kin, 56-61, 111, 113; mother's

brother and sister's son, 56ff.; mediation of, 104; and inheritance, 110;
Vendetta, 103; *See also* Armed conflict
Wa, town of, 4, 7, 11, 12, 13, 71, 106
Wage labour, and migration, 9f., 40, 60n., 110, 112
Water, common rights over, 36
War, 103, 108, 113
War alliance, 98, 103, 104, 112
Wealth, *See* Movable property
Wet season, 1, 61, 31, 32
Widows, 44, 54f., 61, 69, 79, 97
Wife-inheritance, 41, 52, 54, 97; and sister's son, 55, 60, 61; joking between grandfather-grandson, 79
Witchcraft, 40, 98
Xylophones, distribution between Lo and Dagaa poles, 22, 23, 114; funeral, 52, 74, 75; of war, 74, 103, 104
Yakö, 60n., 73, 77, 84, 109; and lineages, 106f.
Zongo, See Trading quarter

For Product Safety Concerns and Information please contact our EU
representative GPSR@taylorandfrancis.com
Taylor & Francis Verlag GmbH, Kaufingerstraße 24, 80331 München, Germany

www.ingramcontent.com/pod-product-compliance
Lightning Source LLC
Chambersburg PA
CBHW070733270326
41926CB00061B/3178